BRUNSWICK COUNTY,

VIRGINIA

WILL BOOKS

Volume 2

Will Books 4 and 5 (in part)
1761 - 1780

Abstracted by
Dr. Stephen E. Bradley, Jr.

INTRODUCTION

The volume to follow is the second in a series of abstracts of Brunswick County, Virginia's will books. An abstract is a summary. Genealogical abstracts serve as a full index to the original. Persons, relationships, land, and features out of the ordinary are included.

Please be aware that these will books contain far more information than merely wills; also included are inventories, estate sales, administrations for those who left no will, accounts current.

This volume covers all of Will Book 4, which is in two parts in the original, and the first 100 pages of Will Book 3.

Each entry has received an assigned number and is indexed accordingly. The number in parentheses at each entry is the original page number. The header on each page indicates which will book. There are five (5) indexes: Full Name, Women's Christian Name, Negro Slave Name, Place Name, and Miscellaneous.

Brunswick County has the good fortune of having an excellent book concerning its history. This volume by Gay Neale is available through the office of the Brunswick County Administrator, and the information to follow is from Gay's careful analysis and research.

The researcher must pay close attention to the years of the transactions, because the Brunswick boundaries have not been constant. The boundaries for the county make a complex story. Brunswick County was formed in 1720, joining on the east the then boundaries of Surry and Isle of Wight counties, and on the west the Blue Ridge mountains, the Nottoway River on the north, and North Carolina on the south. Its original territory included about 12 of Virginia's present counties. Apparently because of the sparse population, Brunswick had no court until 1732; records for the region until 1732 were filed in Prince George County.

Beginning in 1732, Brunswick had its own court and thus records for the region begin in this year. In 1732, Surry County and Isle of Wight County ceded portions to Brunswick on the east. In 1734, a small portion in the north was ceded to Amelia County. In 1746, the present western line of the county was made when the then Lunenburg County was formed to include the region to the Blue Ridge. In 1781, the eastern boundary changed with the forming of Greensville County, and again in 1787 when the south east portion of the county was ceded to Greensville, to make the present borders of Brunswick County.

The whole county was the Parish of St Andrew beginning 1720. In 1754, the parish was divided in two: The land north of the Meherrin River retained the name of St Andrew Parish, and all the land south of Meherrin River became Meherrin Parish.

Brunswick County is fortunate to have its records. Indeed, in my opinion, they are among the best of the early county records. During the American Civil War, several of the surrounding counties experienced grievous record losses: The Yankees liked to burn court houses. When Sherman's army came to Brunswick County Court House, the Clerk of Court had fled, yet had draped his masonic apron over the records. Whoever was in charge of the raiding party must have been a Mason, because blank books were destroyed by having ink poured over them, yet the records were not harmed. Thus Brunswick has her records beginning in 1732.

The source of the abstracts is microfilm made available by the Brunswick County Public Library. My thanks to Pat Ward and the whole library staff for their help and encouragement.

I wish to dedicate this volume to the members and friends of the Lawrenceville United Methodist Church.

1-(1) Appraisal of the estate of *[torn]* as by order dated 20 N..?. Signed by John ...?, Rober[t] ...? 17 Jan ...?. *[Note: Most of document is torn away.]*

2-(2) Will of David(x)Dunn   8 ...? 1769   22 Jan 1770
[Note: Much of document is torn away.]
    To my son ...? Dunn - at age 16 *[torn away]*
    Before my son William *[torn away]*
    Negro fellow Gambo
    To my wife Frances - *[torn away]*
    To my 4 youngest sons David, Drury, *[torn away]*
    To my daughter Betty Dunn - 1 negro girl *[torn away]*
    To Molly Dunn - 1 negro girl Prin...?
Ex.   my wife Frances Dunn, Edward Scarborough, Ishmael Dunn
Wit.   ...? Bowls, Edward Scarborough, Hannah(x)Rawlings
Probate indicates that sd Frances & Ishmael Dunn qualified with William Gee & David Sills their securities; sd Edward Scarborough refused to qualify.

3-(3) Will of James Wortham   8 Jan 1770   26 Feb 1770
[Note: The following also appears as a typewritten copy included in the will book; bold print below is from this typewritten copy.]
    Of Meherrin Parish. "sick and weak in body"
    To my son **William** -
    To my *[torn]* - negro woman Patt & her child Rose; also 1 feather bed called Lucy's bed, etc.
    To my son Edward - 1 negro boy **Andy**.
    To my daughter Mary Minetree - negro boy Marma...?; also my lot at Hoods in the town of *[torn]* in Prince George Co on James River.
    To my son Ch...? - *[torn]*£.
    To my son John - £50.
    To my *[torn]* Elizabeth Wortham - £60.
    To my daughter Anne Wortham - my *[torn]* Cate.
    To my friend & old neighbor Elizabeth Baird widow - £25 "for her attendance on me in time of sickness.
    My executor to sell my land in *[torn]* & North Carolina, as also my livestock & *[household]* & kitchen furniture, & after my debts are paid, the rest to be divided among all my children William Wortham, Edward Wortham, Mary Minetree, Charles Wortham, Elizabeth Wortham & Anne Wortham; also the legacies left to me by my brother Charles *[torn]* death of his widow be sold & the money divided among all my children.
    Probate indicates that William Wortham & Archibald Minet[ree] qualified as excrs with Christopher Mason & William Myrick their securities, that William Huff & Christopher Mason witnessed the will.

4-(5) Appraisal of the personal estate of Charles Edwards Jr dec'd. Appraised by William Smith, Benjamin Blick, John Dugger. Sale of the sd estate. Buyers: James Bennitt, Anne Edwards.

5-(6) Sale of the estate of Charles Edw[ards]. Buyers:

David Andrews	Charles Edwards	Thomas Parrish
Drury Andrews	Charles Edwards Sr	Benjamin Proctor
William Cooper	John Edwards	Nicholas Proctor
Anne Edwards	Isaac Marshall	William Smith

6-(7) Appraisal of the estate of William Short Sr dec'd. Included were negroes: man Ball, lad Buck, boy Dick, boy Jemmy, man Peter, man Pompy, woman Tilder.
    Appraised by Thomas Simmons, Henry Simmons, John Abernathy.

7-(8) Will of Grenow Owen   3 Jul 1769   26 Mar 1770
Of St Andrews Parish
    To my wife Jona - the plantation & land where my house is, during her life & then to be divided among my 4 sons Robert Owen, Richard Brown Owen, Grenow Owen & John Loyd Owen.
Ex.   William Brown, Beverly Brown
Wit.   Drury Birchet Jr, Sarah Brown
Probate indicates that the sd excrs refused to qualify & administration was granted to Daniel Fisher with William Brown his security.

8-(9) Inventory of the personal estate of James Wortham dec'd. Included were negro wench Patt & child, man Mar*[torn]*.

9-(10) Will of John Pettway   29 Jan 1770   *[probate torn]*
Of St Andrews Parish. "sick & weak"
    To my wife Elizabeth - lend to her during her widowhood the use of all my hands; also lend to during her widowhood negroes Harry, Sebubbio, Jacob, Bridget, Ussry, Sarah & Peter.
    To my son Hinchey - 100 acres that I bought from Thomas Dean; also 50 acres where I formerly lived on the south side of Moores Swamp.
    To my son Edward - 150 acres where I now live; also 250 acres on the north side of Moores Swamp below Russells tract; also negro boy Jemmy, & half the man Joe.
    To my son John - 204 acres that I bought from Joshua Mabry; also 162 acres called the pine woods; negro girl Doll; half the man Joe.
    To my *[torn]* - 10 acres, negro girl Moroco, negro Davy.
    To my son-in-law David Smith & his wife Ruth - 7 acres joining Moores Swamp, sd Smith; also negro Sarah & her 2 children Peter & Dorcus.
    To my daughter Frances Pettway - negro boy Nacksey, negro Dilcy, 1 feather bed & furniture.
    To my son-in-law William Watson & his wife Lucretia - negro boy Simon.
    To my daughter Cecilia Pettway - negro boy Umphrey, girl Amca, 1 feather bed & furniture, etc.
    To my 2 daughters Mary Pettway & Amelia Pettway - the 7 negroes I lent to my wife after my sd wife's decease or marriage.

My negro man Sam & my sorrel filly to be sold to discharge my debts; the rest of my estate I give to my wife Elizabeth to educate my daughters Mary & Amelia Pettway.

Other legacies & provisions.

Ex.   my son Edward Pettway

Wit.   Alexander Watson, John Carlos, Joel Mabry

Probate indicates that the sd executor qualified with Frederick Maclin his security.

10-(12) Will of Sarah(x)Hicks   19 Mar 1769   23 Apr 1770

Of St Andrews Parish. "sick and weak"

To my daughter Lucy Seawell - 1 feather bed & furniture, 6 new pewter plates, etc.

To my granddaughter Sarah Hicks the daughter of my son George Hicks - my wearing gold ring.

Other legacies & provisions.

Ex.   my son-in-law Benjamin Seawell, my grandsons Benjamin Seawell & Joseph Seawell

Wit.   Charles Williamson, Thomas Sisson, Judith Williamson

Probate indicates that Benjamin Seawell Jr qualified with Benjamin Seawell Sr his security & that Benjamin Seawell Sr & Joseph Seawell refused to qualify.

11-(13) Will of Frances(x)Pettway   1 Mar 1770   23 Apr 1770

"sick and weak"

To my brother Edward Pettway - negro boy Nackey.

To my brother John Pettway - negro girl Discey.

To my sister Lucretia Watson - 1 bed & furniture.

To my sister Cecilia Pettway - 1 horse, my wearing clothes, 1 gold ring, if she lives to age 21 or marries; should she die before then, then the horse to go to my brother Edward Pettway & the wearing apparel & ring to be given to my sisters at my mother's discretion.

To my sister Mary Pettway - 1 side saddle & bridle.

To my sister Amelia Pettway Pettway - 1 pair of silver shoe buckles, 1 gold ring, silver studs.

Ex.   my brother Edward Pettway

Wit.   Alexander Watson, Braxton Mabry, Seth Mabry

Probate indicates the sd excr qualified with Robert Pettway his security.

12-(14) Will of William Geer   27 Mar 1770   28 May 1770

Of Meherin Parish. "very sick and weak in Body"

To my wife Patty - all my estate & what is due me from my father's will.

Ex.   Thomas & John Maclin of St Andrews Parish

Wit: Arthur Emmerson

Probate indicates that the Thomas Maclin qualified with Francis Young his security.

13-(15) Appraisal of the estate of William Phips as by court order 23 Apr 1770. Appraised by William Macl*[torn]*, Robert Bailey, John Mitchell. Returned to Court 28 May 1770.

14-(15) Account 1766 for the estate of William Ezell dec'd by John Peebles excr. Named:

James Allan	Absalom Atkins	Bailey & Son

Hannah Batte	Hamilton & Co	James Day Ridley
Alexander Bell	John Jeeter	Michael Roberts
John Brewer	William Knight	John Robinson
Peter Brooks	Thomas Massey	Benjamin Rowell
Benjamin Bynum	William Massey	Edward Rowell
Peter Clack	Milnear	John Spence
James Coaker	Cordal Norfleet	Thomas Thomlinson
John Cook	John Peebles Jr	Joshua Thorp
Jonathan Dickson	Dr Thomas Peete	Joseph Tooke
Nathl Edwards Jr	Person & Norfleet	John Wilkinson
William Edwards	John Peirce	Peter Williams
William Elliott	Batt Peterson	Lewis Williamson
John Elzey	John Peterson	Francis Willis
William Evans	Reives	Francis Young
Daniel Fisher	George Reives	

Audited by William Clack, John Flood Edmunds. Returned to Court 28 May 1770.

15-(18) Will of Richard(x)Burnitt   18 Oct 1769   28 May 1770
"sick in body"

To my wife Joice - give to her 1 feather bed & furniture; lend to her cattle & hogs; also lend to her negroes Phillis, Annakey, & Nann, for her lifetime & then they to be divided among my daughters.

To Deborah Burnitt - 1 feather bed & furniture.

To Lucy Burnitt - 1 bed & furniture.

To Daniel Burnitt - negroes Matt & Pompy, 1 horse, 1 gun; also give to him the plantation where I now live after my wife's decease.

To Joice Burnitt Jr - 1 bed & furniture

Ex.   Joice Burnitt Sr, Daniel Burnitt
Wit.   Thomas Ravenscroft, Elizabeth Mosely, Robert(x)Mosely
Probate indicates that Joice Burnett qualified with John Stead her security.

16-(19) Appraisal of the estate of Thomas Harrison dec'd. Appraised by Thomas Morris, James Mason, Robert Powell. William Harrison was admr. Returned to Court 25 Jun 1770.

17-(21) Appraisal of the estate of David Dunn dec'd 26 May 1770 as by court order dated Jan 1770. Included were negroes boy Bobb, Limus, Darcus, Nann, Gambo. Appraised by Richd Caudle, Edward Scarborough, William Harrison. Returned to Court 27 Aug 1770.

18-(22) Appraisal of the estate of John Gilliam dec'd 12 Oct 1769. Included were negroes:

Amy	Hall	Mace	Pompy
Bobbin	Hector	Ned	Que
Dick	Jack	Nutt	Robert
Dinah	John	Patt	Tom

Winney
Signed by Mary Gilliam. Appraised by John Hamilton, Joel Mabry, Hinchey Pettway. Returned to Court 27 Aug 1770.

19-(23) Appraisal of the estate of Richard Burnitt dec'd as by court order dated 28 May 1770. Included were negroes: man Matt, wench Fillis, girl Anake, boy Pompey, girl Nann. Appraised by Nathanael Steed, Robert Moseley, William Jean. Returned to Court 27 Aug 1770.

20-(24) Account for the estate of Richard Shackleford dec'd by Henry Cocke admr. Named: Henry Cocke, Courtney, Henry Howard, James Oliver, Dr Thomas Peete, John Renn.
    Noted were the sheriffs of Mecklenburg & Brunswick. Returned to Court 24 Sep 1770.

21-(25) Appraisal of the slaves of William Avoris dec'd 6 Aug 1770. Named were negro man Stafford & boy Tom. Appraised by Wm Clack, Robert Bailey, Wm Maclin. Returned to Court Oct 1770.

22-(26) Will of James Ingram   18 May 1770   22 Oct 1770
"Sick and Weak in Body"
    To my wife Elizabeth - 110 acres on the south side of Meherin River; negroes George, Ned & Peter; also 1 mare, all my household goods, etc, all during her life & after her decease to the heirs of my body but if none then to my 5 brothers George, Joshua, Richard, Benjamin & Joseph Ingram, except the household goods then to go to my sister Tabitha Gea.
    To William Gee - 50 acres on the north side of Meherin River.
    To my brother Joseph - 1 roan mare.
Ex.   my wife Elizabeth Ingram, my brother Joseph Ingram
Wit.   Thomas Steagall, John Booth, Reuben Booth
Probate indicates that the sd excrx qualified with John Threadgill & William Gee her securities.

23-(27) Anne(x)Massey   8 May 1770   22 Oct 1770
"old and of a Low Estate of Health"
    To my son John Massey - negro boy Ned, the plantation where I now live & 40 acres on the same side of Cattail Creek & if he die without heir then the above to go to my son Richard Massey's eldest son; also to my sd son John I give 2 feather beds & furniture, £10, & 2 cows & calves.
    To my son Richard Massey - the plantation where he now lives & after his death to his eldest son, 1 feather bed & furniture, 2 cows & calves.
    To my daughter Martha Moore - 1 feather bed & furniture, 1 cow & calf.
    To my daughter Tabitha Massey - negro boy Jimmy; should she die without heir, then sd Jimmy to go to my son John Massey; also give to her 1 feather bed, 2 cows & calves, 40 acres, etc.
    To my son William Massey - 10 shillings.
    To my son Hezekiah Massey - 10 shillings.
    To my daughter Sara Jones - 10 shillings.
    The rest of my estate to be divided among my 3 children John, Richard & Tabitha Massey.
Ex.   my sons John Massey & Richard Massey
Wit.   Littleberry Robertson, John Tomlinson, Wilson(x)Shehorn

Probate indicates that John Massey qualified with Littleberry Robertson his security, the other excr having refused to qualify.

24-(29) Will of Isaac Row Walton   19 Jun 1770   22 Oct 1770
Of Meherin Parish. "being weak"
    To my daughter Mary Mabry - negro girl Nann, boy Robbin.
    To my son Henry - the plantation where my father lived to include both sides of Quarrel Swamp as far as the Tarr Kiln Branch & Rocky Branch.
    To my son Daniel - all my lands on the south side of Quarrell Swamp not already devised.
    To my son David - all my land on the north side of Quarrel Swamp above Tarr Kiln Branch.
    To my son Drury - 650 acres on both sides of Rocky Run.
    To my son Isaac Row Wallton - the plantation & land where I now live after the decease of my wife Elizabeth.
    Should any of my above sons die before age 21 or marriage, the land devised to such son to be sold & the money divided among my surviving children.
    To my wife Elizabeth - negroes James, Lucy, Matt, Harculus, Sue, Frank, Jude, Young Jimmy, Ben, Abram, Doll, Young Sifar; also my household & kitchen furniture, my livestock.
    My moiety of the personal estate now in the possession of my mother may be sold at her decease & the money put to interest until my wife's decease.
    The negroes who are to descend to me at my mother's death are to be divided among my 3 sons Henry, Daniel & David; the negroes lent to my wife at her decease are to be divided between my 2 sons Drury & Isaac Row Wallton & my 3 daughters Elizabeth, Fanny & Nancey.
    1 negro devised to me by my father's will to be sold to discharge my part of the claim of my sister Mary Ledbetter.
    My son Daniel to be bound to John Rodgers bricklayer.
    My son David to be bound to Sterling Cato taylor.
    Drury & Isaac are to be bound when of sufficient age.
    Other provisions.
Ex.   Charles Ledbetter, Littleberry Robertson
Wit.   Henry Mounger, John Allen, George Ledbetter, Nathan Harris, John Wallton, Sarah Sisson
Probate indicates that Littleberry Robertson qualified with Henry Ledbetter & John Massey his securities, & that Charles Ledbetter refused to qualify.

25-(32) Will of Brazure Cocke   20 Sep 1766   22 Oct 1770
Of St Andrews Parish. "Sick in Body"
    To my wife Frances - "a Suitable maintainance" for life from the labor of the slaves Sack, Mariah, Patt, Will & Cheney; she to live where I now live with either of her children "as she shall choose."
    To my son William - slaves Tom, Absolom, Phillis.
    To my son Thomas' children - all my title to the negroes I gave to my sd son Thomas.
    To my daughter Elizabeth Holt - slave woman Beck with her increase.
    To my granddaughter Elizabeth Holt - negro girl Amey.
    To my daughter Fanny Oliver - a gold ring.

To my daughter Mary Anderson - negro girl Lucy, & also negro fellow Bowser left to her by my son James' will.

To my daughter Susannah Coleman - negro girl Barbery.

To my daughter Ann Cheek - negro wench Jenny which my son James willed to her; also wench Aggy, my feather bed, etc.

To my daughter Martha Cocke - slaves Jack, Will, Mariah, Patt, Cheney, Frank & Charles; all the household furniture, etc; also negro girl Judy now in the possession of John Oliver.

To Samuel Briggs - all my tools marked with SB.

Ex.   my friends Nicholas Edmunds, Henry Edmunds, my daughter Martha Cocke
Wit.   John Flood Edmunds, Bartholomew Damron, David Roper, James Tarpley
Probate indicates that William Merritt presented the will in right of his wife Martha the sd excrx, with Richard Elliott as security.

26-(34) Will of William Chapman   8 Nov 1770   26 Nov 1770
Of Meherin Parish. "Sick and Weak in Body"

To my son William - all the land where I now live.

To my son John Hamlin Chapman - all the land called Chapman Ford Tract which my brother John Chapman willed to me; also negro boy Charles.

The rest of my estate to be divided among my 4 children William, John Hamblin, Nancy & Elizabeth Chapman. Should my wife Isabellear be "in pregnancy," then that child to have a part of my estate.

Ex.   my brother Benjamin Chapman, my friends William Edwards & Nathaniel Edwards Jr
Wit.   James Day Ridley, James Crutchfield, Richard Hartwell
Probate indicates that Nathaniel Edwards Jr qualified with Benjamin Chapman & William Edwards his securities.

27-(35) Inventory of John Pettway dec'd 22 May 1770. Signed by Edward Pettway Jr excr. Returned to Court 26 Nov 1770.

28-(37) Appraisal of the estate of the Rev Gronow Owen dec'd 24 Apr 1770. Included were negroes: wench Peg, wench Young Peg, boy Bob, boy Stephen. Appraised by John Clack, Thomas Stith, Francis Young. Returned to Court 26 Nov 1770.

29-(38) Inventory of the estate of Frances Pettway dec'd 26 May 1770. Signed by Edward Pettway Jr excr. Returned to Court 26 Nov 1770.

30-(39) Appraisal of the estate of Sarah Hicks dec'd 21 Jun 1770. Appraised by Eldridge Clack, John Simms, Charles Williamson. Returned to Court 26 Nov 1770.

31-(40) Will of James Harwell   8 Sep 1770   25 Feb 1771

To my eldest son Greif - 150 acres on Cope's Creek which I bought from John Robertson; 600 acres in Mecklenburg Co; 400 acres which I purchased from Daniel Carroll & sd Carroll to is live there for his lifetime; 100 acres which I purchased from John Lambert joining sd Carroll; also negro fellows Ned & Lewis & wench Lilly.

 To my second son James - 450 acres where I now live; negro boys Stafford & Peter, wench Jenny; my children & their negroes to live on this sd tract until sd James comes of age, & Jordan Mabry son of Joshua Mabry to live along with my children.

 To my eldest daughter Anna - negro boy Bob & wench Linda.

 To my second daughter Mourning - negro boy Anthony & girl Bett.

 To my third daughter Elizabeth - negro boy Godfrey & girl Phibb.

 To my fourth daughter Sally - negro boy Will & girl Daphney.

 To my fifth daughter Cassander - negro fellow James & girl Younger.

 Other provisions.

Ex. Jordan Mabry, Peter Thomas

Wit. Thomas Cranfurd, Arthur Emmerson, Xpher Mason, Thomas Bedingfield

Probate notes that Peter Thomas was the surviving excr & who refused to qualify; administration with the will annexed was granted to Samuel Harwell with Thomas Stith & Thomas Simmons securities.

32-(42) Appraisal of the estate of Isaac Row Wallton dec'd. Included were negroes:

boy Abraham	man Harculus	woman Lucy
boy Ben	boy Jimmy	man Matt
girl Doll	man Jimmy	boy Robin
woman Fax	woman Judy	woman Sue
woman Frank		

Littleberry Robinson was excr. Appraised by Henry Mounger, Peter Lee, John Phillips. Returned to Court 25 Feb 1771. Noted was an altering of the appraisal amount by court order dated 23 Sep 1776.

33-(44) Will of Nathaniel Edwards Jr 12 Aug 1762 25 Feb 1771

 To my father Nathaniel - all my lands in Virginia for his lifetime & after his decease then to my brother William.

 To my sister Mary Ridley - negro wench Hannah.

 To my sister Rebecca Edwards - negro wench Dinah, boy Abraham, my horse, etc.

 To my brother Benjamin - negro boy Batt.

 To my sister Elizabeth Edwards - negro fellow Archer.

 To my brother Isaac - negro girl Dorcus.

 Other legacies & provisions.

Ex. my father Nathaniel Edwards, my brother William Edwards

Probate indicates that Francis Young & Hinchey Mabry testified to the handwriting; William Edwards qualified with James Wall his security.

34-(45) Appraisal of the estate of Thomas Person dec'd as by court order dated 23 Apr 1770. Included were negroes:

Ben	Cealah	Fillis	Jeffrey
Ben	Dick	Isaac	Jenny
Betty	Dick	Jacob	Jim

Judy	Lucy	Peter	Toney
King	Patt	Rose & child	

Also included were 1 negro wench & 1 child (not named). Returned to Court 25 Apr 1771.

35-(46) Inventory of the personal estate & negroes of Anne Massey dec'd as by court order dated 13 Nov 1770. Included were negroes Ned & Jemmy. Signed by John Massie. Returned to Court 25 Feb 1771.

36-(46) Will of Drury Stith   25 Jun 1770   25 Feb 1771
Of St Andrews Parish.
    "I lay no claim to any part of the Estate my wife Elizabeth Stith was possessed of at our Marriage."
    To my son Drury - all the furniture "belonging to my Hall."
    To my son Buckner - 1100 acres on the south side of Sturgion Run joining Thomas Stith, Henry Morris, Drury Stith, John Loyd, Buckner Stith, *[torn]* Merritt; also slaves Jacko, Frank, Punch, Jude & her children.
    To my wife Elizabeth - 746 acres I bought from Vaughan & Clayton on the south side of Beaverpond Branch, for her lifetime & then to my son Thomas; also 600 acres on the head of Beaverpond Branch joining Clayton, the old road.
    To Robert Laurance's heir - 210 acres on the branches of Loyd's between Morris & Proctor.
    To my daughter Elizabeth Stith - slaves Mag & her child, Milly & her child, Dinah & Suckey, these being "the same Slaves mentioned in my letter to her uncle John Stith."
    I lately purchased 1292 acres from Thomas & William Griffin on both sides of Sturgion Run & sd Griffin has not executed a deed for the same but has given bond for the same; thus I give the sd land as follows: 260 acres to my wife Elizabeth on the south side of Sturgion Run if she pays £140 for it; to my son Edmunds 1032 acres on the north side of Sturgion Run.
    My lands on Jones's Creek & the branches of Blue Stone to be sold to pay my debts.
    Other legacies & provisions.
Ex.   John Coleman, Sterling Edmunds, my wife Elizabeth Stith
Wit.   Nathaniel Roberson, Charles(x)Sadler, William(x)Parsons
Codicil 19 Sep 1770. The 600 acres on the south side of Couche's Run above Drury to be sold to pay my debts. To my wife Elizabeth I give 500 acres joining Kelly, Walker, Edwards, Merritt & Drury Stith. To my son Drury I give my pistols, sword. To Richard Littlepage Lawrance I give 100 acres. Other legacies & provisions. This witnessed by the Rev Thomas Lundie, Henry Simmons, Thomas Edmunds.
Probate indicates that John Coleman & Sterling Edmunds were the surviving excrs & that they refused to qualify *[torn]*.

37-(49) Will of Elizabeth Stith   Jan 1771   25 Feb 1771
"sick and weak in Body"
    To my son Aristotle - my plantation called Fisher's which was part of the 600 acres Col Drury Stith purchased from John Nash, on condition that he give my daughter Sarah at her marriage negro woman Judy & her child; should he refuse, then the land to be sold, sd Sarah to receive the value of

the negroes & my sd son Aristotle to receive the residue; also to my son Aristotle, I give 242 acres on Sturgion Creek which I bought from Thomas Buckland Griffin, on condition that he pay £100 to my daughter Sarah when she is age 21.

To my son Howell - 500 acres which is part of the tract Col Drury Stith purchased from John Nash & the rest that I bought from him; also give to him negroes Tom & Jack, 1 mare, etc.

To my daughter Sarah - negro man Matthew; the residue of my estate not given away.

To my daughter Katherine - 1 stone ring.

To my daughter Charlotte - 1 plain gold ring.

After my decease, my son Howell to go to the care of Sterling Edmunds, my son Thomas to the care of the Rev Thomas Lundie, my daughters Katherine & Charlotte to the care of John Coleman, & my son Edmunds to the care of Thomas Simmons.

Other legacies & provisions.

Ex.　　my friends John Coleman, Thomas Simmons, Sterling Edmunds

Wit.　　Sterling Edmunds, Thomas Edmunds, Thomas Stone

Probate indicates that the sd excrs qualified with Richard Elliott their security.

38-(51) Will of Hugh Hall　　13 Apr 1770　　25 Feb 1771

Of St Andrews Parish. "in a very low state of Health"

To my son Dixon - a bay horse.

To my son William - 1 shoat.

To my wife Mary - lend to her the rest of my estate during her life or widowhood & then to be divided among my 5 sons & daughter.

Ex.　　my wife

Wit.　　George Clack, Elisha Clack

Probate indicates that the sd excrx qualified.

39-(51) Will of William(x)Nance　　17 Nov 1770　　25 Feb 1771

Of Meherin Parish.

To my son Isham - 200 acres in Mecklenburg Co joining Reuben Na*[torn]* & William Fox; also negro fellow Harry, 1 pot, etc.

To my son John - the land where I now live; also 390 acres in Mecklenburg Co joining Drury Malone & Edward Epps; also negro wench Winney, girl Judy, etc.

To my son Reuben - 200 acres where he now lives joining Richard Warthin; also negro boy Cook, girl Luce, etc.

To my daughter Elizabeth Glover - negro girl Phillis, a fourth part of my negro girl Hannah when sold, a horse, 5 sheep.

To my daughter Tabitha Nance - negro fellow Frank, a fourth part of my negro girl, etc.

To my daughter Mary Lanier - negro boy Emmanuel, 5 sheep, a fourth part of my negro girl, etc.

To my daughter Sarah Lanier - £20, negro girl Doll, girl Sarah, a fourth part of Hannah, etc.

To John Lanier - my coat.

Other legacies & provisions.

Ex.　　my 3 sons Isham, John & Reuben

Wit.　　Joseph Floyd, John Nipper, Benjamin Walker

Probate indicates that Reuben Nance refused to qualify & the other 2 excrs qualified with Charles Collier, Joshua Winfield & Josiah Floyd their securities.

40-(53) Appraisal of the estate of Ingram Blanks dec'd. Included were negro wench Nan & child Phillis, fellow Jack, fellow Frank, wench Lidd, fellow Peter. Signed by the excrs Elizabeth Hurst, Penny Hurst, Thomas Morris. Appraised by James Stewart, James Oliver, Nathaniel Mabry. Returned to Court 25 Mar 1771.

41-(54) Will of Richard Caudle   26 Mar 1768   25 Mar 1771
Of St Andrews Parish.
    To my 3 sons William, John & Charles - my land.
    To my son William - negro wench Milly, my still, a mare.
    To my son John - negro boy Sam.
    To my son Charles - negro wench Silvia.
    To my daughter Susanna - negro girl Jenn.
    To my wife - negro Ned, wench Sarah, boy James, & at her death or marriage, the sd negroes & household furniture to be divided among all my children.
    I leave money "to pay for the finishing of a Dwelling House I am no about."
    Other legacies & provisions.
Ex.   my brother Thomas Morass, my wife Mary Caudle
Wit.   William Harrison, Rose(x)Stewart, John(x)Price
Probate indicates that the sd excrs qualified with John Jones & Robert [torn] their securities.

42-(56) Appraisal of the estate of James Ingram dec'd as by court order dated Nov 1770. Included were negro fellow George, fellow Ned. Appraised by Reuben Booth, William Clack, William Maclin. Returned to Court 25 Mar 1771.

43-(56) Will of Samuel White   20 Jun 1769   25 Mar 1771
    To my wife Sarah - during her life or widowhood the use of the plantation where I now live with negro woman Cate, man Jem, boy Roger, & a third part of the livestock & household furniture.
    To my son George - 150 acres where I now live; also negro woman Cate, negro Jem after my wife's decease or marriage; also negro woman Moll & her child Abraham, man Toney, girl Rho...? & half my movable estate, & he to pay to his sister Sarah Mitchell £3 per year "in case she should be left destitute;" should my son George die without heir, then his part of my estate to go to my son John.
    To my son John - negro boy Will, girl Frances, boy Roger after my wife's decease; also Bob & girl Amey, & half my movable estate after my sd wife's decease, & he to pay his sister Sarah Mitchell 40 shillings per year "in case she should be left destitute;" should my son John die without heir then his part of my estate to go to my son George.
    I have already given a full part of my estate to my daughter Hannah Gun, my son William White, & my daughter Sarah Mitchell.
    Other legacies & provisions.
Ex.   my wife Sarah White, my son George White

Wit.   William Shell, ...? Gibbs, Charles(x)Huckebay
Probate indicates that the sd excrs qualified with Allan Love their security.

44-(58) Account for the estate of Ingram Blanks dec'd. Named:

William Avant	Daniel Fisher	John Peter
Thomas Battle	Thomas Harrison	Walter Peter
James Belches	James House	James Stewart
William Bishop	William Knight	Andrew Troughton
Richard Blanks	Joseph Long	Elizabeth Wager
James Buchanan	Elizabeth Lucas	Mary Waldon
James Carter	John Malloby	Benjamin Williams
William Connelly	Thomas Morris	John Willis
Thomas Esell	James Oliver	William Wrenn
William Fear	William Parham	

It was noted that John House was orphan of Lawrance House dec'd.
    Audited by James Maclin, James Wall Jr, Drury Collier. Returned to Court 25 Mar 1771.

45-(60) Will of William Broadnax   22 Apr 1770   25 Mar 1771
"very sick and Weak"
    To my wife Anne - all my estate "to be disposed of as before mentioned by a former Will;" I also devise to her my part of Stephen Drury's estate as by his will dated 10 Jun 1762; all the rest of my estate to "go by my former Will," that is, to my sd wife Anne & to my children "as she shall think proper."
    I give all my right to a piece of land my brother Edward Brodnax purchased for me from Col Theodorick Bland on Stoney Creek & now in the possession of William Brodnax of Dinwiddie Co *[note: the receiver of the land is not clear.]*
Ex.   my son-in-law William Evans, John Brodnax, Anne Brodnax
Wit.   William Lanier, Charles Simons, Nicholas Lanier
Probate indicates that the sd excrs refused to qualify & that James Walker was granted administration with the will annexed with Daniel Fisher his security.

46-(60) Appraisal of the slaves & personal estate of William Nance as by court order dated 25 Feb 1771. Included were slaves:

boy Cook	girl Hannah	girl Lucy	wench Winney
boy Emmanuel	fellow Harry	girl Phillis	
fellow Frank	girl Jude	girl Sarah	

Appraised by Silvanus Stokes, Charles Collier, James Hicks Sr. Returned to Court 22 Apr 1771.

47-(61) Appraisal of the slaves & personal estate of Samuel White dec'd. Included were slaves:

Abraham	wench Cate	man James	Rose	Will
Amy	Frank	Roger	Toney	
Bob				

Also included were negro Moll & child Cate. Appraised by Hezchiah Thrower, Daniel(x)Huff, John

Barker. Returned to Court 22 Apr 1771.

48-(63) Appraisal of the estate of Hugh Hall dec'd. Included were negro girl Cloe, Oliver. Appraised by George Clark, William Boswell, Elisha Clark. Returned to Court 22 Apr 1771.

49-(64) Will of Jane(x)Williams   21 Dec 1777*[sic]*   22 Apr 1771
    To my daughter Lucy Chambless - negro girl Lucey; also 1 feather bed & furniture.
    To my son Seth Williams - negro boy Abram; also 1 cow & yearling, 1 sow & pigs, 1 bed, etc; also negro woman Fib after my daughter Frankey's decease; my sd son Seth to have the care of my 2 youngest children Daniel & Frankey "while they come of age."
    To my daughter Patty Parham - negro boy Sam.
    To my son Charles Williams - 1 mare.
    The residue of my estate is to go to my 2 sons Christopher & Charles Williams.
    Other provisions.
Ex.   my sons Seth Williams & Christopher Williams
Wit.   Rowland Williams, Milly(x)Hyde, Moses Johnson
Probate indicates that the sd excrs qualified with Rowland Williams their security.

50-(65) Appraisal of the estate of Thomas Vinson dec'd as by court order dated 25 Feb 1771. Included were negroes:

girl Annakey	wench Gane	fellow Sam
wench Beck	fellow George	wench Sarah
wench Cate	wench Hannah	boy Solomon
child Charles(sick)	boy James	boy Will
boy Dick	boy Peter	fellow York
fellow Dick	boy Ricks	
girl Dorcus		

Also noted was Cate's only child (not named). Appraised by George Wyche, James Wall Jr, Daniel Cato, Arthur Turner. Returned to Court 22 Apr 1771.

51-(67) Will of William Randle Sr   19 Oct 1770   22 Apr 1771
"in a weak State of Body"
    To my son John - negro girl Jane; all my lands on the north side of Saw Scaffold Branch.
    To my son Coalby - 10 shillings VA.
    To my daughter Anne Tillman - negro boy Cambridge.
    To my son Barnett - negro boy Isaac; the land where I now live on the south side of Saw Scaffold Branch.
    To my daughter Elizabeth Randle - negro girl Violet.
    To my daughter Susanna Jackson - 10 shillings VA.
    To my daughter Oney - negro boy Abraham.
    To my wife Anne - lend to her negro wench Abby during her life & then sd Abby to become the property of my daughter Oney; lend to my sd wife the residue of my estate after my debts are paid & at her decease this to be divided among my son Barnitt & my daughters Elizabeth & Oney.

Other legacies.
Ex.   my wife, my son John Randle
Wit.   Henry Mounger, Benjamin(x)Whealer Sr, Randle(x)Woolsey
Probate indicates that the excr John Randle qualified with Joseph Phips & John Woolsey securities.

52-(69) Appraisal of the estate of Jane Williams dec'd 22 May. Included were negroes: boy Abraham woman Phib, girl Philladay, boy Sam, girl Suckey.
    Appraised by William Brewer, Moses Johnson, Henry Chambless. Returned to Court 24 Jun 1771.

53-(69) Appraisal of the estate of James Wortham dec'd. The only item was negro girl Cate. Appraised by Owen Myrick, John Fletcher, William Huff. Returned to Court 22 Jul 1771.

54-(70) Appraisal of the estate of William Randle dec'd 9 May 1771. Included were negroes: wench Abby, boy Abraham, boy Cambridge, boy Isaac, girl Violet.
    Appraised by William Randle, Benjamin Warren, Benjamin Whealer, Patrick Hall. Returned to Court 22 Jul 1771.

55-(71) Sale of the estate of William Randle dec'd 20 May 1771 by John Randle excr. Named:

Anne Allan	Britain Jones	Charles Smith
Thomas Allan	Charles Ledbetter	Charles Sullivant
Samuel Davis	William Massey	John Swanson
Briggs Goodrich	Elias Morgan	Richard Tillman
Patrick Hall	Joseph Phips	William Vaughan
Thomas Howell	Barnet Randle	John Wallton
Mark Jackson	Coalby Randle	Thomas Ware
Peter Jackson	John Randle excr	John Woolsey
John Johnson	John Seaton	Nathaniel Wray
Thomas Johnson	Burrell Sims	

Returned to Court 22 Jul 1771.

56-(73) Appraisal of the estate of Amos Collier dec'd 19 Jul 1771. Included was negro woman Jenny. Appraised by John Loftin, Robert Rives Jr, Mason Harwell. Returned to Court 22 Jul 1771.

57-(74) Will of Nathaniel Edwards   29 Apr 1771   22 Jul 1771
Of St Andrew Parish. "weak of Body"
    To my wife Jane - 8 beds & furniture "out of which she is to pay the legacies left in Beds to her Children by their Father Anthony Haynes;" also give to her half my pewter & china & earthenware; lend to her for life or widowhood negroes Tim, Brandon & Jemmy(son of Sue), & after her death or marriage I give Tim to my daughter Sarah Edwards, Brandon to my son Isaac Edwards, & Jemmy to my daughter Anne Edwards; also give to my sd wife for her use during her widowhood the negroes given hereafter to my 2 daughters Sarah & Anne Edwards or until my sd daughters are age 21 or marry; I had agreed to give my sd wife £100 per year at my death, but in lieu of that, if she choos-

es, she may use Hixes plantation on the west side of Metcalf's Swamp, & at her death or marriage the sd plantation is to go to my son Isaac.

To my son Isaac - all my lands on the north side of Meherin River; also negroes Old Donum, Old Lucy, Sarah, Donum, & Hamsheir(children of Lucy), Robert Tom, Dick, Lett, Lucy(daughter of Nanny), Dorcas & Godfrey; also my silver spoons marked N.$^{E\cdot}$R.

To my daughter Sarah Edwards - at age 21 or marriage, negroes Old Will, Old Sarah, Flora & her children Bob & Jenny, Ephraim, Peter, Ned, Nanny daughter of Old Lucy, Nanny daughter of Amy, & Peg daughter of Sue; should she die before age 21, then I give Peter & Ephraim to my daughter Mary Ridley, Ned & Pegg to my daughter Elizabeth Willis, & Flora, Sarah & Will to my daughter Ann Edwards, Tim to my daughter Rebecca Jones, Nanny daughter of Lucy & Jenny to my son William Edwards & Nanny daughter of Amy & Bob to my son Isaac Edwards.

To my daughter Ann Edwards - at age 21 or marriage, negroes Mago, Sue daughter of Sue, Cuffey son of Nanny, Patt, Charles Lidia, Milly, Delsey, King & Cloe daughters of Lett, & Sarah daughter of Sarah; should she die before age 21, then I give King & Sue to my son William, Delsey & Charles to my son Isaac, Mago & Sarah to my daughter Sarah Edwards, Patt & Milly to my daughter Mary Ridley, Cloe & Cuffey to my daughter Rebecca Jones, Jemmy & Lidia to my daughter Elizabeth Willis.

To my son William - negroes Old Cuff, Black Moses, Abraham, Dinah & Cuff son of Bess.

To my daughter Mary Ridley - negroes Hannah, Sue & Cuffee son of Sue.

To my daughter Rebecca Jones - negroes Jemmy son of Lucy, boy Sharper.

To my daughter Elizabeth Willis - negroes Yellow Moses, Staffor, girl Clarissia.

To my 2 sons William & Isaac - the reside of my estate after my debts are paid.

Other legacies & provisions.

Ex.   my sd sons William & Isaac Edwards

Wit.   Seymour Powell, Richard Cocke, Hinchey Mabry, Allan Jones

Probate indicates that the sd excrs qualified with Seymour Powell & Sterling Edmunds securities.

58-(76) Appraisal of the estate of John Underwood dec'd 5 Apr 1771. Signed by Elizabeth(x)Underwood admrx. Appraised by John Vinson, Richard(x)Massey, John Doby. Returned to Court 23 Sep 1771.

59-(77) Will of Thomas(x)Jordon   1 Oct 1763   26 Oct 1771

To my son Thomas - negro fellow Jams.

To my daughter Mary Reives - 7 shillings & "no further part of my estate."

To my daughter Hannah Jordon - my fiddle & 5 shillings & "no further part of my estate."

The remainder of my estate, including lands, to be sold, my debts paid, & of the money remaining, a fourth part to go to my son Burrel's children & the other 3 parts to go to my son Thomas, my son Drury, my daughter Jenny.

Ex.   my sons Thomas & Drury

Wit.   Haley(x)Dupree, John(x)Dupree, Robert(x)Dupree

60-(78) Appraisal of the estate of William Phips dec'd 10 May 1770. Appraised by William Maclin, Robert Bailey, John Mitchell. Returned to Court 26 Aug 1771.

61-(79) Sale of the estate of William Phips dec'd 10 May 1770 by William Maclin, Robert Bailey & John Mitchell. Buyers:

Robert Bailey	John McKinny	Elizabeth Strange
Gresham Hagood	John Mitchell	Stephen Strange
Mordicai Hagood	Richard Mitchell	James Wade
Dixon Hall	Thomas Moore	Lazarus Williams
Joseph Ingram	Joseph Phips	Mary Williams
Amy Jackson	John Rose Jr	
James Johnson		

Returned to Court 26 Aug 1771.

62-(79) Will of James(x)Bass   13 May 1768   23 Sep 1771
Of St Andrew Parish. "very Sick and weak"
    To my wife Mary - lend to her the whole of my estate during her life & then as follows.
    To my daughter Mary Emmery - negro Lucy.
    To my grandson James Bass - 1 horse colt.
    The rest of my estate to be divided among all my children except Mary Emmery, but should the sd negro die before she possess her, then she to have an equal part.
Ex.   my wife Mary Bass, Thomas Bass
Wit.   Thomas Rivers, John Wallace

63-(80) Will of Isaac Collier planter   8 Jul 1771   28 Oct 1771
    I lend to my wife Ann for her life & to my daughter Ann Collier while she is single my manor plantation & any part of my land "as they shall think fit."
    To my daughter Ann Collier - negroes Phibby, Annakey, Delsey, Pompy; a feather bed, etc.
    To my son Myhill - negroes James & Daniel, 2 cows & calves, 2 sows.
    To my son Vines - negro boy Dave "that he is already got."
    To my daughter Elizabeth Smith - negro woman Eady "that she has now got."
    To my daughter Judith Hicks - negro girl Eady.
    To my son Thomas - the 45 acres I took up on the south east side of Jack's Branch; etc.
    To my wife Ann - lend to her negroes Nick, Harry, Frank, Patt, Milly, Daphny, etc; after her death, the sd negroes to be divided among my sons Vines, Charles, Isaac & my daughter Elizabeth Smith.
    To my sons Isaac & Myhill - the land I bought from Col Harrison, after my wife's death or my daughter marries; I also give the land I bought from William Smith & the land I took up on the north west side of Jack's Branch, being 630 acres in all.
Ex.   my sons Vines Collier, Charles Collier, Isaac Collier
Wit.   James Trotter, William Hamilton, James Hamilton
Probate indicates that the sd excrs qualified with Benjamin Seawell Jr, Joshua Winfield & Josiah Smith their securities.

64-(82) Appraisal of the estate of Isaac Collier dec'd 30 Oct 1771. Included were negroes:

girl Annakey	Daniel	Daphney	Dilsey

girl Eady	James	woman Patt	boy Pompey
Frank	Milly	Phibby	
Harry	man Nick		

Appraised by Hinchey Pettway, James Trotter, Joel Mabry. Returned to Court 25 Nov 1771.

65-(83) Appraisal of the estate of Nathaniel Edwards Jr dec'd. Included were negroes:

Abraham	Dinah	Hannah	Paymour
Batte	Dorcas	Jemmy	Will
Betty	man Essex	Ned	

Appraised by John Sims, William Randle, John Wallton. Returned to Court 25 Nov 1771.

66-(86) Will of George Carter   21 Apr 1771   25 Nov 1771
Of St Andrews Parish. "Sick and weak in Body"

To my son Charles - negro men Harry & Hal, sd Hal now in the possession of my brother John Carter; should sd Charles die before age 18, then I give sd Harry & Hal to my nephew John Carter son of my brother John; my friend James Hinton to take my sd son Charles into his care & sd negro Harry, to raise my son until my brother John Carter "is settled in such a manner as to take my Son home with him" & then sd John to "take my Son with his Children into his Care."

To my wife Lucy - negro girls Priss, Mill & Nan, & also woman Charity if she does not have to be sold to pay my debts; also 1 mare & colt, saddle & bridle, etc.

The remainder of my estate to be sold to discharge my debts & any remainder to go to my son Charles at age 18; should he die before then, then this to go to my nephew John the son of my brother John Carter.

Ex.   my friends James Wall Jr, James Hinton
Wit.   James Seeroant(?) Jones, James Hinton
Probate indicates that James Hinton refused to qualify but that James Wall Jr qualified with James Wall his security.

67-(87) Will of Adam(x)Sims   8 Dec 1770   25 Nov 1771
Of St Andrews Parish.

To my nephew William Sims the son of John Sims - the plantation where I now live.

To my granddaughter Winny Wyche - £140 or 3 negroes of that value, provided that at age 21 or marriage she agree to the division of her father's estate made by me, Douglass Wilkins & Edmund Wilkins; should she refuse, then the above legacy & other gifts then to go to my 2 granddaughters Rebecca Wilkins & Tabitha Wilkins.

To my granddaughters Rebecca Wilkins, Tabitha Wilkins & Winny Wyche - the residue of my estate.

Ex.   my brother John Sims, Douglass Wilkins, Edmund Wilkins
Wit.   William(x)Farguson, John Sisson, William Edwards
Probate indicates that the sd excrs qualified with Isaac Collier, William Sims, Daniel Nolly & Frederick Maclin their securities.

68-(88) Will of John(x)Price   11 Mar 1772   25 May 1772
Of St Andrews Parish.
    To my daughter Mary Price - my mare, 1 feather bed & furniture, 1 dish, 6 plates, 1 basin.
    To my son Joseph - 1 red heifer 2 years old.
    To my daughter Kathrine Moss - 1 basin.
    To my son William - the rest of my estate & he to pay my debts.
Ex.   my son William Price
Wit.   William Harrison, Ishmael Dunn, Uriah Wright
Probate indicates that the sd excr qualified with Robert Powell & James Balfour his securities.

69-(89) Appraisal of the estate of Capt William Chapman dec'd 12 Mar 1771. Included were negroes:

lad America	boy Jimmy	boy Sam
boy Anthony	wench Little Lucy	girl Silvia
man Archer	wench Lucy	boy Solomon
wench Bess	girl Nan	wench Sue
wench Betty	wench Nan	land Titus
boy Charles	girl Patt	man Will
man Dick	wench Phebe	lad Woodley
lad George	man Roger	
man Jacob	wench Sall	

Also noted were wench Great Lucy & child. Appraised by John Clack, John Sims, William Randle.
Returned to Court 24 Feb 1772.

70-(91) Account 1767 - 1768 for Roger Smith dec'd by John Brewer admr. Returned to Court 24 Feb 1772.

71-(91) Will of Edmund(x)Huling   18 Feb 1772   24 Feb 1772
Of Meherin Parish. "Sick and weak"
    To my wife Mary Huling - all my lands, negroes, stock & household goods during her life, except Peter [&] Pegg & all their children, whom I give to William Betty son of Sarah Betty.
    To my granddaughter Elizabeth Love - all my lands, negroes, stock & household goods that I have given to my sd wife for her life.
    My executor to keep Peter & Pegg & sd Pegg's children until sd William Betty is age 18.
Ex.   friend Hugh Love
Wit.   Nathan Hall, Solomon(x)Wright, Edmond(x)Davis
Probate indicates that the sd excr qualified with Allan Love his security.

72-(92) Appraisal of the estate of the Rev John Nevison dec'd 6 Dec 1769. Included were slaves(13 males & 15 females):

Ben	Cynthia	Gundy	Jacob
Cate	Dick	Isaac	Jammie
Chocolet	Easter	Jack	Joe

Joe	Murreah	Rose	Tabb
Lucy	Patience	Sarah	Willas
Mary	Pegg	Solomon	
Moses	Phillis	Southy	

also Flora & her child Nanny. A large number of books were catalogued. Appraised by William Fanning, Daniel Fisher, William Edwards. Returned to Court 24 Feb 1772.

73-(97) Appraisal of the estate of Stephen Sisson. Included were negroes: boy George, fellow Jack, girl Jenny, boy Joseph, wench Mary, as also 1 girl (not named). Returned to Court 24 Feb 1772.

74-(98) Appraisal of the estate of Simon Clack dec'd 23 Mar 1771. Appraised by John Peebles Sr, George(x)Anderson, James Tomlinson. Returned to Court 24 Feb 1772.

75-(99) Account of the debts paid out of the estate of Christopher Clinch dec'd 1769 - 1770. Named:

John Ballard	Daniel Fisher	Peter Read
James Belcher	John Gray	James Reavis
James Bird	William Holloway	James Day Ridley
Brown	John Jude	Robinson
William Brown	Charles Judkins	Elizabeth Rose
John Carter	William Kimball	William Smith
Clinch	John Lashly	William Stith
Henry Davis	Allen Love	Charles Turnbull
Bowler Dobbins	David Mason	Robert Turnbull
Thomas Clanton	William Mosely	Thomas Harris Williams
James Dyer	Henry Nicholson	Lewis Williamson
Thomas Eaton	John Pearson	Jeremiah Wilson
John Flood Edmunds	Thomas Peete	James Wortham
Nathl Edwards& Son	James Read	
William Evans		

Account of the estate of Christopher Clinch dec'd by Mary Clinch admrx. Named:

Thomas Clanton	William Green	Matthew Myrick
Harwood Clary	Richard Hartwell	John Newell
Edward Clinch	William Holloway	David Reavis
Daniel Coleman	William Huff	James Reavis
William Cook	William Jean	William Smith
Bowler Dobbins	Isaac Ledbetter	Edward Tatum
Gray Edmunds	William Ledbetter	Richard Tilman
Thomas Eaton	James Linch	Thomas Weaver
William Evans	Benjamin Mosely Sr	John Whitby
Martin Forester	Isaac Mosely	Jeremiah Wilson
Briggs Goodrich	Samuel Mosely	
Lucy Gray	William Mosely	

Returned to Court 24 Feb 1772.

76-(101) Appraisal of the estate of Adam Sims dec'd. Included were negroes:

boy Abraham	boy Donum	man Mingo
girl Aggy	man Donum	girl Phillis
boy Ben	boy Fed	boy Stewart
girl Betty	girl Grace	man Tom
boy Cato	boy Harris	man Toney
man Dick	boy Isham	boy Will
woman Dinah	man Jack	woman Zays
boy Doctor	woman Lucy	

Appraised by Francis Young, Joseph Peebles, John Peebles Jr. Returned to Court 24 Feb 1772.

77-(105) Account for the estate of John Howard dec'd by John Ballard admr. Named:

Richard Baker	William Elliott	John Peirce
Elizabeth Belshire	Richard Hardie	Person & Norfleet
William Bennitt	Daniel Harring	Batte Peterson
Edward Cary	Amos Horton	William Peterson
Peter Clark	Robert Howard	Matthew Pope
William Dixon	John McClary	Reuben Wood
Howell Edmunds	Mrs Frances Nelson	George Wyche
Nathl Edwards & Son	John Peebles	
William Edwards	John Peebles Jr	

Noted was that Kathrine Howard was orphan of John Howard; noted also was the widow. Included was quitrents on 347 acres for 1767 - 1770; also an amount was paid to the clerk of York Co; Benjamin Bynum hired Frank.
Returned to Court 23 Mar 1772.

78-(106) Will of John Wrenn   8 Mar 1772   23 Mar 1772
"Sick and weak of Body"
    To my wife Mary - the choice of 1 feather bed & furniture, 1 woman's saddle, 1 chest, etc.
    To my 4 children by my first wife - negro wench Patt to be divided among them when my son Robert Wrenn is age 21 & the sd wench to be hired out until then.
    To my son Robert - 1 gun.
    The rest of my estate to be sold to discharge my debts.
Ex.   Burrel Grigg, Frederick Whittington
Wit.   Howell Whittington, Thomas(x)Wrenn, Charles(x)Davis
Probate indicates that sd Grigg refused to qualify & that sd Frederick Whittington qualified with John Whittington as security.

79-(108) Inventory of the estate of Peter Tatum dec'd. Appraised by Parham, Edward Tatum, Benjamin(x)Bass. Returned to Court 23 Mar 1772.

80-(108) Will of William(x)Doby   21 May 1763   23 Mar 1772
Of Albemarle Parish in Sussex Co.

To my wife Hannah - as much of my land as she can cultivate & the plantation I live on, during her life; also I lend to her negroes Mingo & Rose, etc.

My negro boy Frank who is in the possession of my brother-in-law Charles Gee Jr & my daughter Elizabeth Gee which I gave the possession of to Robert Hancocke dec'd "some years past" to descend to the estate of sd Robert Hancocke & that my sd daughter to be entitled to her part of the value of the sd boy as she is entitled to the other slaves in sd Hancocke's estate.

To my son-in-law John Dillard & to my daughter Mary Dillard - negro boy Arthur.

To my daughter Sarah Crowder & to my son-in-law James Crowder - I lend to them for life my negroes Lewis & Jane, & should my sd daughter have issue, then sd Sarah & James to be vested with the sd slaves.

To my grandson Nathaniel Doby - when he is of age I give him my negro boy Simon, but should he have no issue, then sd Simon to go to my son John.

To my son John - all 320 acres where I now dwell; also my negroes Sue, Moll, Jack & Villag...?, as also the 2 negroes I have lent my wife after her decease, namely Mingo & Rose as also my 2 negroes I have lent to my son-in-law James Crowder & his wife for life, namely Lewis & Jane, provided my sd daughter should die without issue; also all the rest of my estate & he to pay my debts.

Other legacies & provisions.

Ex.   my wife, my son John Doby

Wit.   David Mason, Mary Mason, Henry Gee, John Rives

Probate indicates that Hannah Doby refused to qualify; John Doby qualified with William Edwards & Christopher Mason his securities.

81-(111) Inventory of the personal estate & negroes of William Doby dec'd 15 Apr 1772. Included were 12 negroes:

Amy	Jean	Mingo	Simon
Arthur	Kitt	Moll	Tom
Frank	Lewis	Rachel	
Jack			

Signed by John Doby excr. Returned to Court 27 Apr 1772.

82-(111) Appraisal of the estate of Edward Huling dec'd 10 Apr 1772. Included were negroes:

boy Abraham	boy Hampton	woman Peg
girl Amy	girl Hannah	man Peter
boy Arthur	wench Hannah	girl Pheby
fellow Cato	woman Hannah	girl Phillis
man Ceasar	woman Hester	man Primus
boy Daniel	boy Jemmy	boy Tom
boy Dick	boy Joe	man Will
girl Dinah	girl Milly	

Appraised by Silvanus Stokes, Charles Floyd, Thomas Merriott. Returned to Court 27 Apr 1778.

83-(113) Will of John Peebles   24 May 1770   27 Apr 1772
Of Meherrin Parish.

To my son Henry - the land & plantation where I now live; also my negro man Hall, 1 bed, etc; he to take possession of his estate at age 20.

To my son John - 165 acres which is part of my 538 acre tract.

To my daughter Sarah Jordon - negro wench Hannah provided she pay my daughter Mary Collier £25 VA.

To my wife Frances - 1 feather bed & furniture, 1 side saddle & bridle, a horse; lend to her negro wench Old Hannah as long as she is in Brunswick Co & at her decease or removal I give the sd negro to my son Robert.

My executors to build a house 12' x 16' for my wife "not far distant from the House I now live in," & that she have sufficient cleared land to tend with 1 hand; etc.

The rest of my estate to be sold & the money divided among my sons Robert, Ephraim, Samuel & George Catoe.

Other legacies & provisions.

Ex.   my sons Robert & Henry Peebles
Wit.   James Wall, John(x)Rosser
Probate indicates that Henry Peebles refused to qualify; Robert Peebles qualified with Benjamin Bynum & David Hines his securities.

84-(114) Appraisal of the estate of Martha Embry dec'd. Appraised by Richard Burch, Richard Burch Jr, John Ingram. Returned to Court 27 Apr 1772.

85-(115) Sale of the estate of Martha Embry dec'd 25 Apr 1771. Signed by John Coleman admr. Returned to Court 27 Apr 1772.

86-(115) Will of Edward Smith   28 Mar 1772   27 Apr 1772

To my wife Tabitha - lend to her for life negro wench Sarah, wench Cato, wench Suck, girl Nan, girl Amy, boy Simon; also 6 cows, a steer, 4 feather beds & furniture, etc; & after her death to be divided among my children Richard, Benjamin, Edward, Elizabeth, Sarah, Rebecca, Lucy, Tabitha, & Hannah; also lend to my wife my plantation where I now live & after her death to be divided among my 3 sons Richard, Benjamin & Edward.

To my daughter Mary Moore - 5 shillings.

Frank, Lewis, Peter & Phil & all my other estate are to be sold, my debts paid, & the remainder divided among my aforesaid children Richard, Benjamin, Edward, Elizabeth, Sarah, Rebecca, Lucy, Tabitha & Hannah.

Ex.   my wife Tabitha Smith, my sons Richard & Benjamin Smith
Wit.   William Price, William Harrison, John Maclin Jr, Joseph(x)Tompkins
Probate indicates that sd Tabitha Smith & Benjamin Smith qualified with William Harrison & Nathaniel Malone their securities.

87-(116) Will of John(x)Threadgill   16 Sep 1771   27 Apr 1772
Of St Andrews Parish. "Sick and weak of body"

To by wife Annabel - lend to her all my cattle, my grey mare, my hogs, etc, during her widowhood; I lend to her my plantation for her life.

To my sons William & John - my land joining the river upon their paying £24 to Randolph Threadgill & George Threadgill.

To my son Thomas - the first colt of the grey mare.

To my son George - my sorrel mare.

To my son Randolph - my grey mare after my wife's death or marriage.

To my daughter Elizabeth Stone - 2 sheep.

The rest of my estate I lend to my wife during her life or widowhood & then to be divided among my 5 sons William, John, Thos, Randolph & George.

Ex.   my wife, my sons William & John Threadgill

Wit.   William Gee, William Watson, George(x)Steagall

Probate indicates that William Threadgill qualified with John Threadgill & George Twitty securities.

88-(118) Will of Richard Burch   6 Feb 1764   27 Jul 1772
Of St Andrews Parish.

To my wife Jane - my household golds, cattle & hogs; lend to her slaves Harry & Bess for life.

To my son Richard Burch Jr - 254 acres where I now live, my water mill; negroes Jack, Sarah & Jemmy, & negro woman Bess.

To my daughter Mary Mason - negroes Humphrey, Hannah, Frank, Harry, Sarah, & Tony.

To my daughter Elizabeth Lanier - negroes Lucy, Hannah, Philic & Judy; also negro man Harry after her mother's decease.

Other legacies & provisions.

Ex.   Richard Burch Jr, Charles Mason & Wm Lanier

Wit.   Thomas Stith, John(x)Mason, George Clayton, Richd Elliot, William Merritt

Probate indicates that Richard Burch & Charles Mason qualified with Richard Mason & Thomas(?) Butler their securities.

89-(120) Account 1770 for the estate of Richard Sullivant by John Ballard Jr admr. Returned to Court 27 Jul 1772. Named: William L...?. Returned to Court 27 Jul 1772.

90-(120) Inventory of the estate of Richard Sullivant 16 Apr 177 by John Ballard Jr admr. Returned to Court 27 Jul 1772.

91-(121) Account 1762 for the estate of Hinchey Mabry. Named:

Thomas ...?	Charles Duncan	Anne Mabry
Joseph Bishop	Simon Foster	Burwell Lucy
Russell Blackley	Briggs Goodrich	Daniel Mabry
Nicholas Blanks	Edward Goodrich	James Mabry Jr
Patt Bradley	Samuel Gordan	Joel Mabry
John Clack	Thomas Gunn	Joshua Mabry
Thomas Collier	Henry Harris	Nathaniel Mabry
William Connelly	Thos Jackson	Frederick Macling
Isham Daniel	John Jones	James Macling
John Taylor Duke	John Knight	Isham Moore

Henry Morriss	John Ragsdale	James Troter
Parham's excrs	John Rivers	Wood Tucker
Matthew Parham	John Roberson	John Williamson
David Peoples	William Roberson	Joseph Williamson
John Peoples	Moses Smith	John Willie
Joseph Peoples	William Thornton	
John Petway	John Tilman	

Also noted was Old Juno. Returned to Court 27 Jul 1772.

92-(123) Account 1757 of the estate of Michael Wall dec'd by Rebecca Hall admrx. Named:

James Bennett	Joseph Hensley	Wm Verell
John Bruce	John Jackson	Maj James Wall
Joseph Carter	Harwood Smith	John Wall
John Chapman	Stith & Clack	John Wall Jr dec'd
Dunlop & Co	Littleton Tazewell	Benjn Waller
Christopher Gadsden	John Tompson	

Also noted was the personal estate in South Carolina. Audited 27 Jan 1772 by David Mason. Returned to Court 27 Jul 1772.

93-(125) Appraisal of the estate of James Goodrum dec'd. Included was negro man Charles. Appraised by Thomas Lanier, Joseph Carter, William Brent. Returned to Court 27 Jul 1772.

94-(127) Appraisal of the estate of John Price dec'd 22 Jul 1772. Appraised by Wm Harrison, Jesse Edwards, Joseph Wilkes. Returned to Court 27 Aug 1772.

95-(128) Will of William Davis   17 Sep 1771   24 Aug 1772
"Sick in body"

To my wife Martha - the use of my land while she is single until my son John Davis is age 21 & then I lend to her half of my sd land during her life or widowhood; also lend to her negroes Jo & James during her life or widowhood & then they to be sold & the money divided among my children.

To my son John - half my land when he is age 21 & after the death or marriage of my wife I give him the other half of my land; also negro girl Tab at age 21.

To my daughter Nancy Davis - negro girl Grace at age 18.

To my daughter Mary Davis - negro girl Dinah at age 18.

The residue of my estate after my debts are paid I lend to my wife during her life or widowhood.

I appoint my wife Martha Davis guardian to my 3 children, namely, John, Nancy & Mary.

Other provisions.

Ex.   my wife, my brother Benjamin Davis

Wit.   Amy(x)Tompson, Dedmund Row, John Jones

Probate indicates that the sd widow renounced all right under the will, that Moses Quarles & Peter Tompson were her securities, & an order for letters of administration with the will annexed was given.

96-(129) An additional account of the estate of Hinchey Mabry dec'd. Named:

Alexander	William Gower	John Ogburn
Peter Blan	Harrison	Parham's excr
Pat Bradley	Jackson	Butts Parham
Gray Briggs	Thomas Jackson	John Peeples
Philip Burrow	Richard Kelto	William Roberson
John Butts	Lewis Lanier	Henry Simmons
William Davis	Daniel Mabry	Joseph Tatum
Charles Duncan	Nathaniel Mabry	Daniel Weldon
Robert Gee	John Maclin	
Abell Gower	Henry Morriss	

Returned to Court 28 Sep 1772.

97-(131) Will of William(x)Wood   5 Feb 1772   28 Sep 1772
"sick of body"
    My debts should be paid. My plantation, negroes, stock & household furniture should be sold & equally divided among all my children.
Ex.   my son William Wood
Wit.   Henry Haley, Ben Bynum, John Medearis, James Haley
Probate indicates that the sd excr qualified with Haley Dupree & Ben Bynum his securities.

98-(132) Account 1760 for John Ingram Jr dec'd by Mrs Elizabeth Steagall excrx. Named:

Dr Courtney	Jeremiah Ingram	William Mitchel
Benjamin Ingram	Salley Ingram	Alexander Pool
George Ingram	William Ingram	John Tippit
Hannah Ingram	Allen Love merchant	
James Ingram		

Included were negroes: Tom age 10; the hire of Jane for 7 years; the hire of Sue for 6 years.
Audited by William Thornton, John Jones, William Clack. Returned to Court 28 Sep 1772.

99-(133) Will of John Williams   28 Feb 1770   23 Nov 1772
Of Meherrin Parish.
    To my son Frederick - 5 shillings sterling.
    To my son James - £10 at age 21.
    To my son John - £10 at age 21.
    To my daughter Susannah Williams - a feather bed & furniture & a cow & a calf at age 21 or she marries.
    To my son William - £10 at age 21.
    To my son Silas - £10 at age 21.
    To my daughter Betsey Williams - a feather bed & furniture & a cow & a calf at age 21 or she marries.
    To my wife Elizabeth - lend to her for life or widowhood the residue of my estate of every kind; after her decease, my lands, negroes, livestock & all my estate to be sold & the money divided

among my surviving children excepting my son Frederick.
Ex.   my wife Elizabeth, my son James, William Brown
Wit.   Hugh Love, Allan Love, John Matthis
Probate indicates that James Williams & William Brown qualified 24 Nov 1778 with Reuben Nance & John Minter their securities.

100-(135) Will of George Rives   19 Dec 1772   25 Jan 1773
Of Meherrin Parish.
    All my lands are to be sold.
    To my son Benjamin - negro man Peter, girl Fib.
    To my son William - negro man Roger, girl Winney, £110, 1 feather bed & furniture.
    To my daughter Franke Rives - negro woman Diner, boy Dick, £30 VA.
    To my wife Sarah - the use of the residue of my estate both real & personal during her widowhood & then to be divided among all my children Elizabeth Massey, Ann Peeples, Ben Rives, William Rives, Franke Rives.
    My children to be free at age 16 & to possess their estate at that age.
Ex.   my son-in-law Wm Massey, my son Wm Rives
Wit.   William Fox, Thomas Massey, Benjamin Sykes
Probate indicates that William Massey qualified with Wm Edwards & Benja Sykes his securities.

101-(137) Appraisal of the personal estate & slaves of Wm Davis dec'd as by court order dated 28 Sep 1772. Included were negro woman Jeen, Joe, Grace, Tabb. Appraised by Charles Collier, Vines Collier, Josiah Smith. Returned to Court 23 Nov 1772.

102-(138) Will of John Lifsey   17 Jul 1772   23 Nov 1772
Of Meherrin Parish. "Sick and week of body"
    To my son Benjamin - my right to an entry of land joining the late Robt Jones Esqr, Drury Cook, & William Powell; also £50, my negro man George.
    To my son Wm - the plantation where my father formerly lived with the tract where I now live joining Thos Smith & Thos Morris; also my negro boy Harry.
    To my son John - the plantation where I now live with the land not before bequeathed to my son Wm; also to my son John I give my negro Anthony.
    To my daughter Anne - my negro girl Rachell.
    To my daughter Rebeckah - my negro Jamey, but should my sd daughter die without issue, then the sd negro to be returned to my estate to be divided among my children.
    To my daughter Jane - my negro girl Judy, boy Taffey, after my debts are paid.
    To my wife - the residue of my estate real & personal during her lifetime in order to maintain & educate my children; after her decease, the sd estate to be divided among my surviving children.
Ex.   my wife, my son Benjamin Lifsey, my friend Dr James Day Ridley
Wit.   James Day Ridley, John Wyche, Archd Dancey
Probate indicates that Marthy Lifsey & Jas Day Ridley qualified to execute with James Balfour & David Mason their securities.

103-(140) Will of John(x)Denton   24 Nov 1772   28 Dec 1772
Of St Andrews Parish. "sick and week"

My debts are to be paid. My lands, stock, & the rest of my estate are to be sold & the money put to interest & divided among my children as they arrive at age 21: My sons Jessee, John, Benjamin & James Denton.

Ex.   John Whittington, Thomas Denton, James Maclin
Wit.   Benjamin Goodrich, Mary(x)Renn, Rebecca(x)Prince
Probate indicates that the sd excrs qualified with Charles Williamson, Benjamin Goodrich & Daniel Fisher their securities.

104-(141) Appraisal of the estate of George Carter dec'd 22 Jan 1772. Included were negroes Harry, Hannah, Charity & her child, Priss, Milley. Appraised by James Wall, William Parham, Charles Lucas. Returned to Court 25 Jan 1772.

105-(145) Appraisal of the estate of Benjamin Edwards. Appraised by John Dugger Sr & Benjamin Bennett. Returned to Court 25 Jan 1773.

106-(146) Appraisal of the estate of John Wmson dec'd 11 Dec 1772. Appraised by James Wall, Wm Brewer, John(x)Rosser. Returned to Court 25 Jan 1773.

107-(147) Account for the estate of Benjamin Edwards dec'd by John Edmunds admr. Named:

Benjamin Blick	Henry Fort	Richd Kirkland
Charles Edwards	Benjamin Hargrove	Benjamin Proctor
Edward Fisher	John Jones	Francis Young
Mr Fisher	Kenneday	

Returned to Court 23 Jan 1773.

108-(147) Will of Thomas Blick   14 Jul 1762   23 Mar 1773
Of Dinwiddie Co.

To my wife Mary - all my estate both real & personal & she to pay my debts.
Ex.   my wife
Wit.   Peter Jones, Charles Butterworth, Robert Birchett
Probate indicates that Charles Butterworth deposed that he signed a document but that sd Thomas Blick did not state that it was his will; thus the will was proved by Peter Jones 26 Apr 1773 where the sd excrx qualified with Isaac Marshall & Scarbrough Penticost as her securities.

109-(148) Will of William(x)Davis   23 Mar 1773   26 Apr 1773

To my son William - the land I now live on; also negro fellow Jack, wench Tab.

To my son Charles - my negro wench Lusey, boy Frank.

The rest of my negroes to be divided among John Davis, Federick Davis, Jessee Davis, Thomas Davis, Patty Rosser; the rest of my estate to be divided between William Davis & Charles Davis.
Ex.   William & Charles Davis
Wit.   David Rosser, Ben Cheatham, Eads Smith

Probate indicates that William Davis qualified with John Brewer & Benjamin Rives as his securities.

110-(148) Will of Richard Brown   16 Feb 1773   26 Apr 1773
Of St Andrews Parish. "sick and weak in body"

 To my wife Frances - lend to her negroes Robin, Moses & George, & the plantation I now live on during her life; give to her negroes Janey, Doll, Ding, Penny, Will & Tom; also give to her my household furniture, horses, cattle, hogs & sheep in Brunswick Co, & also all my stock on the plantation in North Carolina where my son Richard now lives.

 To my son William - give to him after my wife's decease negroes Robin.

 To my son Richard - negroes Simon & Burwell.

 To my son Lewis - the land I now live on & negro Moses, after my wife's decease; also give to him negroes Davy & Chaney.

 To my son Beverly - negro Jerry; also after my wife's decease I give him negro George.

 To my son John - negro Jack.

 To my daughter Jeaney Harrison - negro girl Dinah.

 To my daughter Sarah Daniel - negro girl June.

 To my daughter Sucky Butt - negro girl Mina.

 To my daughter Mary Sexton - negro girl Amey.

 To my daughter Francis Brown - negroes Judy, Ben & Winny.

 The remainder of my estate to be divided between my wife Francis & my son Lewis Brown.
Ex.   my wife Frances Brown, my son Lewis Brown
Wit.   Wm Richardson, Nathaniel Richardson, Thos Stith
Codicil. 16 Feb 1773. My daughter Elizabeth Wright & my daughter Edna Tarpley to be paid 1 shilling sterling each "and no more." Same witnesses.
Probate indicates that the sd excrs qualified with Thomas Stith & William Richardson as their securities.

111-(150) Will of Richard Cocke   2 Nov 1770   26 Apr 1773
Of Surry Co. "sick and weak"

 To my brother Thomas Cocke - my plantation in Brunswick; also my share of the profits from the store kept my William Edwards of Hicke's Ford under the firm of William Edwards & Company; should there be a loss in the sd trade, then the above land to be sold to pay my proportion.

 To my brother Lemuel Cocke - a mare, 1 bed & furniture left to me by my mother, my wearing apparel.

 To my sister Betty Lucas - my gray horse.

 To my uncle John Cocke - my silver watch.

 Any other of my estate to be divided between my 2 brothers Lemuel & Thomas & my sister Anne Cocke after my debts are paid. My negroes are to be kept on the plantation until my brothers & sisters come to age 21.
Ex.   John Cocke Jr, my brother Lemuel Cocke
Probate indicates that Lemuel Cocke qualified with James Buchanan, James Balfour & James Wall his securities.

112-(152) Inventory of the personal estate & negroes of George Rives dec'd 4 Feb 1773. Included were negroes: Dick, Dinah, Fib, Jame, Peter, Roger, Sam, Win.
Signed by William Massey. Returned to Court 26 Apr 1773.

113-(153) Appraisal of the estate of John Wren dec'd. Included was 1 negro wench (not named). Appraised by Thos Morris, Nathl Mabry, Benja Williams. Returned to Court 26 Apr 1773.

114-(154) Account 1769 of the estate of John Peterson dec'd by Batt & John Peterson excrs. Named:

John Avent	Daniel Fisher	Seymour Powell
Thos Bedingfield	Joshua Jones	Michael Roberts
John Bland	John Lovesey	Edward Rowell
John Brewer	Chiseland Morris	Thomas Smith
Miles Cary's estate	John Peoples	Thomas Thweat
William Cato	Batt Peterson	Wm Turner
James Dunlop	Briggs Peterson	William Vaughn
Wm Edmunds	Frances Powell	Saml Westbrook
Nathl Edwards & Son	Jno Peterson	John Wilkinson
Joseph Ellis	Mrs Peterson	
Wm Eppes		

also named was negro Sam. Noted was a sale in Southamton.
Audited by David Mason, James Wall. Returned to Court 26 Apr 1773.

115-(155) Will of John(x)Melton   26 Mar 1773   26 Apr 1773
Of St Andrews Parish. "sick and weak of body"
To my wife Mary - lend to her the land & plantation where I now live, with all the rest of my estate real & personal, during her lifetime or widowhood; after her decease the sd land, plantation & personal estate to be divided "amongst as many of my children as shall be then alive."
Ex.   Burrill Grigg, Henry Bailey
Wit.   Drury Stokes, Henry(x)Bailey

116-(156) Will of Samuel House   7 Aug 1769   24 May 1773
Of Meherrin Parish. "sick and weak"
To my wife Mary - the occupation & use of my plantation where I now live during her life or widowhood; at her decease or marriage, I give the sd land & plantation to my youngest son John; should he not arrive to age 21, then this legacy to be sold & the money divided between my 2 youngest daughters Rebecca House & Lucy House.
To my daughter Rebecca House - 1 feather bed & furniture.
To my daughter Lucy House - 1 feather bed & furniture.
Other provisions.
Ex.   my wife Mary House, my son Lawrence House, William House
Wit.   Xpher Mason, David Blalock, Isaac Roberson, James Williams
Probate indicates that the Mary House & Lawrence House qualified with William Williams & William Blalock their securities.

117-(158) Appraisal of the estate of Exum Williamson dec'd 17 Jun 1767. Included were negroes:

David	Ned	Primus	Silvey
Hannah	Patience	Rose	Tim
Judey	child Peter	Sall	
Moses			

Appraised by Urvin Brown, Nathl Hicks, Benjamin(x)Rives. Returned to Court 24 May 1773.

118-(159) Will of Daniel Carrell   3 Apr 1773   24 May 1773

To my son George - 1 coat & "westcoat."

To my grandson Daniel Carrell - 1 coat & "westcoat."

To my wife Sandal - all my estate consisting of livestock & 1 horse, beds, furniture, etc, with my whole estate, during her lifetime & after her decease to fall to Peter Goodwin.

Ex.   Mark Jackson, Henry Jackson Jr

Wit.   Henry(x)Jackson Sr, Mary(x)Jackson

Probate indicates that the sd excrs refused to qualify & that administration with the will annexed was granted to Peter Goodwin with Henry Jackson Sr his security.

119-(160) Will of John Batten(x)Dobyns   26 Oct 1772   22 Mar 1773

Of St Andrews Parish.

To my son John - 100 acres where I now live joining Mathews, Martin & Williams, 1 feather bed & furniture, on condition that he pay to my cousin Frances or Jessee Brumbelow £7.

To my son Moses - my plantation of 100 acres where I now live joining Stith & Atkinson, 1 bed & furniture & 1 mare, & he pay to his sister Anne £3.

To my son Charles - 100 acres between the lands given to my above named sons, 1 bed & furniture, & he to pay to his sister Rachel £3.

To my daughter Anne - the bed & furniture I now lie on.

To my daughter Rachel - 1 bed & furniture.

To my daughter Betty - £2s10.

The rest of my estate to be sold & divided among my following children: John, Moses & Charles.

Ex.   my 2 sons John & Moses Dobyns, Hugh Williams

Wit.   Mary(x)Wright, John Wright, Richard Littlepage

Probate indicates that Moses Dobbins qualified with John Duggar his security, that John Dobbins & Hugh Williams refused to qualify; a further probate action took place 26 May following.

120-(161) Will of Robert Nicholson   6 May 1773   28 Jun 1773

My land & plantation where I now live on Couches Run to be sold & the money applied to pay my debts.

To my niece Martha Stith - negro girl Temp.

To my wife Rebecca - to have the use of the rest of my estate both real & personal until the child she is now pregnant with comes to age &, if a son, then I bequeath to him 727 acres in Mecklenburg Co on both sides of Collin Creek, but if a daughter then the sd land to be divided between my wife & my sd daughter; if either a son or a daughter, then my slaves & personal estate to be divided between my wife & my sd child at lawful age after my debts are paid; should the sd child die before

lawful age, then I give to my wife Rebecca all my estate real & personal.
Ex.   my friend Thomas Stith, my wife Rebecca
Wit.   Elizabeth Stith, Mariania Stith, Thos Stith
Probate indicates that the sd excrs qualified with Nathaniel Harrison, Alexander Watson, Frederick Burdge & Buckner Stith Jr their securities.

121-(162) Will of Judith Thweatt   12 Oct 1770   28 Jun 1773
"very sick"

     To my daughter Mary Brown - my right to the 2 negroes Mathew & Anthony that my husband John Thweatt left my daughter Mary.

     To my daughter Elizabeth Birchett - my right to the negro wench Doll that my husband John Thweatt left my daughter Elizabeth.

     To my granddaughter Frances Brewer - negro boy Peter.

     To my granddaughter Nancy Goodwin - negro boy Ned.

     To my daughter Elizabeth Birchett - my negro wench Moll.

     To my son-in-law Urvin Brewer - the balance of his account to me "for to be an Equal part in my Funeral Expences."

     To my daughter Judith Goodwin - the residue of my estate real & personal.
Ex.   James Goodwin
Wit.   Isham Lundy, Elizabeth(x)Foster, Benja(x)Rives
Probate indicates that the sd excr qualified with William Battes his security.

122-(164) Appraisal of the estate of William Davis dec'd as by court order 26 Apr 1773. Included were negroes:

wench Beck	fellow Jack	girl Rachel
Bett	wench Jane	Sela
Daniel	wench Lucy	wench Tabb
boy Frank	wench Moggy	boy Will
Harry	girl Phibe	

Appraised by David Rosser, Eades Smith, Ben Cheatham. Returned to Court 28 Jun 1773.

123-(166) Account of the estate of Thomas Vinson dec'd by Zebulin ...? admr. Named:

John Atkinson mercht	Daniel Fisher	John Tomlinson
Jno Ballard	David Mason	Arthur Turner
William Batts	John Peoples	James Wall Jr
Richard Bell	Purdie & Dixon	Joseph Williamson
Daniel Catoe	Jno Rives	Robert Williamson
Wm Cook	Michael Roberts	George Wyche
Edwards & Company	Major Tiller	Peter Wyche
William Evans	James Tomlinson	

Audited by Wm Clack, Fredk Maclin. Returned to Court 28 Jun 1773.

124-(167) Account for the estate of Martha Embry dec'd by Jno Coleman admr. Named: Roger Atkinson, John Coleman, Thos Edmunds, Robert Lucy, Rev Mr Lundie, Jno Wilkinson, Frank Woodow.

    Returned to Court 26 Jul 1773.

125-(168) Will of Peter(x)Adams   23 Apr 1773   26 Jul 1773
Of St Andrews Parish.

    To my wife Ann - I give to her all my estate after my debts are paid except my land & negroes; I lend to her the use of my land & negroes during her lifetime.

    To my nephew William Adams - all my land provided he lives to have an heir, but if he should die without an heir, then I give the same to Frederrick Maclin & his brothers John, Thomas & William Maclin.

    To Elizabeth Maclin wife of James Maclin - negro boy Joe.

    To Amey Clements wife of Thomas Clements of Sussex Co - negro girl Christian.

    To Frederick Maclin & his 3 brothers John, Thomas & William Maclin - the remainder of my negroes, being Hannah, Doll, Arter, Charles, Bob & Bowling, after the death of my wife.

Ex.   my wife Ann Adams, Frederick Maclin, Thomas Maclin
Wit.   Benja Simmons Sr, William Redding, Jesse Butts

126-(169) Will of Arthur Dellihay   (no date)   23 Aug 1773
Of St Andrews Parish.

    To my wife Sarah - my whole estate real & personal during her widowhood.

    To my sons John & Edmond - my land after the decease or widowhood of my wife Sarah.

    To the unborn child - if a son, then my land to be divided among the 3.

    To my daughters - my personal estate after the decease or widowhood of my wife.

Wit.   John B. Goldsberry, Ichabod Marchall, Thomas Parrish
Probate indicates that Edward Tatum was granted administration with the will annexed with Sarah Dellilhay & Wm Brent his securities.

127-(170) Appraisal of the estate of Daniel Carrell dec'd. Appraised by Benja Harrison Jr, John Brewer & James Harrison. Returned to Court 23 Aug 1773.

128-(171) Appraisal of the estate of Thomas Blick dec'd 8 May 1773. Included were negroes: wench Nann, man Sharper, young wench Suck, man York.

    Appraised by John Clack, Edward Robinson, Robert Hicks. Returned to Court 23 Aug 1773.

129-(173) Sale of the estate of Simon Clark dec'd 1771. Buyers:

George Anderson	Peter Clarke	Justain Knot
Wm Bennitt	Robert Clarke	Henry Mitchell
Benja Bynum	Winifred Clarke	Jno Peoples
Sterlling Catoe	Wm Edwards	Robert Peoples
Henry Clarke	John Jeter	Wm Pride
Joshua Clarke	Jno Johnson	James Rosser

James Tomlinson   James Vinson
Jno Turner   Wm Wren
Returned to Court 23 Aug 1773.

130-(175) Account 1771 for the estate of Simon Clarke by Justain Knott admr. Named:

George Anderson	Joshua Clarke	Robert Peoples
William Brewer	Wm Edwards	James Tomlinson
Sarah Brooks	Mary Fennell	Capt Jno Turner
Henry Clarke	Jno Johnson	

Audited by Tho Stith, James Maclin. Returned to Court 23 Aug 1773.

131-(175) Appraisal of the estate of James Harwell dec'd 2 Mar 1771. Included were slaves:

child Anthony	Dinah	James	Sambo
Bess	Fanny	Moll	Stafford
Bett	Frank	Ned	Younger
child Bob	Godfrey	Peter	
Dick	Goliak	Pheby	

& also Linda & her child Daphney. Appraised by Allan Love, Hezekiah Thower, Thomas Bracey, John Barner. Returned to Court 23 Aug 1773.

132-(178) Account 1770 for the estate of James Harwell dec'd by Samuel Harwell admr. Named:

Jesse Abernathy	James Harwell	Nathaniel Megs
Thomas Betty	Mark Harwell	William Merritt
Benjamin Blick	Mason Harwell	Mrs Richard Morris
Gray Briggs	Mourning Harwell	Anne Pattillo
Jere Brown	Richard Harwell	Austin Pattillo
Neil Buchanan Sr	Sally Harwell	Nancy Pattillo
Mathew Carlos	Alexander Horsburgh	Benjamin Pennington
Charles Collier	Henry Jackson	John Robertson
Thomas Crawford	James Jackson	William Robertson
Mary Davis	Wm Jeans	Charles Simons
Alexander Donald	Michael Jones	John Steed
John Douglass	William Jones	Thomas Stith
William Douglass	George Lang	Richard Taylor & Co
Martha Gladish	Buckner Lanier	George Twitty
Thomas Harrison	David Lanier	R. Walker
Betsey Harwell	Lemuel Lanier	William Walker
Cassandra Harwell	Richard Locke	Alexander Watson
Elizabeth Harwell	John Loftain	Joshua Winfield
Frederick Harwell	William Loyd	
Greif Harwell		

Noted was 1140 acres. Audited by Tho Stith, John Clack, Ben Hicks. Returned to Court 23 Aug 1773.

133-(181) Will of David(x)Sims   29 Jun 1773   27 Sep 1773

My lands on the north side of Grassey Pond road that leads to the court house to be sold to discharge my debts.

To my wife Elizabeth - lend to her all my lands on the south side of the Grassey Pond road that leads to the court house during her life & after her death to be sold & then divided between all my children; also lend to my sd wife all my negroes during her life, reserving a maintenance for all my children as long as they live with her or are single & after her death to be divided between all my children.

Other provisions.

All 4 of my sons are to be bound out & 2 of them to a "chear maker." All my children are to be schooled & my 4 sons "to be well schooled."

Ex.   William Sims, Edmund Wilkins

Wit.   William Malone, Anne(x)Malone, Nancy(x)Colleir

Probate indicates that the sd excrs refused to qualify & that administration with the will annexed was granted to James Mason with Daniel Fisher & Peter Pelham his securities.

134-(182) Will of William(x)Bishop   12 Aug 1771   27 Sep 1773

Of St Andrews Parish. "very sick & weak in body"

To my nephew John Bishop son of my brother James Bishop & his wife Mary - 90 acres that I now live on.

To my nephew James Bishop son of my brother James Bishop - my long gun.

To John Lawrence son of Jesse Lawrence - my Brunswick gun.

To William Dunn - 1 cow & calf, 2 pewter dishes, 6 pewter plate.

To Jarimy Bishop - all my wearing clothes & Virginia cloth.

To my sister-in-law Elizabeth Fawn - £5.

To my nephew the aforesd John Bishop son of my brother James Bishop - the remainder of my estate consisting of hogs, cattle, 2 mares, household furniture, plantation tools & money, & sd John Bishop is to pay my debts.

Ex.   my nephew John Bishop

Wit.   Thomas Morris, John Lawrence, Anness(x)Lawrence

Probate indicates that the sd excr qualified with Thos Morris & John Lawrence his securities.

135-(184) Account 1773 of the estate of Chs Edwards Jr dec'd. Named:

Joseph Andrews	John Clack	Joseph Peebles
Joseph Bennitt	widow Anne Edwards	Joseph Phipps
Reuben Bennitt	Mathew Edwards	William Smith(R Creek)
Thomas Blick	John Edwards Jr	Litt Stanback
Gray Briggs	Benjamin Haregrove	

Noted were the clerk & goaler of Dinwiddie. Returned to Court 27 Sep 1773.

136-(185) Account 1771 - 1772 for Capt Nathl Edwards dec'd by William Edwards excr. Named:

John Ambrose	Jno Bland	Theoderick Bland
Jno Ballard	Richard Bland	Niel Buchanan

Charles Buckner	Frederick Green	Mr Pendlton
Jesse Burnett	Andrew Hamilton	Walter Peter
Chapman	Jno Hamilton & Co	Procter
Benjamin Chapman	James Hinton	Dr James Day Ridley
Will Chapman	Peter Jackson	Robertson's excrs
Thomas Crawford & Co	John Jourdan	Edward Robinson
Cunningham & Co	Richard Kelly	Littleberry Robinson
William Edwards & Co	Nathaniel Laffoon	William Sims
Richard Elliott	Allan Love	Henry Taylor
Graves Eves	Hinchey Mabry	Jammy Wall Sr
Daniel Fisher	John Maclin	Peter Ware
Edward Fisher	Col Davis Mason	Augustine Willis
Thomas Gholston	William Mason	John Wray
Gilliam's excrs	Archd Middlemost	Young & Pocke
Briggs Goodrich	Peter Pelham Jr	

John Maclin [apparently] purchased negro boy Jammy; noted was the sheriff of Southampton; also noted was the estate of Col Nathl Edwards.

Audited by Wm Starke, D. Fisher, James Wall. Returned to Court 22 Nov 1773.

137-(187) Account 1763 for James Northcross dec'd. Named:

Jno Colleir	Mr Secretary Nelson	George Purdie
Isaac Edwards	Mary Northcross	Dr James Day Ridley
Richard Hanson	William Parham	Richard Taylor
Samuel Lucas	Walter Peter & Co	
Capt David Mason	Leonard Powell	

Joseph Burnett was guardian to Mary Northcross & Martha Northcross.

Noted was Leonard Powell who made the coffin & also a coffin for a little girl.

Audited by Wm Starke, D. Fisher, James Wall, as by court order dated 27 Sep 1773. Returned to Court 22 Nov 1773.

138-(187) Appraisal of the estate of Saml House dec'd 25 Jun 1773. Appraised by Jordan House, Hezekiah Thower, Ben Hicks. Returned to Court 22 Nov 1773.

139-(189) Will of John(x)Fennell   26 Oct 1768   22 Nov 1773
Of Meherrin Parish.

To my wife Elizabeth - the Quarter plantation & 5 negroes Patty, Will, Amy, Jacob & Rose, during her life & after that I give the sd land & negroes to my son Isham; also lend to my sd wife 5 cows, 2 feather beds & furniture, etc, for her lifetime & after that I give the same to my son Isham.

To my son Isham - the remainder of my estate after my debts are paid, provided he arrive to age 21 or marries; otherwise I devise all my estate to the elder son of my son Sith Fennell.

Ex.   my wife Elizabeth Fennell, my son Isham Fennell, John Dorson
Wit.   George Wall, William Wall, James Wall

140-(190) Will of Robert Read   25 Sep 1766   24 Jan 1774
Of Essex County.

The land my father William Read left me to be divided between my 2 brothers John & Lewis Read & my brother Lewis is to have the manor plantation.

To my sister Anner Read - negro woman Rhode.

To my sister Mary Read - negro boy James.

To my sister Susannah Mathis - negro boy David.

To my brother Jno - my riding horse, saddle & bridle, all my wearing apparel.

To my brother Lewis - my other horse.

To my sister Anner - my breeding mare.

To my sister Mary - my mare fold.

To William son of James Quarles, to Thomas son of William Read, to Catharine daughter of Thomas Manning, to Betty or Elizabeth daughter of William Mathis, & Molley Read daughter of Thomas Read - £5.

To my friend James Quarles - £5 VA.

The rest of my estate to be divided among John, Lewis, Anner & Mary Read.

To Susannah Mathis - my negro boy David.

Ex.   James Quarles
Wit.   Hugh Williams, Richard Ramsay, John Quarles

141-(191) Will of Thomas(x)Underwood   18 Oct 1773   24 Jan 1774
"very sick and Weak in Body"

To my wife Elizabeth - all my estate during her lifetime or widowhood & afterward then the sd land to my son[s] William & Sammons Underwood; William's to join the lower line of Tomlin's Run, Harrison, Second Branch, Drury Going, & all above that branch to belong to my son Sammonds.

Ex.   friend Richard Hay, my wife
Wit.   Edward(x)Freeman, Richard(x)Mason, Avey(x)Mason
Probate indicates that sd Elizabeth Underwood refused to qualify, that sd Richard Hay qualified with David Sills & Richard Mason his securities.

142-(192) Will of William Turner   28 Nov 1773   24 Jan 1774
Of St Andrews Parish. "Sic & weak of Body"

All my negroes now in possession to be kept on the plantation where I now live for 10 years beginning 1 Jan after this date & the profits therefrom to pay my debts & to support my wife & children.

After the term of 10 years, my estate is to be divided between my wife & my children John, Pattsey, Jennitt & Rebeccah by my 2 friends Jno Turner & Wm Peterson.

If the child my wife is now pregnant with is delivered, then the sd child to have the use of £200 from my estate after the above 10 year term.

Ex.   friends Jno Turner, Wm Peterson
Wit.   James Day Ridley, Richard Clifton, Nicholas(x)Smith
Probate indicates that the sd excrs qualified with Benja Bynum & Robt Dupree their securities.

143-(193) Account 1773 for the estate of Jno Underwood dec'd by James & Betty Solomon. Named:

David Adams	Jno Doby	Richard Massey
Jno Ballard	Nathl Edwards	Thomas Massey
Peter Brooks	Wm Edwards & Co	William Massey
Sarah Brooks	James Goen	Jno Peeblees
Clack Courtney	Richard Hay Jr	
Crawford & Co		

Noted was the sheriff of Mecklenburg. Audited by David Mason, Alexr Watson. Returned to Court 28 Feb 1774.

144-(194) Will of Thomas(x)Mitchell   1 Jan 1774   28 Feb 1774
"Weak in body"

 To my daughter Lucy Nolly - negro girl Sarah, woman Esther.

 To my son Locket - negro man Davey, boy Mingo, 175 acres where I now live.

 To my daughter Mary Mitchell - negro woman Aggy, girl Milley.

 To my daughter Dorothey Mitchel - negro woman Nutt, girl Little Moll.

 To my wife Ann - lend to her for life negro woman Moll; also £6 yearly for life for the hire of negro Jack or as long as the sd Jack should live to be paid by my son Locket, & then I give the sd Moll to my daughter Mary Mitchell.

 Other provisions.

Ex.   my son Locket Mitchell

Wit.   James Maclin, Joel Smith, Wm Raney

Probate indicates that the sd excr qualified with Peter Pelham Jr & ...miah(?) Nolly his securities.

145-(195) Will of Thomas Simmons   22 Jan 1774   28 Feb 1774
Of St Andrews Parish. "sick of Body"

 To my wife Ermine - Lewis, ...?.

 The remainder of my estate to be sold to pay my debts & the remainder divided among my wife Ermine, Henry & Benjamin Simmons.

Ex.   my wife Ermine, Henry & Benjamin Simmons

Wit.   Thos Lundie, Wm Edwards, Wm Short

Probate indicates that Henry Simmons & Benjamin Simmons qualified with Wm Edwards & Jno Flood Edmund their securities. On 26 Sep 1774, Ermine Simmons qualified with John Flood Edmunds & Henry Tazewell her securities.

146-(196) Sale of the estate of Phillip Penn dec'd by Thomas Penn admr. Buyers:

Bartholomew Dameron	Richard Lanier	Jno Read
Abner Greenwood	Mary Penn	David Roper
Jno Hightower	Moses Penn	Wm Tulley
Thos Hightower	Thomas Penn	Jeremiah Wright
Wm Holloway	James Quarles	Robt Wright
James Jones	Moses Quarles	

It was noted that Mary Penn bought 1 negro wench & child (not named), that Moses Penn bought

1 negro girl (not named). Returned to Court 28 Mar 1774.

147-(197) Appraisal of the estate of Philip Penn as by court order dated Sep 1773. Included were 1 negro girl, 1 negro wench & child (not named). Thomas Penn was admr. Appraised by Hugh Williams, Charles Mathis, David Roper. Returned to Court 28 Mar 1774.

148-(198) Appraisal of the estate of Richard Morris dec'd 23 Mar 1774. Included were negroes Batt & boy Ned. Signed by Susanna Morris admrx. Appraised by Tho Stith, Drury Stith, Nathl Burdge. Returned to Court 28 Mar 1774.

149-(200) Appraisal of the estate of Jno Williams dec'd as by court order dated 1763. Included were negroes: wench Betty, boy Dick, girl Doll, boy George, boy Jack, girl Judy, boy Matt, woman Meter, man Ned.
    Appraised by Wm Maclin, Jno Gresham, Jno Russell. Returned to Court 25 Apr 1774.

150-(201) Will of Robert(x)Clarke   (no date)   25 Apr 1774
"Sick and weak in Body"
    After my debts are paid, I wish that my estate "may Lie until my Youngest child comes of age" & then to be sold & divided, after my wife Susannah has her dower right, among my son[s] Willey, Robt, Mial, & my daughter Deliah Clarke.
Ex.   Haley Dupree
Wit.   Fredk Davis, Peter Clarke, Henry Clarke
Probate indicates that the sd excr qualified with John Brewer & Peter Clarke his securities.

151-(201) Account 1773 - 1774 for the estate of Thomas Blick dec'd by Scarbrough Penticost. Named:

Benja Blick	Thomas Johnson	Henry Morris
Charles Butterworth	Allan Love	Edward Robinson
Elisha Clarke	Rev Thomas Lundie	Thomas Stith
Charles Edwards	Federick Maclin	
Jno Edwards	Jno Mitchell	

Returned to Court 25 Apr 1774.

152-(202) Inventory of the estate of Jno Williams dec'd. Included were negroes: Betty, Dick, Doll, George, Jack, Jesse, Mater, Moll, Ned.
    Signed by Frances Bailey. Returned to Court 25 Apr 1774.

153-(202) Will of John Parker   21 Sep 1771   23 May 1774
"sick & weak in body"
    To my wife - the plantation & ordinary house of 100 acres where I now live, 2 feather beds & furniture, etc, during her life or widowhood, & out of the profits of the ordinary she shall erect a brick chimney in my dwelling place with a fire place in the sd chimney for each room; I give to her negro man Luck, 1 desk, etc.

All my land on both sides of Stoney Creek to be sold & the money divided among 4 of my children, namely, Elizabeth, John, Starling & Thomas, & the money to be at interest until they arrive at age.

To my daughter Elizabeth - negro girl Pheby at age.

To my son John - negro man Will who is to be hired out until my sd son is of age.

To my son Starling - negro man Young Eaton.

To my son Thomas - negro woman Rachel; if my lands on Stoney Creek are not sold, then Rachel to be sent there to the Quarter, but if my land is sold, sd Rachel to return to my wife for 4 years or to be hired out at my wife's decease until my son Thomas is of age.

To my son Sterling - the plantation of 100 acres & ordinary house where I now live after the decease or widowhood of my wife.

To my sons John & Thomas - 200 acres joining where I now live which I purchased from Rives, to be divided when they are of age.

To my son William - negro girl Patt now in his possession.

To my daughter Anne Rogers - negro girl Alse now in the possession of her husband Wm Rogers.

To my daughter Nancy - negroes Cate & Dick.

To Grief Birchett - £10 VA, provided my wife abides by this will.

To my son Wm - £10 VA from the sale of my Stoney Creek lands.

Negro boy Peter to be sold by my executors to go toward discharging my debts; the balance of my estate to be sold to discharge my debts & any remainder to go to my 4 children Elizabeth, John, Sterling & Thomas.

Other provisions.

Ex.   friend Thomas Rives
Wit.   Henry Edmunds, Tho Briggs, Moses Dobbins, Hensley Grubbs, Henry Briggs, Frederick Briggs, Thomas Edmunds

Probate indicates that the sd excr refused to qualify, that Jane Parker the widow renounced all benefit she might have under the sd will; the sheriff was ordered to take the estate "into his hands and Dispose of the same as the Law Directs."

154-(204)Will of John(x)Wray   11 May 1773   23 May 1774
Of Meherrin Parish. "weak of Body"

To my wife Frances - lend to her my best feather bed & furniture & my mare during her lifetime & then to be divided as follows:

To my son Nathaniel - 1 shilling.

To my son Jno - 1 shilling.

To my daughter Rebeccah Culver - 1 shilling.

The land where I now live & the residue of my estate to be sold & then as follows:

To my daughter Mary Wray - 50 shillings.

To my grandson Benjamin Wray - 50 shillings.

And the remainder to be divided between my wife Frances & the remainder of my children, namely, my son James Wray & my daughters Avas Miz'd & Edy Miz'd.

Should my mare prove with foal, then my wife to comply with my agreement with my neighbor

Jno Powell & deliver to him the foal of the sd mare at age 1 & sd Powell to pay 40 shillings.
    Other provisions.
Ex.   my son James Wray
Wit.   Benja Johnson, Jno Powell
Probate indicates that the sd excr qualified with Jeremiah Mize his security.

155-(205) Will of John(x)Ogborne   Jan 1774   23 May 1774
Of St Andrews Parish.
    To my son William - 150 acres joining Wm Stith, Beaver Pond Branch.
    To my son Jno - 150 acres joining Wm Stith, Benja Whiteley, John Ingram, bridge road.
    To my wife Tabitha - the use of the land & plantation where I now live, as also the use of negro wench Judy, & all my stock, tools, etc, all during her lifetime & after her death the sd land & plantation & wench Judy & stock, etc, to be divided among my sons James, Harry, Benjamin, Charles, & Mathew.
Ex.   my son William Ogborne & James Ogborne
Wit.   Peter Cocke, Benjamin Whiteley, John Niblett
Probate indicates that the sd excrs qualified with Wyatt Williams & Robt Moris their securities.

156-(206) Appraisal of the estate of Thomas Underwood dec'd 5 May. Signed by Richard Hayes Jr excr. Appraised by Thomas Burnett, Edward Freeman, Peter Freeman. Returned to Court 23 May 1774.

157-(206) Account for the estate of Benjamin Edwards dec'd by John Edwards. Named:

Blick	Benja Hargrove	Peter Pelham
Benjamin Blick	John Jones	Benjamin Procter
Charles Edwards	Kannedy	Henry Truett(?)
William Edwards	Richard Kirkland	Francis Young
Edward Fisher	James Mason	
Mr Fisher	Samuel Mason	

Returned to Court 27 Jun 1774.

158-(207) Will of Elizabeth Webb widow   12 Feb 1774   23 Jul 1774
    To my son Micah Webb - 1 feather bed & furniture, my negro boy Jacob.
    To my son John Webb - negro boy Brandon.
    Elizabeth Gilliam to have the use & labor of negro boy Sam during her lifetime & after her decease I give sd Sam to my grandson William Gilliam.
    My daughter Mary Birdsong to have the labor of my negro girl Fillis for her lifetime & after her decease I give sd Filis to be divided among my daughter Mary Birdsong's children.
    The remainder of my estate I give to be divided among my son John, my son Micah, & my daughter Elizabeth Gilliam.
    To my daughter Winford Boseman - my clothes; all the household goods & hogs, etc, that is in my daughter Winney Boseman's possession to be for her use & benefit during her lifetime & after her decease I give this to my granddaughter Winey Boseman.

Ex.   my son John Webb
Wit.   Drury Dunn, James Johnson, Joseph Harris
Probate indicates that the sd excr qualified with James Johnson & John Robinson his securities.

159-(209) Will of Joseph Andrews   20 May 1774   22 Aug 1774
Of St Andrews Parish. "Very sick and weake of Body"
    To my wife Elizabeth - 1 feather bed & furniture "whereon she lies," 1 iron pot & pot rack, etc.
    To my son John - my pistols & holsters, 1 small chest of drawers.
    To my son David - 1 set of blacksmith tools.
    The rest of my estate I leave to my wife during her life or widowhood & then to be divided
among my 3 youngest children Clabon, Mary & Jesse Andrews.
    To my daughter Hannah Barnes - 1 shilling.
    To my daughter Sarah Proctor - 1 shilling.
    To my son Benjamin - 1 shilling.
    To my daughter Anna - 1 shilling.
Ex.   my son John Andrews, my wife
Wit.   Thomas Procter, Mary Campbell, Elizabeth Page
Probate indicates that the sd excrs qualified with Thomas Procter & David Peoples their securities.

160-(211) Inventory of the estate of Thomas Mitchell dec'd by Lockett Mitchell. Included were negroes:

Agga	Jacky	Mingo	Sarah
Dava	Little Noll	Moll	
Ester	Milley	Nutt	

Returned to Court 22 Aug 1774.

161-(212) Appraisal of the estate of Thomas Read as by court order dated Feb 1774. Included were
negroes: Alicke, Bridget, Rochel, Sam.
    Sarah Read was admr. Appraised by Hugh Williams, Richard Ramsey, John Quarles. Returned
to Court 22 Aug 1774.

162-(214) Appraisal of the estate of Arthur Dillehay dec'd. Appraised by Benjamin Bass, Parham,
Nathaniel Tatum. Returned to Court 22 Aug 1774.

163-(215) Account for the estate of Thomas Person dec'd by Jesse Williamson admr. Named were
Secretary Nelson, Capt John Turner. Slaves were noted but not named.
    Returned to Court 22 Aug 1774.

164-(216) Inventory & sale of the estate of Charles Gordan dec'd with Nancey Gordan admr. Buyers:

Dudly Clarke	Abner Granwood	William Lanier
James Fisher	Mining Harrup	Wm Mathis
John Goalston	Richard Lanier	Jacob Miller
Elizabeth Gordan	Robin Lanier	Moses Quarles

| Thomas Richardson | Thomas Rieves | David Vaughn |
| William Rideout | Capt Buckner Stith | |

Signed by Thomas Richardson. Returned to Court 22 Aug 1774.

165-(217) Will of John Spraborough   15 Jul 1774   26 Sep 1774
"Very sick & weak in Body"

To my wife Jothen - lend to her all my movable estate that I do not give to my 2 sons James & John during her life & at her decease to go to my son Archulus.

To my son James - the plantation with 175 acres where he now lives; also 1 cow & calf, 1 feather bed & furniture.

To my son John - the remaining part of the land where my son James lives which will be 175 acres after my son Archelous has 50 acres from the tract; also 1 cow & calf, 1 feather bed & furniture.

140 acres of my land joining Batts, Joshua Dewberry & Brewer, to be sold & the money I lend to my sd wife.

To my daughter Ann Spraborough - 1 cow & calf, feather bed & furniture.

Ex.   my wife
Wit.   Rubin Addams, William Garner

Probate indicates that the sd excrx qualified with John Spraborough & William Garner her securities.

166-(219) Appraisal of the estate of Thomas Laurance. Appraised by Thomas Morris, Nathaniel Mabry, Henry Baley. Returned to Court 26 Sep 1774.

167-(220) Sale of the estate Thomas Laurance Sr 28 Nov. Buyers:

John Atkeison	Burrel Grigg	John Laurance
Henry Bailey	Frederick Grigg	James Mason
John Bishop	Benjamin Harrison	Isaac Melton
John Dungion	Laurance House	Limelick Sandifur
William Fryer	Ann Laurance	

Returned to Court 26 Sep 1774.

168-(222) Account 1773 of the estate of Thomas Laurance. Named were Richard Blanks, John Laurance admr, Richard Northross. Returned to Court 26 Sep 1774.

169-(223) Appraisal of the estate of John Denton 7 Jan 1773. Appraised by John Whittington, Thomas Denton, James Maclin. Returned to Court 26 Sep 1774.

170-(225) Account 1772 - 1773 for the estate of John Denton. Named:

James Balfour	John Hamilton	William Walker
Mary Cagebrook	James Maclin	Frederick Whittington
Thomas Denton	James Oliver	John Whittington
William Edwards	Rebeccah Prince	

Noted was the sheriff of Dinwiddie; quitrents paid on 417 acres; the sale of 274 acres; the sale of 140 acres.

    Audited by John Whittington, Thomas Denton, James Maclin. Returned to Court 26 Sep 1774.

171-(226) Account 1773 for the estate of John Wren dec'd by Frederick Whittington. Named:

John Atkeison	John Laurance	Benja Williams
Richard Cock	James Mason	Francis Wrenn
William Colony	Drury Stokes	Joel Wrenn
Rebeccah Corral	Penrod Vaughan	
Samuel Grigg	William Walker	

Returned to Court 26 Sep 1774.

172-(227) Appraisal of the estate of William Bishop 25 Jun 1774. Appraised by John Laurance, Benjamin Williams, Nathaniel Mabry. Returned to Court 26 Sep 1774.

173-(229) Will of John Maclin   8 Jun 1771   28 Nov 1774
Of St Andrews Parish.

    To my son Frederick - I confirm to him all former gifts that I have made him; also give to him negro man Sam, 1 colt, with the balance of his account.

    To my son John - I confirm to him all former gifts that I have made him; also give to him negro man Frank, a book case, a mare, with the balance of his account.

    To my son Thomas - I confirm all former gifts that I have made him; also give to him negro girl Fanny, a young mare, with the balance of his account.

    To my son-in-law Matthew Parham - I confirm all former gifts that I have made him & his wife Rebeca; also give to him the balance of his account.

    To my son-in-law James Maclin - I confirm all former gifts that I have made him & his wife Elizabeth; also give to him negro man Jack & sd Jacks's wife Hannah & her daughter Chloe, & £10 VA.

    To my son Wm - provided he shall live to age 21 or have issue, I give to him negro man Bob & his wife Juno, boy Harry, boy Cyrus, boy Fill, girl Milley, girl Phillis, & my half of negro man Tony; also 2 beds & furniture, etc, the plantation I now live on with its land excepting 1 acre including the grave yard, 200 acres called Round Meadow, ...? acres lying near the court house, 300 acres on the long slash which is the half between James Maclin & myself; should my sd son William not arrive to the age of 21 or not have issue, then all that I have given him to be divided between my 3 sons Frederic, John & Thomas; my sd son William to enjoy the estate immediately after my decease & I leave the care & management of him & his estate to my excrs.

    To my daughter Amy Maclin - should she live to age 21, marries, or has issue, then I leave to her negro man Tom & his wife Sarah & all her children, namely, Isaac, ...?, Miner, ...?, & her choice of 1 bed & furniture, etc; should she die before age 21 or marries, then I wish this legacy to descend to my daughter Susannah Maclin; my daughter Amy to enjoy the estate immediately after my decease & I leave the care & management of her & her estate to my excrs until she is age 21.

    To my daughter Susannah Maclin - should she live to age 21 or marries, then I leave to her negro woman Sue & her daughter Silvia, woman Bess & all her children, namely, Arter, Tab, & Hannah; also 1 good bed & furniture, £50, etc, with reversion to my daughter Amy Maclin, & my sd daughter Susannah to enjoy the estate immediately after my decease.

Should both my daughters Amy & Susannah die before age 21 or are married, then their legacies to be divided between their surviving brothers.

To my sons Frederick, John, Thomas, William, *[torn]*, Matthew Parham - all my *[torn]* in ...? Pitsilvania Co, & my son John to have the first choice. *[Note: At the preceding ellipsis, Augusta has been pencilled in at some time, obliterating the underlying word, yet the next word is definitely Pitsilvania.]*

The rest of my estate I leave to my 3 sons Frederick, John & Thomas.

Ex.   my 3 sons Frederick, John & Thomas

Wit.   *[torn]*, James *[torn]*, Michael Wall, Robert *[torn]*

Probate indicates that Frederick Maclin & Thomas Maclin qualified with John Maclin & William Maclin their securities, & that John Maclin refused to qualify to execute.

174-(236) Appraisal of the estate of Bowler Dobbin dec'd. Included were 1 negro wench, 2 fellows (not named). Appraised by Owen Myrick, Saml Hartwell, John Maclin. Returned to Court 28 Nov 1774.

175-(238) Account 1774 for the estate of John Howard. Named: John Ballard, Benjn Benson, Peter Clark, Reuben Hood, Catey Howard, Jane Howard, Mary Howard, Rachel Howard, Saml Howard.

Also noted were the hires of negroes Bob, Frank & Nan. Returned to Court 28 Nov 1774.

176-(239) Account of the debts paid from the estate of Christopher Clinch dec'd. Named:

James Adamson	John Gray	Joshua Poetress
James Baind	John Linch	Josiah Randall
Gray Briggs	Edward Marks	George Tarkill
John Clack	Ellic Morgan	Rebeca Taylor
John Crawson	Benja Person	Samuel Yeargin
Bowler Dobin	Joshua Poarch	

Returned to Court 28 Nov 1774.

177-(241) Sale of C. Clinch's estate. Mary Clinch bought negroes: girl Becky, man Butcher, girl Nan, boy Will.

Returned to Court 28 Nov 1774.

178-(241) Will of Henry(x)Cook   13 Nov 1772   25 Jul 1774
Of Meherrin Parish.

To my daughter Sarah Rives - 10 shillings.

To my daughter Mary Lanier - 1 negro boy (not named).

To my daughter Anne Lowd - negro wench Lucy.

To my son Drury - negro wench Mureah & her child Simon.

To my son John - negro man Manser.

To my daughter Betty Peeples - £10.

To my grandson Burwell Cook son of John Cook - negro boy Bob, but should my sd grandson die before age 21 or marries, then sd Bob to be sold & the money divided between all the children my son John shall have living at that time.

To my grandson John Cook - negro boy June, when my sd grandson is age 21, but should my sd grandson die before age 21 or marries, then sd June to be sold & the money divided between all the children my son Drury Cook may have living at that time.

To my grandson Thomas Cook son of Henry Cook - negro girl Sall, when he is age 21, but should my sd grandson die before age 21 or marries, then sd Sall to be sold & the money divided between my 2 granddaughters Mary Cook & Sarah Cook, daughters of my sd [son] Henry Cook dec'd.

To my grandson Sterling Cato - negro wench Celah.

To my son Drury - negro girl Patt.

The plantation where I now live to be divided between my 2 sons John & Drury.

To my wife Elizabeth - her choice of 1 feather bed & furniture; also negro girl Rachel.

The residue of my estate to be sold & the money divided among my 2 sons John & Drury & my 3 daughters Mary Lanier, Anne Lowd & Betty Peoples.

Ex.   my son-in-law David Peoples
Wit.   Wm Edwards, Wm Vaughan, Henry Lanier, William Maclin
Probate indicates that the sd excr qualified with Jehue Peoples & Hubard Peoples his securities.

179-(244) Will of Joshua(x)Clack   27 Nov 1774   23 Jan 1775
Of Meherrin Parish. "sick & weak of body"

To my son Peter - 17 acres joining Cain Branch, Peter Clack, Joshua Clack; also 1 cupboard.

To my grandson Willie Clack son of Robert Clack - 50 acres joining Robert Clack dec'd, Drury Clack; but should my sd grandson die without issue, then I give the sd land to my son Henry.

To Jeftan(?) Knott - the remaining part of the land where he now lives not already given to him.

To my wife - lend to her during her widowhood the plantation where I now live with the use of all the land from the Cain Branch up the Spring Branch; also negroes fellow Jim & wenches Libbie, Grace, Moll, Fillis; as also 10 cattle, etc.

To my son Henry - after my wife's death or marriage I give to him my plantation & all the rest of my land & the mill; also my negro wench Phillis & her child Will & her future increase on paying my wife 10 barrels of corn per year.

To my grandson Simon Clack - negro boy Dick; should my sd grandson die under age & without issue, then sd Dick to go to the 2 "Natural and Reputed Children of my son Simon Clack Dec'd," namely, Mildred Fennell daughter of Mary Fennell & Elizabeth Jeffries daughter of Winehfield Jeffres "afterwards Winehfield Clack."

To my grandchildren Milley Clack, Joshua Clack, Nathaniel Clack, Sue Clack, Peter Clack, Rebaca Clack, orphans of Nathaniel Clack - £2 each, to be paid at my wife's death.

William Evans to be discharged from all debts due me.

Kirby Moody to be discharge from all debts due me.

All the rest of my estate to be sold.

After my wife's death, the part lent to her may be sold & divided among my sons Peter, Joshua & Henry Clack, Elizabeth Mitchell, Susannah Step, Amy Nott, Sarah Tomlinson.

Ex.   my 2 sons Peter Clack & Henry Clack
Wit.   George Wyche, Batt Peterson, John Pritchett
Probate indicates that Peter Clack qualified with John Pritchett & Lewis Dupree his securities.

180-(247) Will of Charles Collier   4 Oct 1773   23 Jan 1775
Of Meherrin Parish. "Sick and weak of Body"

    To my daughter Elizabeth Harris -1 shilling sterling.

    To my daughter Ann Moody - 1 shilling sterling.

    My wife is to be maintained out of my estate during her life or widowhood.

    To my son John - 1 bed & furniture.

    To my son Henry - 1 bed & furniture.

    The remainder of my estate to be divided between my son Jon Collier & Lucy Wilson.

Ex.   my 2 sons George & John Collier

Wit.   Richard Woodroof, John Brewer, John Woodroof

Probate indicates that the sd excrs qualified with James Johnson & John Hill their securities.

181-(248) Will of Reubin Booth   6 Dec 1774   23 Jan 1775
"Sick and weak in Body"

    To my wife Rebecca - the use of all my land during her widowhood; give to her negroes Grant, Tom, Young Sue, Peter & Jim, during her widowhood; also give to negroes Bob & Patt, half my household & kitchen furniture, & half my stock of horses, hogs & sheep.

    To my nephew Wm Maclin - negro Stafford, after his mothers's death.

    To my daughter Nancy - the rest of my estate after my debts are paid, should she arrive to age 18 or marries, but should she die before age 18 or marries, then this legacy to be divided among my brother John Booth, my sister Mary Hill, my nephews George Booth son of George Booth, Wm Booth son of Giliam Booth, & my niece Lucy Gilliam Booth daughter of Thomas Booth.

    The estate lent to my wife shall go to my daughter Nancy at the marriage or death of my wife, but should sd Nancy not be living, the estate to be divided as the other legacy to my sd daughter Nancy.

Ex.   my wife Rebecca, my brother George Booth, my brother Gilliam Booth

Wit.   John Jones, Lewis Collier, William Clack, John Mitchell

Probate indicates that the sd excrs qualified with Richard Elliott & William Walker their securities.

182-(250) Appraisal of the estate of Thos Washington dec'd. Included were negroes:

Ben	Jeffree	Silvia
Bob	girl Marandy	girl Sue
fellow Cato	Moses	Will
Dick	Peter	girl Winney
wench Hannah	Rose	

& also wench Abigail & her son Lewis, wench Vilot & her son Charles, Bett & 3 children, Pegg & 4 children, Tabb & 4 children.

    Appraised by Owen Myrick, Wm Holloway, John Person. Returned to Court 23 Jan 1775.

183-(252) Appraisal of the estate of Thomas Washington in Surry Co. Included were negroes: Clarisa, Dafney, Dinah, Jacob, James, Mingo, Peter, Roger, Surry, & also Bridget & her 2 children Weldon & Sall.

    Appraised by Wm Clinch, Nathiniel Nicholson, Nathiniel Schell. Returned to Court 27 Feb 1775.

184-(254) Appraisal of the estate of Charles Collier dec'd 9 Feb 1775. Appraised by John Rosser Jr, Richard Woodrough, John Brewer as by court order dated 23 Jan 1775. Returned to Court 24 Apr 1775.

185-(257) Sale of the estate of Charles Collier dec'd. Buyers:

Henry Adams	Richard Garner	Richard Mason
Henry Brewer	William Garner	Wm Rivers
John Brewer	James Harris	Thomas Shalton
George Collier	John Hill	Jas Sprabrough
John Collier	Henry Holt	Thomas Williams
Lucy Collier	James Johnson	
Oliver Day	Simon Lane Jr	

Returned to Court 24 Apr 1775.

186-(261) Sale of the estate of Henry Collier dec'd 9 & 10 Feb 1775. Buyers: Thomas Camp, George Collier, John Collier, John Gilham, John Hill, John Sprabrough.
     Returned to Court 24 Apr 1775.

187-(261) Appraisal of the estate of Joseph Andrews dec'd. Appraised by Thomas Sadler, John Ross Jr, Thomas Proctor as by court order dated Aug 1774.

188-(263) Appraisal of the estate of John Fennil Jr dec'd. Included was "1 old negroe woman" (not named). Appraised by Isham Lundie, Lewis Dupree, Wm Wommacke as by court order 10 Jan 1775. Returned to Court 24 Apr 1775.

189-(265) Account for the estate of John Fennill Jr dec'd by Isham Fennill admr. Noted was John Tomblinson's estate. Returned to Court 24 Apr 1775.

190-(265) Appraisal of the state of John Chavis Weldon dec'd 26 Sep. [Appraised by] John Dunkley, Joseph Crook, Henry Maclin. Returned to Court 26 Oct 1761.

191-(266) Account of the estate of George Tillman dec'd by Mary Tillman excrx. Named were Mr Butler, John Tillman. Noted was "his fathers Estate;" also noted was "the negroe Doctor"[Note: Is *Doctor* here a name or an occupation?]
     Audited by Thomas Butler, John Edmunds. Returned to Court 23 Nov 1761.

192-(267) Will of Ingram Blanks   20 Nov 1761   25 Jan 1762
Of St Andrews Parish. "Sick & Weak of Body"
     To my wife Eliza - lend to her the plantation where I now live, negro wench Nan, fellow Peter, during her lifetime & after her death I give the plantation(from the Quag Branch that divides the old plantation & the plantation where I now live down Anter Dam Swamp to the mouth of Little Meadow) to my son Wm, it being 90 acres.
     To my son James - all my land of 90 acres between William Bishop's line & Quag Branch.

To my son John - the remainder of my land between Dividing Branch & my son Wm, being 90 acres.

To my sons John & William - the 2 negroes lent to my wife, after her decease: John to have Peter & William to have Nan.

To my son James - negro fellow Jack.

To my son John - the child my negro wench Lid is now with if alive; if not, then I give to him the first live child sd Lid brings.

To my daughter Nancy Blanks - sd negro wench Lid; should she die without heir, then sd Lid to return to my estate to be divided among all my children.

To my daughter Suckey Blanks - negro fellow Frank; should she die without heir, then sd Frank to return to my estate to be divided among all my children.

To my daughter Mary Blanks - negro girl Phillis; should she die without heir, then sd Phillis to return to my estate to be divided among all my children.

To my wife Elizabeth - lend to her 4 cows & calves, household goods, etc, for her life & then to be divided between my son John & my son Wm.

All my estate not bequeathed away to be sold to pay my debts & if there is any surplus, then I give £10 to my daughter Mary Blanks & the remainder to be divided among all my children.

Ex.   my wife, Thomas Morris

Wit.   William Bishop, Thomas Morris, Richard Blanks

Probate indicates that the sd excrs qualified.

193-(271) Appraisal of the estate of Thomas Moore as by court order dated 24 Aug 1761. Appraised by Moses Vinson, Daniel Cato, James Powell. Returned to Court 24 Jan 1762.

194-(272) Appraisal of the estate of Joel Winfield dec'd 21 Oct 1761 as by court order dated 28 Sep 1761. Included were dec'd negroes Gloster, Sam & Chloe. Also included were living negroes: Dicky, Frank, James, Lucy, Sall, Toney. Appraised by Benjamin Lanier, Silvanus Stokes, Josiah Floide. Returned to Court 22 Feb 1762.

195-(274) Will of Nathiniel(x)Johnson   13 Oct 1761   22 Mar 1762
"very Sick and weak"
    To my son Arthur - 150 acres joining Owen Myrick.
    To my son John - the remaining part of my land & plantation where I now live.
    To my daughter Tabitha Johnson - 50 acres on Quarrel Swamp joining Henry Johnson & Jeconias Randle.
    My cattle, hogs, horses, household goods, & all the rest of my estate to be sold to pay my debts & the money remaining to go to my wife Wincey.
Ex.   my wife Wincy Johnson, Harrod Clary.
Wit.   Owen Myrick, John(x)Letbetter, Harrod Clary

196-(276) Appraisal of the estate of Tobias Moore dec'd. The only item listed was 1 horse. Signed by John Vinson admr. Appraised by Moses Vinson, James Powell. Returned to Court 22 *[word omitted]* 1762.

197-(276) Appraisal of the estate of Ambrose Smith dec'd. Appraised by Henry Lee, William Barrow, Richard Branscomb. Returned to Court 22 Mar 1762.

198-(278) Will of Michaiel Young Jr   5 Feb 1762   22 Mar 1762
Of St Andrews Parish. "Sick and Weak of Body"
    My wife Lucy, my father Michaiel Cadle Young Sr & my mother Temperance Young to live on the tract I bought from Samuel Wiggins on Poplar Creek, for their lives & after their decease to be the property of my nephew Michaiel Young son of Francis Young.
    To my wife - all my household furniture & stock.
Ex.   my wife Lucy Young, my brother Francis Young
Wit.   Jn Paisance, Francis Young, Phillip Singleton, Federick Rives, Thomas Young
Probate indicates that sd Francis Young qualified to execute with Reuben Bennit & Thomas Young his securities.

199-(280) Account for the estate of John Bittle dec'd by Jacob Barnes as by court order dated 20 Mar 1762. Named:

Drury Bynum	Nicholas Nelson	John Tilloe
John Dupree	Cordial Norflet	William Turner
Nathiniel King	Joseph Scott	
Kirby Moody	William Taylor	

Noted was the sheriff of Southampton.
    Appraised by Daniel Fisher, Thomas Twitty, John Ruffin Jr. Returned to Court 23 Mar 1762.

200-(281) Will of William Smith   11 Nov 1761   26 Apr 1762
Of Meherrin Parish. "Sick and weak"

    To my son Moses - my young gray mare, saddle & bridle, 1 sow & pigs, my little gun.

    To my son Aaron - my yellow mare, 2 sow & pigs, my Brunswick gun.

    To my wife Susannah - lend to her the use of my plantation, livestock, corn & tobacco, & all my estate during her [lifetime] & at her decease to be disposed of as follows:

    To my son Thomas - 1 feather bed & furniture, 1 cow & calf.

    To my son William - 100 acres.

    The rest of my estate after my wife's decease & after my debts are paid is to be divided among all my children, but excepting my son William.
Ex.   my wife Susannah Smith
Wit.   Christopher Mason, Thomas Smith, Pheeby Smith
Probate indicates that the sd excrx qualified with Christopher Mason & Thos Smith her securities.

201-(283) Appraisal of the estate of Mathew Waldin dec'd. Appraised by Thos Morris, Nathl Mabry, Daniel Mabry. Returned to Court 26 Apr 1762.

202-(284) Appraisal of the estate of Nathiniel Johnson dec'd as by court order dated 22 Mar. Appraised by Owen Myrick, Harrod Clary, John Johnson. Returned to Court 26 Apr 1762.

203-(287) Appraisal of the estate of Hinchey Mabry dec'd. Included were negroes:

Archer	Hall	boy Nero	man Shagg
Bett	Hector	Oro	Tom
David	Jimm	Rippin	
Dinah	Milley	Sam	

Appraised by John Maclin, Edward Goodrich, Frederick Maclin. Returned to Court 27 Apr 1762.

204-(291) Appraisal of the personal estate of Sarah Hurst dec'd as by court order dated 26 Apr 1762. Appraised by Wm Thompton, Robert Hicks, William Vaughn. Returned to Court 24 May 1762.

205-(292) Will of James Harrison   16 Mar 1762   24 May 1762
Of St Andrews Parish. "sick and Weak of Body"

    To my wife - my plantation during her widowhood & at her marriage or decease the sd plantation to be rented yearly until my 2 children are age 18 & then to be divided between my daughter Rebecca Harrison & my daughter Dolley Harrison; I also lend to my wife 2 cows & calves, 1 yearling, 2 sows & pigs, 7 large killable hogs, 3 pewter dishes(2 of which were given to her by her father), etc, & after her decease or marriage to be sold & the money used to school & maintain my children.

    To my daughter Dolley Harrison - the first live child that is born to my negro girl Sender, also 1 small gilt trunk, at age 18 or marries.

    To my daughter Rebecca Harrison - the sd negro girl Sender & to possess her at age 18 or marriage.

    To Thomas Harrison - 150 acres on Hixes Swamp, provided he pay to Howell Whittington "what I was to give for the said Land."

The remaining part of my estate to be sold to pay my debts & any residue to go to maintaining my children.

Ex.   my wife, Thomas Harrison

Wit.   Thomas Morris, James Blanks, John Renn

Probate indicates that sd Thomas Harrison qualified with James Stewart & Benja Williams his securities. Probate also indicates that Sarah was the wife of sd James Harrison.

206-(295) Appraisal of the estate of Thomas Wood dec'd 22 Mar 1762. Signed by Robert Lundie admr. Appraised by Nathl Hicks, James Parham, John Brayham. Returned to Court 24 May 1762.

207-(296) Inventory of the estate of Thomas Thomas dec'd 29 Jun 1762 as by court order dated 25 Aug 1760. Appraised by Thomas Lindsey, Thomas Stone, Phillemon Lucy. Returned to Court 29 Jun 1762.

208-(297) Appraisal of the estate of Charnel Hightower dec'd as by court order dated 26 Apr 1762. Included were negroes:

Adam	Guy	Lydia	Robin
Cate	Harvey	Moll	girl Winney
George	Jack	boy Ned	
Grace	Jenny		

Sarah Hightower was admr. Appraised by Lewelling Jones, William Averiss, John Henia(?). Returned to Court 26 Jul 1762.

209-(300) Account for the estate of George Brewer dec'd by Lewis Parham excr. Named:

James Bennit	Thomas Meggs	John Smith
Alley Brewer	Margret Powel	Robert Smith
Nicholas Brewer	John Person	Peter Vinsent
Wm Brewer	James Powell	Rebecca Wall
John Johnson	James Ridley	
John Mallerby		

Noted was the inventory "of my fathers Estate."

Audited by Robert Champbell, Nathiniel Wyche. Returned to Court 26 Jul 1762.

210-(301) Account for the estate of Charles Singleton dec'd by Thos Singleton. Named were Daniel Fisher, Phill Singleton, Robert Stark.

Appraised by Thomas Butler, John Powell, Thomas Collier. Returned to Court 26 Jul 1762.

211-(302) Appraisal of the estate of George Brewer Jr. Included was negro boy Will. Appraised by John Vinson, Daniel Cato. Returned to Court 26 Jul 1762.

212-(303) Account 1762 for the estate of George Brewer Jr dec'd by John Brewer admr. Named: Alse Brewer, John Brewer, John Hunt, Thomas Morris, Lewis Parhams's excrs, Dr James D. Ridley, James Wooddall.

Audited by Robert Champbell, Nathiniel Wyche. Returned to Court 26 Jul 1762.

213-(304) Account for William Hammond. Noted was a balance due John Hammond. John Hammond made oath to the account 9 Nov 1756 before Wm Covington. Returned to Court 23 Aug 1762.

214-(305) Account 1756 for Elizabeth Hammond dec'd by Charnel Hightower Sr. Noted was "1 years schooling of your Daughter." Sworn to 25 Mar 1758 before Charles Mathews & Peter Jones. Returned to Court 23 Aug 1762.

215-(305) Account for the estate of Wm Lashley dec'd by Thomas Clanton excr. Named: William Brewer, Daniel Fisher, Richard Hyde, Alan Love, Josiah Randle.
    Noted were 4 poll taxes in 1761. Audited by Daniel Fisher. Returned to Court 26 Aug 1762.

216-(306) Account for Daniel Jackson dec'd. Named:

John Barlow	Lewis Jackson	Burrel Lucy
John Chapman	Raif Jackson	John Maclin
John Clack	Samuel Jackson	Daniel Nolley
William Clack	Thomas Jackson	Nehemiah Nolly
Thomas Ingram	Nick Jarrot	Moses Pondrey
Daniel Jackson	John Jones	Robinson
Bethiah Jackson	John Jones merchant	Benjamin Sewell
John Jackson	Joseph King	Stephen Sisson
John Jackson excr	Robert Lanier	Hew Williams
John Jackson Jr	Thomas Lanier	

Audited by Thomas Butler, Henry Nicolson. Returned to Court 27 Sep 1762.

217-(308) Appraisal of the estate of Richard Thomas 11 Aug 1761. Appraised by David Abernathy, Charles Abernathy, James Harwell. Returned to Court 27 Sep 1762.

218-(309) Appraisal of the estate of Richd Thomas 11 May. Appraised by Wm Harrison, James Boy, Richard Cordle. Returned to Court 27 Sep 1762.

219-(310) Account for the estate of Wm Powell dec'd by John Lifsey excr. Named: Nicholas Brewer, Jeremiah Brown, Theophilus Fields, Anthony Irby, Secretary Nelson, John Persons, James Powell.
    Noted was quitrents on 383 acres; John Brewer was excr of George Brewer dec'd. Returned to Court 25 Oct 1762.

220-(311) Will of William Martin   1 Jul 1762   22 Nov 1762
"very weak of Body"
    To my spouse Mary - all my estate during her life & after her decease to be divided among my children, excepting the land, which I bequeath to my son Henry.
Ex.   my sons William Martin & Abraham Martin.

Wit.   William Brown, John Brown, Benjamin Burrell
Probate indicates that the sd excrs qualified 23 May 1763 with Henry Martin & Jonathan Williams their securities.

221-(312) Will of Archibald Gray   17 Oct 1762   22 Nov 1762
   To my mother - for her lifetime the labor of my negro girl Joan & her issue.
   To my brother John Gray - my horse & saddle, & he to fulfill his promise to me to dispose of my wearing clothes & the legacies "after which as my Sisters Catharine Ramsey, Mary Smith, and Honour Westbrookes each already Blest with a Compleasency of Worldly Estate to live on."
   The residue of my personal estate to be divided among my brothers John & Watson Gray & my sister Ann Gray.
   My negro girl Jane & her issue to be divided among my 2 brothers John & Watson & my sd sister Ann, after my mother's decease.
Ex.   my brother John Gray
Wit.   Wm Buckhanan
Probate indicates that at court in Sep 1763 John Gray qualified with Simon Turner his security.

222-(314) Will of William Parham   14 Jan 1763   28 Feb 1763
"very sick"
   To my brother James - 190 acres which is the plantation where I now live; also my negro wench Phib; £50 out of the legacies left *[torn]* my brother John Parham.
   To my brother John - £50, 1 feather bed & furniture, 6 pewter plates, 1 dishes, 5 cattle, etc.
   To Absalom Atkinson - 4 barrels of corn.
   The remainder of my estate to be divided between my brother[s] John & James Parham.
   To my sister Frances Parham - 2 cows, my white mare, etc.
   To Benjamin Forden Andrews - 5 shillings.
   Other legacies & provisions.
Ex.   my 2 brothers James Parham & John Parham
Wit.   Lewis Dupree, Urvin Brown, John Dupree
Probate indicates that John Parham qualified with Lewis Dupree & Christopher Mason his securities.

223-(317) Will of William Samford Sr   3 Feb 1762   28 Feb 1763
"Sick and weak of Body"
   To my daughter Ann Road - 1 bed & furniture, her first choice.
   To my daughter Hannah Samford - 1 bed & furniture, her second choice.
   To my son Urvin - 1 shilling.
   To Elisha Robinson & his son Thomas - 1 shilling.
   To my daughter Sarah Simmons - 1 shilling.
   To my daughter Mary Morgan - 1 shilling.
   To my son William - the tract of land where I now live & my water grist mill, & all the rest of my personal estate "in Consideration of his . . . Discharging my Just debts."
Ex.   my son William, Hugh Williams
Wit.   Josiah Ogbourn, William Ogburne, Henry Blanks

Probate indicates that William Samford qualified with Joseph Bishop & Mathew Bishop his securities.

224-(319) Account for the estate of Richard Russell by John Russell admr. Named: Joseph Andrews, John Bailey, William Clark, Howell Collier, John Taylor Duke, Allan Love, William Williams.
    Audited by John Maclin, Thos Twitty Jr. Returned to Court 28 Feb 1763.

225-(320) Account 1762 for the estate of Morgan McKeney dec'd. Named:

Capt Richard Bank	Nicholas Edmonds	Thos Merritt
George Booth	David Gunter	John Phenix
Wm Christian	Maj Frederick Jones	Hugh Williams
George Dearding	Sarah Jones	Joseph Wrenn
John Dunkley	Thomas Jones	
Moses Dunkley	Henry Maclin	

Noted were the widow & 3 children (not named).
    Audited by Hugh Williams, Lewelling Jones. Returned to Court 28 Feb 1763.

226-(321) Appraisal of the estate of James Harrison dec'd as by court order dated 23 May 1762. Included were 2 negro wenches & children (not named). Appraised by John Maclin, Lemuell Lanier. Returned to Court 1 Mar 1763.

227-(323) Will of Amy Gilliam   30 Nov 1760   28 Mar 1763
Of St Andrews Parish. "very Sick and Weak of Body"
    To my sister Martha Gilliam - 13 negroes who are already in her possession:

Amy	Eagg	Nutty	Sarah
Betty	Grace	Patt	Subbabo
Cue	Hector	Robin	
Dinah	Jack		

    I also give to my sd sister Martha Gilliam 1 mare, hogs, cattle, my wearing apparel, etc.
Ex.   my sister Martha Gilliam
Wit.   Mychaiel Cadle Young, Mary Vaughn, Wm Vaughn
Probate indicates Michaiel Cadle Young proved the will & who also deposed that sd Wm Vaughn & Mary Vaughn dec'd subscribed their names to the sd will.

228-(325) Will of Edward Clanton   24 Feb 1763   28 Mar 1763
    To Sarah Johnson daughter of Moses Johnson - negro woman Lucy; should she die without heir, then I give her to David Johnson younger son of sd Moses Johnson.
    To my brother Thomas Clanton - negro fellow Jack.
    To Edward Clanton son of sd Thos Clanton - my plantation that I bought from William Hardin.
    To Miss Elizabeth Hunt of Sussex Co - negro wench Dinah, boy Simon.
    To my brother Charles Clanton - all my wearing apparel.
    To my friend Mary Clinch - a black horse.
Ex.   Christopher Clinch

Wit.   Christopher Clinch, Thomas Washington, Sarah Washington
Probate indicates that sd Christopher Clinch qualified with Thomas Peete & John Fletcher his securities.

229-(327) Will of James Parham   13 Oct 1762   28 Mar 1763
"Sick and weak"
    To my brother William - negro fellow Skipper; £12s7p4 which sd William borrowed from me.
    To my sister Frances Parham - negro woman Joan; also 1 bed & furniture, all the new feathers; also "a Christian like maintenance out of my Estate to be provided by John Parham from time to time."
    To my brother John - 300 acres where Thomas Scott lives; also 4 negroes Toney, Dick, Roger & Jacob; also 2 feather beds & furniture; also 450 acres where I now live & the 200 acres I bought from Jeremiah Brown & the 50 acres that I bought from George Reives & the 100 acres that was divided to Mathew Parham by the will of John Peterson of Isle [of] White Co; also the rest of my estate & he must pay my debts.
    Other legacies.
Ex.   my brother John Parham
Wit.   Wm Elliott, George Wyche, Wm Bosman, Henry Williams
Probate indicates that sd John Parham qualified with John Peterson & George Wyche his securities.

230-(330) Will of William Mitchell   14 Feb 1763   28 Mar 1763
Of St Andrews Parish. "Sick and weak"
    The land where I now live to be sold to pay my debts.
    My land in Edgecomb Co in North Carolina near the town of Tarbrough & all the rest of my estate to be divided between my wife Mary & my son Olph; should either my wife or my son die without issue, then the survivor of each to enjoy the whole; should they both die without issue, then the whole to be divided between Wm & Thomas Stanback sons of George Stanback.
Ex.   George Stanback
Wit.   Andrew Troughton, Wm Owen, James Troughton
Probate indicates that George Standback qualified with William Thornton & Wm Clack his securities.

231-(332) Will of Mary Wall   3 Feb 1762   28 Mar 1763
    To my son George Wall - £40 at age 18, & should he die before that age then to my daughter Mary Wall.
    To my son Urvin Brown - my cupboard & tea kettle.
    To my daughter Betty Cooke - 1 bed & furniture in her possession; also my copper kettle.
    To my daughter Mary Wall - 4 negroes Moll, Jack, Jemmy & Patt; should she die before age 18, then the sd negroes to go to my son George Wall & Burrell Cooke son of Betty Cook; also to my sd daughter I give the rest of my estate.
Ex.   John Cook
Wit.   Nathl Hix, Frederick Davis, Harmon Rives
Probate indicates that the sd excr qualified with John Peebles & Wm Rives his securities.

232-(333) Account for the estate of Tobias Moore dec'd by John Vinson excr. Named: Jeremiah Brown, Daniel Cato, John Cato, John Johnson, Walter Pitts, James Powell, James Day Ridley, Thos Shepherd, Moses Vinson.

Audited by Thomas Buttes, Burwell Lanier. Returned to Court 25 Apr 1763.

233-(334) Appraisal of the estate of Wm Brown dec'd 8 Apr 1763. Signed by Lewis Williamson admr. Appraised by Benjamin Rives, Timothy Rives, Wm Rives. Returned to Court 23 May 1763.

234-(336) Will of Mary Clack   23 Apr 1763   23 May 1763
Of St Andrews Parish. "Sick and Weak"

To my son John Clack - my 2 negro fellows Great Jack & Old Dick, for his lifetime & at his decease then to my grandson James Clack.

To my son Wm Clack - my negro wench Great Frank & her child Grace.

My negro wench Nan & her 3 children Isaac, Robin & Abram are to be sold by my excrs to pay my part of a debt due to my son-in-law Robert Ruffin on a mortgage given by my dec'd husband; should Nan & her 2 children Robin & Abraham be sufficient to pay my debts, then I give sd Isaac to my grandson Eldridge Clack.

Ex.   my 2 sons John Clack & Wm Clack
Wit.   William Lindsey, William Raney, Patrick Hall
Probate indicates that the sd excrs qualified with James Parham & Thomas Twitty Sr their securities.

235-(338) Inventory of the estate of Wm Parham dec'd. Included was negro wench Tib. Signed by John Patten. Returned to Court 27 Jun 1763.

236-(339) Inventory of James Parham dec'd. Included were 5 negroes: Dick, Jacob, Joan, Roger, Toney. Signed by John Pattain. Returned to Court 27 Jun 1763.

237-(341) Appraisal of the estate of William Lashley dec'd as by court order dated 28 Jun 1757. Included were 2 negro fellows, 1 wench & 1 boy (not named). Appraised by George Wyche, John Roper, Thomas Morris. Returned to Court 27 Jun 1763.

238-(345) Appraisal of the estate of James Northcross dec'd 13 Jul 1763. Signed by W. Edwards admr. Appraised by John Carter, James Wall Jr, Henry Anderson. Returned to Court 25 Jul 1763.

239-(347) Will of Joseph Harrison   8 Mar 1763   28 May 1763
Of St Andrews Parish.

To my daughter Nanny Chappell - negro girl Phillis.

To my son William - negro man Sharper, 1 bed & furniture, 1 colt.

To my son Daniel - negro girl Sarah, boy Ambross, 1 feather bed & furniture, 1 mare.

To my son Benjamin - negro woman Patt, 1 feather bed & furniture.

To my son Simmons - negro girl Judith, 1 feather bed & furniture.

To my daughter Patty Harrison - negro woman Ginney, 1 feather bed & furniture.

To my wife Elizabeth - all my cattle, hogs, sheep, horses, & all my other estate not given away;

negro man Tom to be sold & the money given to my sd wife.
Wit.   Joseph Carter, Daniel Harrison, Frederick Maclin
Probate indicates that sd Carter proved the will on 28 May 1763, that sd Maclin proved it 25 Jul following, & that Elizabeth Harrison was granted administration with the will annexed with John Peeples & Wood Tucker her securities.

240-(349) Appraisal of the estate of Mary Wall dec'd as by court order dated 28 Mar 1763. Included were negroes Jack, Jemmy, Moll, Patt. Signed by John Cooke.
    Appraised by Nathiniel Hix, John Dittisfor, John Parham. Returned to Court 22 Aug 1763.

241-(352) Account for the estate of Daniel Jackson dec'd by Bethiah Jackson & John Jackson excrs. Named were John Jackson, Nehemiah Nolly. Returned to Court 22 Aug 1763.

242-(353) Will of Robert Champbell   30 Apr 1763   22 Aug 1763
Of St Andrews Parish. "Sick and weak of Body"
    To my wife Mary - negro wench Anekey, 2 of my best feather beds & furniture, 1 black horse, 1 of my best cows & calves.
    To my son Walter - all my land & plantation called the Roaring Rock on the north side of Meherrin River in Luningburg Co; also 250 acres "on which their has been a plantation" which my brother Walter bought from Philemon Brown.
    To my son Colin - all my lands joining the court house which my sd brother Walter purchased from Stephen Drury & old Amos Timms.
    Should my wife choose to live on my plantation on Meherrin River, then my son Walter shall not hinder her in so doing; should she choose to live where she now lives, then my son Collin shall be under the same restraint as his brother Walter; my wife to have all the rents & profits of all my lands until my sd 2 sons arrive to age 21.
    To my wife & children to be divided equally among them - 3 negroes Arthur, Moll & Sall with their increase; these sd 3 negroes my brother died possessed of, after which Col John Wall took them "into his possession under a pretention of a lent to my brother and since the Decease of the said John Wall are now in the possession of his son James Wall as also thir said Increase."
    To my sd wife - I give all the rest of my personal estate during her lifetime & after her decease this to be divided among my 5 children.
    Other legacies & provisions.
Ex.   my friends Wm Thornton, John Clack, Wm Clack
Wit.   John Turbyfill, John Rose Jr, John Turbyfill Jr

243-(356) Appraisal of the estate of Joseph Harrison. Included were negroes: boy Ambross, woman Fillis, woman Jane, girl Judith, woman Pall, girl Sarah, man Sharper, man Tom.
    Appraised by John Butts, Joseph Carter, Frederick [torn]. Returned to Court 26 Sep 1763.

244-(359) Will of Henry Embry   14 Jul 1762   26 Sep 1763
Of St Andrews Parish.
    To my wife Martha - lend to her for life the use of 1 moiety of the land where I now live & all

the houses, excepting those where my son Henry lived, & 1 barn; also lend to her all my negroes & livestock on my sd plantation for 2 years after my decease, & after 2 years I further lend to her the sd stock & the 6 negroes Mingo, *[torn]*, Marrear, Amy, Luckenny, *[torn]*.

To my daughter *[torn]* Embry - after my wife's decease I leave the above sd moiety of land where I now live & half my livestock.

To my granddaughter Mary Embry - the other moiety of land where I now live which is that part of the land on which her father Henry Embry lived, provided she claim no other part in the lands her sd father died owning but relinquish the same; should she refuse to do so, then I will the sd land to be divided between my granddaughter Mary & Sarah Embry; also give to my sd granddaughter Mary the negroes Sarah & Moll with their increase; also 1 feather bed & furniture, etc, after my wife's decease.

To my daughter Mary Maritt - lend to her a moiety of my land on Sturgeon Run & after her decease I give the sd moiety to my grandson Henry Maritt, provided he lives to age 21 & have issue, but should he die without issue, then I give the sd moiety to my grandson Henry Embry.

To my grandson Henry Maritt - the moiety of my land on Sturgeon Run, provided he live to age 21 & has issue, but should he die without issue, then I give this moiety to my grandson Henry Embry.

To my daughter Mary Maritt - lend to her for life the negroes Pompey, Cate, & Little Mingo, also 1 desk, etc, & after her decease to be divided among my grandchildren she now has living; also lend to her for life after my wife's decease the negroes Mingo, Ceazor, Murear & Amy & afterward to be divided among my grandchildren which she now has living.

To my granddaughter Sarah Embry - a tract of land on the Great Branch of Wa...? Creek where Thomas Walker now lives; also give to her negro Anekey & her increase; give to her after my wife's decease negroes Luckenny, Little Ceazor, a feather bed & furniture, etc.

To my granddaughter Martha Elliott - negro Dillo; also give to her after my wife's death 1 feather bed & furniture.

To my granddaughter Ermin Embry - 1 feather bed & furniture after my wife's decease.

To my grandson Wm Embry - 400 acres in Luningburgh Co where my son William lived at the time of his death & which is the first survey I made on R...? Creek; also 200 acres joining the same which I purchased from Nathaniel Thomas Jones & is devised to my grandson William by his father's will, provided my sd grandson Wm Embry will at age 21 make an absolute title to my grandson Henry Embry to all the lands devised him by his father's will as well as to a proportionate part of the negroes devised in sd will; & my sd grandson William Embry makes his sisters Ermin, Martha & Elizabeth Embry a title to the negroes devised to them by his father's will, as well as a title to them for a share of the negroes undivided by his father's will; & my sd grandson make an absolute title to Elisha Brooks for that part of 119 acres devised to him by his father's sd will; should my sd grandson refuse to comply with giving the titles to my sd grandchildren Henry, Ermin, Martha & Elizabeth, & also to Elisha Brooks, then I devise the sd 400 acres where my son Wm Embry lived at his decease & also the sd 200 acres joining it to my grandson Henry Embry; should my grandson Wm Embry die before he can confirm the above titles, then my grandson Henry Embry to make good & confirm the titles to his sisters Ermin, Martha & Elizabeth, & also to Elisha Brooks; & should sd Henry refuse to do so, then I devise the sd 400 acres & the sd 200 acres to my granddaughters Ermin, Martha & Elizabeth.

To my son Wm Embry's children - negroes Harray, Tarla, Nelley.

To my grandson Wm Embry - 1 case of bottles & a large Bible.

To my grandson Henry Embry - 1 chest of drawers, a large looking glass.

To my daughter-in-law Elizabeth Embry - lend to her during her widowhood all the estate as directed in her husband's will.

Should both my granddaughters Mary & Sarah Embry died without lawful issue, then the land & negroes before devised to them may descend to my grandson Henry Embry

Other legacies & provision.

Ex.   my daughter Mary Maritt, Richard Burch

Wit.   Edward Kent, Isaac Wall, Henry Wall

245-(368) Will of John Williams   9 Dec 1762   26 Sep 1763

"Sick and weak in Body"

All my estate to be kept together by my executors until my son Wyatt arrive to age 21 & then to be divided between my wife Frances & my 3 children Wyatt Williams, Susanny Williams & John Williams.

To my wife Frances - the use of my 2 negroes Ned & Mater, for her lifetime, but the increase of the wench Mater from this time forward to be divided between my daughter Susannah & [my son] John.

To my son Wyatt - negroes Betty, Matt & Dick; also my land in Granvil Co North Carolina to be sold & the money given to my sd son Wyatt, & that £100 be made up from my debts for his use.

To my son John - my plantation where I now live; also negro girl Judy & boy George.

To my daughter Susannah Williams - negro girl Doll & boy Jack; also 1 gold ring now in the possession of my sister Sarah Hopkins.

Ex.   Capt Thomas Twitty, my wife Frances Williams

Wit.   Molly Twitty Jr, Mary Twitty, Thomas Twitty Jr

Probate indicates that the sd excrs qualified with Wm Thornton their security.

246-(370) Will of George Simms   3 Jun 1763   26 Sep 1763

Of Meherrin Parish. "sick and weak"

To my son Nathl - all my land between Lightfoot's line that was formerly Col Benjamin Harrison's, on a prong of Deep Branch, joining the westward road, Old Shop Branch.

To my son Zachariah - all my land without the south side of Pole Bridge Branch, joining the cart path.

To my son Bartlet - after his mother's decease I give to him my manor plantation & its land below the cart path, joining the land purchased from Robt Taylor & joining my 2 sons Nathl & Zachariah.

To my son Burrell - all my land on the upper side of the branch below Burwell's line, & sd Burwell not to have any part of my estate that I leave to be divided among all my children.

To my son William - 250 acres purchased from Robert Taylor; also the remaining part of the land on the upper part of the cart path, joining my son Burwell, Dividing Branch, Cold Water; also give to sd Wm negro boy Johnson, girl Fibb, boy Roger; after his mother's decease, I give him my best bed & furniture, etc, & he not to have the land or receive the legacies until age 21 & should he die without issue then the land above to be sold & the money divided between my children then living, but excepting my son Burwell.

Ex.   my son Milington Simms

Wit.   John Clack, William Chapman, Wm Clack

Probate indicates that the sd excr qualified with Wm Clack, Thomas Lyall & Adam Sims his securities.

247-(374)Will of John Chapman   12 Apr 1763   24 Oct 1763
Of Meherrin Parish.

   To my wife Anne - negroes Charles, Sarah & Hagar.

   To my daughter Mary - negroes Bett, Phillis, Will & Roger.

   To my brother William - the land give to me by my mother as by indenture in Brunswick Co.

   To my wife Ann - the residue of my estate of whatsoever kind.

Ex.   my wife Anne Chapman

Wit.   John Vinson, Edward Robinson, John Robinson

248-(376) Will of John Ingram   3 Mar 1762   28 Nov 1763
Of Meherrin Parish.

   To my wife Hannah - negro fellows Dick, Phill, Daniel & Davy; also woman Judith; all stock & household goods "as she shall have occasion of during her Life or widowhood;" after her decease, to be divided among my children.

   To my son Samuel - negro boy Moses & whatever estate of mine in his hands.

   To my son John - in his lifetime negro Tom, & since my sd son is deceased, the sd boy to be disposed of according sd John's will.

   To my grandson Jeremiah Ingram son of my sd son John dec'd - £5 for the education of my sd grandson.

   To my son James - 50 acres on the north side of Meherrin joining my son George's land with 100 acres, being part of the tract where I now live.

   To my son George - 177 acres on the north side of Meherrin River, which is part of the land I bought from Daniel Taylor.

   To my son Jesse - 300 acres in Granvil Co North Carolina which I bought from John Zacharie; also negro man Charles, & half the stock on the sd land.

   To my son Joshua - 300 acres in Luningburg Co which is part of 600 acres I bought from John Smith.

   To my son Richard - 300 acres in Luninburg Co which is the other part of the sd 600 acres I bought from Smith.

   To my son Benjamin - 350 acres in Luninburg Co joining Bates & House, which I purchased from Henry Bates & Wm Davis; also £15 to make his land equal with the others.

   To my son Joseph - the manor plantation with 50 acres on the north side of Meherrin River which is part of the land I bough from Daniel Taylor, after his mother's decease & when he is age 21.

   My personal estate to be divided among my children James, George, Joshua, Richard, Benjn, & Joseph Ingram & my 2 daughters Elizabeth Vaughan & Tabitha Gee, including what they have already received; the following negroes also to be divided among them:

girl Cate	boy Hall	woman Nan
boy Ceazer	boy Isham	girl Patt
man Frank	man Jim	boy Peter
man George	girl Letty	

Ex.   my wife Hannah Ingram, my 2 sons James Ingram & George Ingram
Wit.   Wm Lindsey, Elizabeth Robinson, John Tippitt

249-(380) Appraisal of the estate of Wm Adams dec'd. Included were negroes: wench Amy, girl Barthshab, wench Janey, girl Orpha, girl Sarah, girl Sue. Appraised by Eads Smith, William Davis.
        Returned to Court 28 Nov 1763.

250-(382) Appraisal of the estate of John Ingram Jr dec'd as by court order dated 28 Jul 1760. Included were negroes Jack, girl Jenny, Tom, & woman Sue & her child Pegg. Signed by James Ingram excr. Appraised by Wm Maclin, John Marshall, Samuell Marshall. Returned to Court 28 Nov 1763.

251-(384) Appraisal of the slaves & personal estate of John Chapman dec'd as by court order dated 12 Oct 1763. Included were negroes: Bett, man Charles, Hagar, Judy, Phillis, Roger, Sall, Will.
        Appraised by Adam Simms, John Jones, John Robinson. Returned to Court 28 Nov 1763.

252-(386) Appraisal of the estate of Edward Clanton dec'd. Included were negroes fellow Jack, woman Dinah, boy Simon. Returned to Court 23 Jan 1764.

253-(387) Will of William Fox   22 Dec 1763   23 Jan 1764
"sick and weak of Body"
        To my daughter Betty Ren - negro girls Patt & Abby.
        To my daughter Lucy Robinson - negro boy Toney.
        To my son William - the land joining Licks Bog, Log House Branch; negro Jona, woman Nan, boy Frank; cattle, a horse, etc; negro boy Dick.
        To my son Thomas Avent Fox - the land I hold on the lower side of Log House Branch; negro boys Tom & Jacob, girl Beck.
        To my son John - the plantation I live on; negro girl Amy, Lucy, boy Charles.
        To my daughter Mary Johnson - negro boy Robin.
        To my daughter Sarah Fox - negro boy Nat.
        To my daughter Noona Fox - negro boy Daniel.
        To my daughter Lucy Robins - 20 shillings.
        To my wife Sarah - lend to her negroes Great Jimmy, Little Jimmy, Dinah, all the household goods & stock during her widowhood & after her decease I give Great Jimmy & Dinah to my son William & Little Jimmy to my son John.
        After my decease, all my household goods & stock to be sold & the money divided among all my children except Wm Fox.
Ex.   Thomas Vinson, my wife Sarah Fox, my son Wm Fox

Wit.   John Birdsong, John Sones
Probate indicates that Thomas Vinson & Wm Fox qualified with Christopher Mason, George Wyche & Benjamin Rowell their securities.

254-(392) Inventory of the estate of William Fox dec'd as by court order 14 Feb 1764. Included were 19 negroes:

Aby	Dick	Jinny	Pat
Amy	Dinah	Little Jimmy	Robin
Beck	Frank	Lucy	Tom
Charles	Great Jimmy	Nan	Toney
Dan	Jacob	Nat	

Signed by excrs Thomas Vinson & Wm Fox. Returned to Court 27 Feb 1764.

255-(393) Will of Wm Read   31 Dec 1762   27 Feb 1764
Of St Andrews Parish.

    To my son Thomas - negro boy Elleck already in his possession.
    To my son Robert - my plantation & land where I now live; also negro girl Rhoda.
    To my son Wm - negro fellow Dick.
    To my daughter Frances Stone - 1 shillings.
    To my daughter Catharine Quarles - negro Sam.
    To my daughter Elizabeth Read - negro girl Ruth.
    To my son Robert - all my estate real & personal in this dominion not hereafter mentioned.
    The remainder of my estate to be divided between Robert Read, Catharine Quarls, Elizabeth Read, Susannah Matthews, John Read, Anna Read, Mary Read & Lewis Read.
    My son Robert to have the bed I bought from John Miller.
    To my wife Elizabeth - lend to her during her lifetime or widowhood all my estate above mentioned, & should she die or marry before my son John come to age 21, then my estate to be in the care of my excrs until my son John is age 21.
Ex.   my son Robert Read, James Quarles
Wit.   Hugh Williams, Moses Quarles, Lewis Quarls
Probate indicates that the sd excrs qualified with John Quarls & Thomas Briggs their securities.

256-(395) Account 1761 for the estate of John Drew dec'd by Willis Roberts. Named were Col Edmds, Robt Jones. Noted was a legacy left Thos Stith by Richd Park dec'd.
    Audited by Benjamin Lanier, George Deardan. Returned to Court 28 Feb 1764.

257-(396) Account for the estate of Littleton Tazewell dec'd by Joseph Gray admr. Named:

Jepthah Atherton	George Cain	Wm Hunter
Wm Barlow	Col Eyeres	Dr Jameson
Wm Bishop	Mr Field	John Jones
John Blow	D. Fisher	Capt Maclin
Jno Bowdin	John Gee	James Martin
Gray Briggs	Samuel Gordon	Anthony Metcalf

Wm Newsom	Benjn Ruffin	Wm Thweatt
Lewis Parham	John Shalton	Rebecca Wall
Capt Patarson	Henry Simmons	Wm Watkins
Dr Peete	Thomas Simmons	John Watlington
Rev Mr Pendie	Griffin Stith	Col John Willis
Halcot Pride	Tazwell	Mr Wright
James Ransom	John Tazwell	

Noted were the portion for the Rev Mr Nevison's wife, the legatees of Mrs Sophia Tazwell, a legacy left to John Tazwell by his father.

Audited by Benjn Ruffin, Samuel Blow, Richard Kello. Returned to Court 26 Mar 1764.

258-(399) Appraisal of the estate of Jacob Jones dec'd. Appraised by John Brewer, Roger Smith, Richd Branscomb. Returned to Court 28 Mar 1764.

259-(400) Will of Henry Cook   21 Jan 1764   23 Apr 1764

To my wife Elinor - all my land from the mouth of Hollow Branch to the creek; also negro girl Belinder, all my household goods & stock, all my debts & accounts.

To my son Thomas - 330 acres where I now live, after my wife's decease; also my negro boy Andrew.

To my daughter Mary Cook - negro boy Collins, 1 feather bed.

To my daughter Salley Cook - negro girl Lucy.

I lend negroes Tom, Nan & Ariala to my wife during her lifetime & after her death they then to be divided among my 3 children; my wife to have the use of the 3 negroes to the charge of raising them to the time or marriage or the age of 20.

Ex.   my wife Elinor Cook, Thomas Vinson, Moses Vinson
Wit.   Henry Brown, Thomas Davis, Wm Burt, Wm Bird

260-(402) Appraisal of the estate of Robert Champbell dec'd. Included was 1 negro woman (not named). Appraised by John Read, Thomas Proctor, Robert Proctor. Returned to Court 28 May 1764.

261-(404) Account for the estate of James Harrison dec'd. Named:

Richard Blanks	Wm Parham	Wm Ren
Jno Austin Finney	Thos Peete	Moses Smith
Thomas Harrison	David Pennington	George Stanback
Wm Harrison	Walter Peter	
James Oliver		

Audited by Thos Morris, Pen^y. Hurst. Returned to Court 28 May 1764.

262-(405) Will of Thomas Kirkland   28 Apr 1764   25 Jun 1764

To my eldest sister Mary Fuqua - my oldest negro.

To my brother Wm - all my "tolls & Cloaths" & £20.

To my brother Benjn - my youngest negro boy.

To my youngest sister Elizabeth Kirkland - my mare & £10.

To my mother Ann Kirkland - £15.

The remainder of my estate to be divided among my brothers & sisters.

Ex.   my brother Wm Kirkland, Samuel Fuqua

Wit.   James Hall, James Allan, Wm Hunnicutt, Wm Simmons

263-(406) Appraisal of the estate of Joseph Bishop dec'd. Included was negro boy Sam. Appraised by Wm Stith, John Ogbon. Returned to Court 25 Jun 1764.

264-(408) Appraisal of the estate of Wm Mitchell dec'd Jun 1763. Appraised by Frederick Stanback, Benjn Blick, John Clack. Returned to Court 24 Jul 1764.

265-(410) Account for the estate of Drury Bynum dec'd by John Little. Named: Elizabeth Bynum, James Gatt, James Lanier, John Peoples, Georg Purdie, Thomas Williamson.

    Noted was a legal proceeding in NoHampton Co North Carolina; the clerk of Southampton.

    Audited by Will Person, Wm Blunt, Wm Thweatt. Returned to Court 25 Jul 1764.

266-(411) Appraisal of the estate of Wm Martin dec'd. Included were negro man Boatswain & wench Hannah & her child. Appraised by Robert Briggs, Philemon Lasy, James Lindsey. Returned to Court 27 Aug 1764.

267-(413) Sale of the estate of John Wall dec'd. No buyers named; included was the sale of 1 old negro fellow (not named).

Account for the estate of John Wall dec'd. Named:

Richard Burch	Jiles Kelley	John Stundy
Richd Burch Jr	Henry Maclin	George Turnbull
Thomas Dewberry	Col John Maclin	David Wall
Dunkley	Charles Mason	John Whittington
John Harwell	Wm Pinnell	John Winfield
John Hays	Wm Scoggin	
James Ingram	Wm Smith	

Audited by Allan Love, Pen^y Hurst. Returned to Court 27 Aug 1764.

268-(416) Appraisal for the estate of George Sims dec'd as by court order dated Sep 1763. Included were negroes:

Annakey	girl Dorcass	boy Peter	Tom
Beck	boy Johnson	boy Roger	boy Tom
boy Bob	Paul		

Appraised by Isaac Row Walton, Wm Chapman, John Walton. Returned to Court 27 Aug 1764.

269-(418) Will of Benjamin Chapman Donaldson   9 May 1774   22 May 1775

    To my daughter Sarah Hines - the use & occupation of all my land that I have not before given away by deed or deeds; also the use & profits of the slaves Isle of Wight, Surry, Jack, Jacob, Hannah, Judy, Voluntine, Austine & Tom; after her decease I give the sd land to my grandson Sterling Hines

& the negroes to be divided among all her children; a bond I have from Nathl Wyche for £63 I deem may be used to purchase a young negro wench who is to be divided as the above sd slaves.

To my grandson Donaldson Turner - 1 mare colt, my household furniture, 6 cows & calves, 6 sows & pigs.

To my daughter Elizabeth Turner - £3.

To my daughter Mary Dupree - £2.

To my granddaughter Elizabeth Dupree - £3.

To my granddaughter Hannah Rives & Ann Hines - £2 each.

To George Wyche - 1 ring of 20 shillings value.

To Nancy Wyche, Rebecca Wyche, Rebecca Dupree, Elizabeth Dupree, Hannah Hines & Elizabeth Wyche - to each a ring of 10 shillings value.

Ex.   Nathiniel Wyche, Thomas Turner Jr

Wit.   Isham Fennell, Henry Dupree, Thomas Dupree

Probate indicates that the sd excrs refused to qualify & that David Hines was appointed administrator with the will annexed with Thomas Dupree & Frederick Davis his securities.

270-(420) Appraisal of the estate of John Parker dec'd 1 Apr 1775 as by court order dated Jul 1774. Included only were negroes Will, Rachel & her child Alec, Cate, Van, & 1 unnamed.

Appraised by Sterling Edmunds, Henry Edmunds, John Gilliam. Returned to Court 22 May 1775.

271-(421) Appraisal of the estate of Col Drury Stith dec'd 20 Mar 1771. Included were,

Aggy	Frank	Lewis	Sarah
Amy	Hannah	Mag	Sarah
Betty	Jack	Milley	Scipio
Bob	Jacko	Molley	Suckey
Charles	Jamey	Nanny	Sunkey
Daniel	Joe	Punch	Tom
Dick	John	Robin	Will
Dinah	Judy	Sall	
Fanney			

Signed by Thos Stith admr. Appraised by Nathiniel Harrison, Buckner Stith Sr, George Walker, Samuel Harwell. Returned to Court 26 Jun 1775.

272-(432) Sale of the estate of Ricd Morris 6 Apr 1774. No buyers named. Signed by Susannah Morriss admrx. Returned to Court 26 Jun 1775.

273-(434) Appraisal of the estate of Robt Nicolson dec'd 1 Jul 1773. Included were negroes:

Aggy	Bob	Jupiter	Sampson
Amy	David	Milly	Sue
Beck	Dick	Nan	Temp
Ben	Isaac	Ned	Will
Bett	Jack	Patt	

Signed by Thomas Stith & Rebecca Nicolson excrs. Appraised by Benjamin Blick, Buckner Stith

Jr, Zebulon Lewis, Frederick Burgess. Returned to Court 26 Jun 1775.

274-(439) Will of Richard Branscom   7 Mar 1775   24 Jul 1775
Of Meherrin Parish. "Sick and Weak of Body"

To my son Thomas - 100 acres where he now lives, from Narrow Branch to Haw Branch & not touching the low grounds of Duglass Run.

To my son Richard - 200 acres on the south side of Uper Spring Run, which is part of the tract I sold to Robert Williamson; also his 1 first choice of my beds & furniture.

To my son John - 200 acres where I now live after the death of my wife Sarah; also 1 feather bed & furniture.

To my daughter Sarah Branscom - 1 feather bed & furniture, 1 loom & geer.

To my wife Sarah - lend to her for life all the rest of my estate & after her death my estate to be divided among my 3 children Richard, John & Sarah, but should any of these 3 marry before I die, then "they shall not come in for any part of my Estate lent to my said wife . . . ."

If Wm Richardson does not pay for a tract of land that he purchased from me, then the sd land to be sold & the money divided among my 3 children Richard, John & Sarah.

Ex.   my wife Sarah Branscom, my son Richard Branscom
Wit.   Wm Goodrich, Edward Goodrich Jr, Wm Furgason
Probate indicates that the sd excrs qualified with Duglass Wilkins their security.

275-(441) Will of Henry Wilson   24 Sep 1774   24 Jul 1775
Of St Andrews Parish.

To my 2 sons James & Henry - 430 acres in Maclinburgh Co on the south side of Mountain Creek.

To my son James - negro man Peter.

To my daughter Martha Dunkley - lend to her for her life negro boy Arthur & 1 bed; at her death, the sd negro boy to go to my grandson Henry Dunkley.

To my daughter Mary Nash - lend to her for her life negro boy Harry & at her death I give the sd negro to my grandson John Nash.

To my son John - negro boys Moses & Aaron &, at my wife's death, also negro girl Rose, provided my sd son does not charge my estate for a former account, but if does, then 1 of the sd negroes to be sold to discharge the debt.

To my son Henry "if he should return" - negro girl Pheby; should he not return, then the sd negro to remain in the possession of my wife during her lifetime & then to be divided among the rest of my children.

To wife - lend to her for her lifetime negroes Sam, Solomon, Phillis, Holley, Rose & Viny, & Phibby if my son Henry should not return; also all my stock & household furniture, excepting the beds already given; at my wife's death, all my estate not already given to go to my children; also lend to her for life the plantation where I now live.

To my son John - the land & plantation where he now lives & at my wife's death I give him the land & plantation where I now live.

Ex.   my wife, my son John Wilson
Wit.   Hugh Williams, John Quarles

Probate indicates that John Wilson qualified with John Lattimore & Jacob Willis his securities & that the sd excrx refused to qualify.

276-(444) Will of Elizabeth Walton   12 Feb 1771   24 Jul 1775
    To my grandson George Sims - £10 at age 21.
    To my granddaughter Sarah Sims - £10 at age 21.
    To my grandson Isaac Row Sims - £10 at age 21.
    To my daughters Mary *[torn]* - *[torn]*
    To my daughter Kathrine Harris - my sealskin trunk that I keep my clothes in.
    The residue of my estate to be sold & the money divided into 4 parts & 1 part given to the children of my son Isaac Row Walton, & the other 3 parts divided among my 3 now living children John Walton, Mary Letbetter & Katharine Harris.
Ex.   Henry Munger, Littlebury Robinson
Wit.   *[torn]*
Probate indicates that David Stokes & Sarah Stokes were 2 of the witnesses; that the sd excrs refused to qualify & that administration with the will [annexed] was granted to George Letbetter with Gideon Harris & Briggs Goodrich his securities.

277-(446) Will of Absalom Harwell   3 Nov 1774   25 Sep 1775
"Sick and Weak in Body"
    To my wife Anne - 1 young mare, all my hogs & sheep, all my household furniture, my crops.
    To the child my sd wife is now pregnant with - 1 gun, 1 silver watch.
    To my father Samuel - my old black horse.
Ex.   my brother Samuell Harwell
Wit.   Thos Short, Thos Stith
Probate indicates that the sd excr qualified with Wm Walker & John Jones his securities.

278-(448) Will of George Clack   9 Oct 1773   25 Sep 1775
Of St Andrews Parish.
    To my wife Purdence - I give to her for life the use of my plantation where I now live on the south side of Great Creek, joining Rollings & Peter Wms; also the use of negroes Jack, Smith & Bocer, & also my livestock.
    To my son George - negroes Tom, Friday, Cloe, Juno & Peter; also give to him after my sd wife's death the above mentioned tract of land.
    To my son Elisha - I give to him after the death of my sd wife the 3 negroes given for her use.
    To my daughter Prudence Courtney - negro boy Daniel.
    To my daughter Mary Bass - negro boy Voluntine.
    To my son Randle - negroes Austin, Will & Abby.
    To my daughter Patience Wyche - negro wench Cull.
    The remainder of my estate to be sold after my sd wife's death & the money divided among all my children, namely, Mary Bass, Randle Clack, Elisha Clack, Tempy Stokes, Prudence Courtney, Patience Wyche & George Clack.
    The estate devised to my son Randle to remain in the hands of my executors until sd Randle

"shall appear and make or Demands of his Legacies;" should he be dead & never makes a demand, then his legacy to be divided among my executors.

Ex.   my 2 sons Elisha Clack & George Clack

Wit.   John Clack, Henry Robinson, James Clack, Mary Robinson, Patty Clack.

Probate indicates that sd Elisha Clack qualified with Thos Bass & Thos Gholson his securities. Sd George Clack qualified 22 Apr 1776 with John Williams, Thomas Bass & Lewis Scarborough his securities.

279-(451) Account for the estate of Charles Gorden dec'd by Anne Richerson admr. Named:

Benjamin Blick	Rawley Hightower	Thos Stith
Wm Brent	John Hobbs	Maj Thos Stith
James Corner	Barthm Ingram	Richard Taylor
Martha Dunkley	John Ingram	Charles Vaughan
Sterling Edmunds	Jiles Kelley	David Vaughan
Thos Edmunds	Lewis Lanier	George Walker
John Edmundson	Richard Lanier	Isham Westmoreland
James Fisher	Wm Lanier	Edmund Wilkins
Robert Gee	Frizzell Maclin	John Williams
John Goldston	Mary Merritt	John Wright
Abner Greenwood	Henry Moss	Solomon Wynne
Joseph Harper	John Quarles	
John Hightower	Thos Rives	

Audited by Hugh Williams, Robert Lanier as by court order dated Aug 1774. Returned to Court 25 Sep 1775.

280-(453) Sale of the estate of Thos Washington dec'd in Surry Co 6 Dec 1774. Buyers:

John Austin	Caleb Ellis	James Nicholson
Wm Bailey	Jonathan Ellis	Owen Preston
Wm Bailey Jr	Jas Gilcrist	James Rae
Wm Blunt	Etheldred Gray	Nathl Sebrell
Joseph Cheatham	Thos Holt	Wm Spratly
Benjamin Clary	Henry Howard	Sarah Washington
Lemuel Cock	Wm Jorden	Henry White
George Cooper	Jorden Judkins	Nicholas Wilson
John Cooper	James Kee	Hubbard Wiott
Archibald Dunlap	Benjn Mooring	
Cabell Ellis		

Returned to Court 25 Sep 1775.

281-(456) Account for the estate of Thos Person dec'd by Jesse Williamson admr. Named were John Ballard, Secretary Nelson, Capt John Turner.

Returned to Court 25 Sep 1775.

282-(457) Inventory & sale of the estate of Henry Cook dec'd 23 Aug 1774. Buyers:

John Anderson	Morris Floid	John Pritchett
Burwell Bass	Thos Floid	Moses Rives
Drury Bass	John Guter	Edwd Rowell
Samuel Bass	Jacob Harris	John Shearling
Henry Brown	Nathl Hix	Eades Smith
John Brown	John Jeeter	John Taylor
Jesse Butt	Joel Knight	James Tomlinson
Daniel Catoe	Justin Knott	John Tomlinson
Daniel Catoe Sr	James Lanier	Lucas Tomlinson
Sterling Catoe	Thos Low	John Turner
Benjn Clack	John Mackintire	Henry Wall
James Clack	Kirby Moody	Wm Wammock
Wm Clack	John Morgan	Henry Williams
Drury Cook	David Peeples	Robert Wms
Henry Cook	Ephraim Peeples	Henry Williamson
Jane Cramore	Robert Peeples	James Williamson
Lewis Dupree	Batt Peterson	Robert Williamson
Wm Epps	John Peterson	George Wyche
William Evans	Solomon Poarch	John Wyche
Hardy Fennell	Andrew Prince	

Returned to Court 25 Sep 1775.

283-(464) Appraisal of the estate of Henry Wilson dec'd 1 Aug 1775. Included were negroes:

Aaron	Moses	Phillis	Will
Hall	Old Solomon	Rose	
Holly	Phibby	Sam	

Appraised by George Walker, Benjamin Ingram, Robert Lanier.

John Wilson the excr reported Richard Hanson had made a purchase from sd Henry Wilson & that Joseph Jones was indebted to the sd Henry Wilson. Returned to Court 25 Sep 1775.

284-(468) Appraisal of the estate of Henry Wilson dec'd in Maclinburg. Included were negroes Peter & Arthur. Appraised by Henry Deloney, John Ballard Jr, Samuel Marshall Jr. Returned to Court 25 Sep 1775.

285-(469) Inventory of the debts due by bond & open account to George Rives "found at his Disease." Named:

John Booth	Daniel Hawkins	Thos Massie
Benjamin Bynum	John Johnson	Humphrey Morgan
Hen Cook	James King	John Morris
Joshua Dewberry	Wm Knight	James Odonnally
John Dobie	John Lovesay	William Peeples
Joseph Finch	John Massie	John Peterson

Ambrus Proctor	John Smith	Aaron Vinsent
Simon Rives	William Smith	Thomas Williamson
Wm Rives	John Tomlinson	
Jesse Roland	Joseph Tuke	

Signed by Wm Massey. Returned to Court 23 Oct 1775.

286-(471) Will of John(x)Rosser   25 Feb 1775   23 Oct 1775
Of Meherrin Parish.

To my son David - the land where I now live provided sd David shall allow his mother Elizabeth Rosser for life sufficient lands to work 2 hands & 1 room in the house.

To my wife Elizabeth - lend to her for life negro Will & then I give sd Will to my daughter Rebecca Tomlinson; also lend to my sd wife for life negro wench Janey & then I give sd Janey & her increase to my daughter Elizabeth Rosser; also lend to my sd wife for life 1 horse & saddle, 1 bed & furniture, 2 cows & calves, etc, & then all to be sold & the money divided among my 4 sons John, James, Thomas & Benjamin.

To my son David - negroes Robin & Little Jenny, 1 bed & furniture.

To my son Benjamin - negro boy Toby, 1 bed & furniture, 1 horse & saddle.

To my daughter Sarah Rosser - negro girl Cate, 1 bed furniture.

To my daughter Mary Davis - negro girl Frances, £10 VA.

To my daughter Elizabeth Rosser - 1 bed & furniture.

To my daughter Rebecca Tomlinson - £4 VA.

To my son John - the land he lives on.

The rest of my estate & negroes Pat & Phoebe to be sold & the money, after my debts are paid, is to be divided among my 4 children David, Benjamin, Sarah & Elizabeth.

Ex.   John Rosser, David Rosser
Wit.   James Wall Jr, Mary Wall
Probate indicates that the sd excrs qualified with James Wall Jr & John Turner their securities.

287-(473) Will of William(x)Williams   16 Jan 1773   23 Oct 1775
Of St Andrews Parish. "weak in Body"

To my wife Mary - the use of the house where I now dwell with the plantation, negroes, stock, & all my household furniture, during her widowhood.

To my son Matthew - negro woman Lucy, 1 violin & 1 copper kettle after my wife's death.

To my son Lazarus - negro girl Doll, 1 sword, scabbard & belt.

To my son William - after my wife's death, I give him the house, land & plantation where I now live, as also negro Dick, 2 cows & calves, etc.

To my daughter Amy Jackson - 260 acres allotted for her joining Matthew Williams, William Johnson & Daniel Taylor.

To my brother Benjamin Williams of Southampton Co - all the lands in Southampton which my father Nicholas Williams desired he should have; also my right to negro woman Martha & her increase which my sd father desired sd Benjamin to have.

The remainder of my estate to be divided among my 4 daughters Ann Johnson, Martha Bennitt, Sarah Phips, & Amy Jackson, after the death of my sd wife, & my 3 sons Matthew, Lazarus & William to make the division among my sd daughters.

Ex.   my 2 sons Lazarus Williams & William Williams

Wit.   Lazarus Williams, Edward Goodrich, John Strange, Alexr(x)Burdge

Probate indicates that William Williams qualified with John Mitchell & John Rose his securities.

288-(475) Appraisal of the estate of Samuel Wright dec'd. Appraised by Owen Myrick, John Warren, Laurence Howse. Returned to Court 27 Nov 1775.

289-(476) Will of John Rives   20 Aug 1775   22 Jan 1776

"Sick and Weak"

    To my wife Elizabeth - negroes Jane, Tillar, Criss, Arthur, Fred, London; also 1 side saddle, etc.

    To my father - all the rest & residue of my estate after paying my debts.

    My wife to pay all the debts that she "corrected before I Married her out of her Legacy."

Ex.   my wife Elizabeth Rives, my father Benjamin Rives

Wit.   William Fox, William Lundy, Lucas Tomlinson

Probate indicates that Benjamin Rives qualified with Henry Turner & William Lundy his securities, & that sd Elizabeth Rives refused to qualify.

290-(478) Inventory of the estate of William Williams dec'd 24 Nov 1775. Included were negroes Dick, Lucy & her child Bob, Doll, Ben, Fred.

    Signed by William Williams acting excr. Returned to Court 22 Jan 1776.

291-(479) Will of Harmon(x)Rives   3 Jan 1776   22 Jan 1776

"very Sick and Weak in Body"

    To my cousin Benjamin Rives - all my whole estate after my debts are paid; should there be no such heir, then my estate to be divided among my brother William Rives' children.

Ex.   my brother William Rives, Benjamin Rives

Wit.   Patty(x)Gulley, John Jeter

292-(481) Will of Howell Briggs   13 Jul 1774   22 Aug 1774

Of St Andrews Parish.

    To my wife - lend to her for life or widowhood my land & plantation where I now live.

    To my daughter Betsy - after my wife's death or marriage, I give to her my land & plantation where I now live, but should my sd daughter die without issue, then my nephew Jesse Briggs son of Thomas Briggs should have my sd land.

Ex.   my father-in-law John Quarles

Wit.   Hugh Williams, Thomas Briggs, Saml Briggs

Probate indicates that the sd excr qualified with Moses Quarles & David Roper his securities; will was further proved 26 Feb 1776.

293-(482) Appraisal of the estate of Richard Branscomb dec'd 2 Nov 1775. Appraised by William Goodrich, William Barrow, William Forgason Sr. Returned to Court 26 Feb 1776.

294-(484) Appraisal of the estate of Absalom Rose dec'd 22 Feb 1776. Appraised by James Wall Jr, Seymour Powell, Thos Llewellin. Returned to Court 25 Mar 1776.

295-(484) Appraisal of the estate of Thomas Griffis[*in margin:* Griffith] 8 Feb 1776. Appraised by Peter Freeman, George Woodroof, Thomas Eaves. Returned to Court 25 Mar 1776.

296-(485) Will of Urvin Brown   23 Sep 1775   22 Apr 1776
Of Meherrin Parish. "very sick"
   To my wife Mary - lend to her all my estate until my son Burwell comes of age or she marries &, at either event, my personal estate should be divided, reserving to my sd wife negroes Matt, Anthony, Abby, Mary & Winney, with 2 feather beds; & after her decease, the sd negroes to be divided among my surviving children.
   After my son Burwell comes of age, then John Turner, James Wall, & James Wall Jr are to make an equal distribution of the residue of my negroes & their increase among my surviving children.
   To my son Burwell - the land & plantation where I now live, provided he comes to age 21 or marries & has issue; should he not, then my sd land to be sold & the money divided among my surviving children.
   To my wife - 1 bay mare I bought from Henry Bass.
   Other legacies & provisions.
Ex.   my wife Mary Brown, my friend John Maclin
Wit.   James Wall, Nathaniel Hicks, George Wyche
Probate indicates that the sd excrs qualified with Charles Stewart & John Brodnax their securities.

297-(487) Will of Samuel Tewell   1 Mar 1776   22 Apr 1776
"As I have listed in the standing Army for the space of two Years to defend my Country if it should be please God that I shou'd get killed or Die I give my negroe Boy Dick to my Sister Jane Tewell and her Heirs for ever. I leave my negroe fellow Bob to be sold to pay my just Debts and the Balance to John Tewell for ever. I leave my Stock of Cattle and Hogs and Feather Bed and Colt to Matthew Davis. I leave my Mare and black Horse to Matthew Tewell.
   Probate indicates that since there was no witness, that Shadrack Alfriend testified to the handwriting & thus the will was proved.

298-(487) Appraisal of the estate of John Rives dec'd 3 Mar 1776. Included were Jane & her 2 children; wench Criss; boy Arthur; wench & child Tiller.
   Appraised by James Allen, Benja Sykes, John Jeter. Returned to Court 22 Apr 1776.

299-(488) Appraisal of the estate of Penny Hurst dec'd 25 May 1776. Appraised by Nathl Mabry, Benja Williams, Nathaniel Malone. Returned to Court 27 May 1776.

300-(489) Will of Samuel Pincham   3 Nov 1773   24 Jun 1776
Of St Andrew Parish.
   To Henry Anderson of Amelia Co - the land & plantation where I now live; as also the tools, house & kitchen furniture except a desk which I give to my grandson Samuel Pincham; also to sd

Henry Anderson I give slaves Jeff, Swan, Doll, Patt & Ben on condition that sd Anderson will permit my daughter Mary Roberts to enjoy all the sd premises during her lifetime & after her death I give the sd land where I now live to my grandsons Samuel Roberts & Thomas Roberts.

All the slaves mentioned above to be divided among the children of my daughter Mary Roberts that shall be living at her death, as well as the stocks, etc.

To my granddaughter Rebecca Roberts - negro girl Sarah.

To my granddaughter Jane Roberts - negro girl Silvia.

To my grandson Samuel Pincham - all my ready money after my debts are paid & all the money due me by bond or otherwise.

To my son Peter - all the rest of my estate both real & personal not otherwise disposed of, during her lifetime & after his death I give to my grandson Samuel Pincham all lands not otherwise disposed of; the slaves & personal estate given to my sd son Peter to be divided among his children at his death.

To Elizabeth wife of my sd son Peter - to enjoy the use & profits of my mill in Amelia during her life after the death of my sd son.

Ex.   Peter Pincham, Benjamin Ward, Henry Dennis

Wit.   William Stith, Mason(x)Bishop, William Bishop, Daniel Apperson

Probate indicates that Henry Dennis qualified with Christopher Haskins his security.

301-(491) Will of George Clayton   19 Oct 1775   24 Jun 1776
Of Dinwiddie Co & Bristol Parish.

To my son Brittain - 200 acres in Charlotte Co which I purchased from Col Drury Stith.

Ex.   my son Brittain, William Abernathy

Wit.   Peter Jones, John Clayton, John Short

Probate indicates that Brittain Clayton qualified with John Clayton his security.

302-(492) Appraisal of the estate of Absalom Harwell dec'd 29 Nov 1775. Appraised by David Abernathy, Nathan Pepper, James Harwell. Returned to Court 22 Jul 1776.

303-(492) Account for the estate of Hugh Hall dec'd. Named:

William Allen	Mrs Edwards	Charles Hynes
William Brodnax	Francis Eppes	Samuel Meggott
Jesse Brown	William Fortune	Joseph Proctor
Elisha Clarke	James Greenway	Lewis Scarborough
Thomas Cranfield mer.	Mr Hall	George Woodroof
Arthur Edwards	John Hoomes	

Noted was the clerk of Southampton; also noted was the "sale of the Personal Estate after the second marriage;" negro Chloe was hired for 1773. Returned to Court 26 Aug 1776.

304-(494) Appraisal of the slaves & personal estate of Reuben Booth dec'd 24 Jan 1775. Included were slaves:

Ben	Delee	Fred	Great Tom
Bob	Doctor	Great James	Little James

Little Tom	Old Sue	Sender	Will
Natt	Patt	Stafford	
Ned	Peter		

as also Young Sue & child.

   Signed by the executors Rebecca Booth, George Booth, Gilliam Booth. Appraised by Rawleigh Hightower, Lewis Collier, George Steagall. Returned to Court 26 Aug 1776.

305-(496) Appraisal of the estate of George Clarke dec'd 27 Oct 1775.Included were negroes:

woman Abby	man Jack	man Smith
woman Boker	girl Juno	boy Val
girl Cull	man Peter	boy Will
boy Daniel	boy Orson	

Appraised by Richard Pilkinton, Daniel Fowler, John Crews. Returned to Court 26 Aug 1776.

306-(497) Will of William Moseley   29 Nov 1771   26 Aug 1776
Of Meherrin Parish.

   To my son Levy - the plantation of 150 acres where I now live after my wife's decease, joining Thoms Clanton on the lower side of Lizard Creek, Little Creek.

   To my wife - 1 bed & furniture, 1 horse & side saddle, 1 iron pot, etc, for her lifetime.

   All my personal estate to be divided among all my children.
Ex.   my 2 sons William Moseley & Samuel Moseley
Wit.   Edmund Webb, William Holloway, Thomas Clanton, Edward Clanton
Fully probated 23 Sep following. Probate indicates that the sd excrs qualified with Benjamin Moseley & John Beck their securities.

307-(498) Appraisal of the estate of John Rosser dec'd 4 Nov 1775. Included were [negroes]: girl Cate, girl Frances, Little Jenny, Patt, Phoebe, Robin, Toby, William, & Old Jenny & child.

   Appraised as by court order dated 23 Oct 1775 by James Wall Jr, Thos(x)Morris Sr, George Wyche. Returned to Court 25 Nov 1776.

308-(500) Will of Samuel Lucas   4 Dec 1776   27 Jan 1777
"sick and weak"

   To my wife Rebecca - I give to her 1 black work horse, 1 bay horse, 2 beds & furniture, etc, negro boy Anthony; also lend to her the use of the plantation where I now live with 400 acres, & also negroes Nero, Lucy, Judy, Chloe, Bess & Tom, all my stock, etc.

   To my son William - all my land in Mecklenburg Co; also negro woman Nan, woman Dinah, girl Suck, man Peter, boy Will, boy Tom, boy Steporey, boy Aleck, & all other things I have given him.

   To my daughter Becky Lucas - negro woman Aggy, girl Fib, girl Flora, boy Frank, boy Harry, boy Peter, girl Peggy; also 2 beds & furniture, 1 side saddle.

   To my son John - all the residue of the land where I now live not lent to my wife for life, & at her death I give him the whole tract of 800 acres; also negro woman Phillis, boy George, boy Ben, boy Haley, girl Nanny, boy Joe, girl Judy, girl Hannah; also 2 beds & furniture, 1 mare, 1 gun; at my wife's decease I also give to my sd son John negroes, Tom & Lucy, 1 walnut table, etc.

To my daughter Sally Lucas - if she lives to age 21 or marries, then I give to her negro woman Lydia, girl Cuba, boy Peyton, boy Bob, boy Abram, girl Lucy, girl Sukey, boy Lewis; also 2 beds & furniture; I also give to my sd daughter Sally after my wife's death negro woman Bess; should she die before age 21 or marriage, then what I have given to her to be divided among my surviving children.

To my son William - after my wife's decease negro man Nero, woman Judy.

To my daughter Becky Lucas - after my wife's decease negro woman Chloe.

The rest of my estate to be divided among my 4 children William, Rebecca, John & Sally Lucas.

I leave the care of my daughter Sally Lucas & her estate to my wife until my sd daughter is age 21 or marries.

Ex.   my 2 sons William & John Lucas

Wit.   Alexander Watson, William Chapman, Robert Pettway, John Denton, Jesse Denton

Probate indicates that the sd excrs qualified.

309-(503) Appraisal of the estate of William Moseley dec'd as by court order dated 23 Sep 1776. Appraised by William Holloway, John Pearson, Thomas Clanton. Returned to Court 27 Jan 1777.

310-(504) Will of Jesse Abernathy   20 Mar 1776   24 Mar 1777

To my sister Clarissa Abernathy - 1 sorrel filly.

My livestock, household furniture, & my negro wench Jenny to be sold & my debts paid; any remainder to go to my brothers & sisters.

Ex.   my father David Abernathy, my brother Liles Abernathy

Wit.   Thomas(x)Wade, William Butler, John Caudle

Probate indicates that the sd excrs qualified, that the witnesses to the will were in the Continental Army, that David Abernathy testified to the handwriting, that Richard Elliott was security for the sd excrs.

311-(505) Will of Arthur Turner   15 Feb 1777   24 Mar 1777

"weak in Body"

My land in Southampton that I purchased from John Ruffin & my land on Congaree River that I purchased from Colin Person are both to be sold to pay my debts &, should there be a lack, my executors to sell such things "as they think most convenient" to pay all my debts.

To my son Donaldson, my son John, & my daughter Milly Turner - all the remainder of my estate to be divided among them; should either of my sd children die without issue, then the division to be among the survivors; should they all die without issue, then I give it to my brother Thomas Turner.

Ex.   Philip Person, Colin Person, Thomas Turner

Note added: If my sd children all die without issue, then my negro girl Patience to go to my sister Dorcas Clifton for her lifetime & then to descend as mentioned above.

Wit.   David Hines, John McLemore, James McLemore

Probate indicates that Thomas Turner qualified with David Hines his security.

312-(506) Inventory of the estate of Samuel Lucas dec'd. Included were 30 negroes (not named). Signed by William Lucas Jr & John Lucas. Returned to Court 24 Mar 1777.

313-(507) Will of Sarah(x)Wyche   15 Nov 1776   24 Mar 1777

To my sister Tabitha Lucas - during her lifetime I give her the use & profits of negro wench Hannah & boy Ned; after my sd sister's decease, I give sd Hannah & sd Ned to be divided between my nephews Nathaniel Lucas & Edmund Lucas; also to my sd sister for her life, I give to her the use & profits of the residue of my estate & at her decease to be divided between my sd nephews Nathaniel & Edmund Lucas or their survivor.

My will is that Charles Lucas Sr "shall never lay any Claim or Title to any of the above Legacies nor never to be called any part of his Estate."

Ex.   Frederick Lucas

Wit.   Charles Edmunds, Rebecca Lucas, Robert Pettway, Charles Lucas Jr

Probate indicates that the sd excr qualified 26 May following with Charles Lucas Jr his security.

314-(509) Will of Charles Stewart   20 Mar 1777   24 Mar 1777

"Sick and Weak"

To my mother Elizabeth Stewart - negroes Will, Harry & Phoebe, during her lifetime & after her decease they to be divided among all my sisters.

My horses are to be sold & the money applied to my debts, & any surplus to be divided among my sisters Nancy Rives, Rebecca Stewart, Elizabeth & Sally Stewart; after "the Death of my mamma and Grand Mamma," all my lands on the north side of Otterdam Swamp are to be sold & the money divided among my sd sisters; also the land on the south side of Otterdam Swamp in which Mrs Irby has a lifetime right may be sold immediately & the money divided among my sd sisters; all the rest of my estate is to be divided among my sd sisters "upon their finding a proper Mainenance during her life, for Mrs Robinson."

Ex.   friends John Rives & Mordecai Jones

Wit.   Henry Tazewell, Nathl Newsom, Richd Stewart

Probate indicates that the sd excrs qualified with Daniel Fisher & John Jones their securities.

315-(510) Will of Joseph(x)Phillips   4 Jan 1777   26 May 1777

"sick and weak in Body"

To my wife Elizabeth - lend to her all my estate during her life or widowhood; after her marriage or death, all my estate to be sold & the money divided among all my children then living.

Ex.   Beverly Brown, my wife Elizabeth

Wit.   William Lindsey, Michael(x)Singleton, Thomas Hightower

Probate indicates that the sd excrx qualified with Joseph Greenhill & Michael Singleton her securities.

316-(511) Appraisal of the estate of John Ingram dec'd. Included were negroes: lad Ben, child Fanny, boy James, wench Judy, girl Lucy, wench Moll, wench Patt, boy Peter, child Sall.

Also included was 1 wench (not named).

Appraised by Edward Goodrich, Owen Strange, Robert Bailey. Returned to Court 26 May 1777.

317-(512) Will of Sarah(x)Powers   10 Dec 1776   23 Jun 1777

"being sickly and weak"

To my sister Lydia Powers - negro man Davy.

To my brother-in-law Stephen Barns - £20 "to be laid out in bringing him up as my Executors shall Think most proper."

To my sister Lydia Powers - the remainder of my estate of all kinds.

Ex.   my sister Lydia Powers, Owen Myrick

Wit.   Owen Myrick, George King, Joel(x)Woolsey

Probate indicates a further probate on 28 Jul following & Owen Myrick refused to qualify.

318-(513) Will of Rebecca Wall   3 May 1777   28 Jul 1777

Of Meherrin Parish. "weak in Body"

To my son Benjamin - all the land I am possessed of.

To my sons Michael & William - whatever appears to be due me from them on a settlement.

The remainder of my estate to be sold, excepting my wearing clothes which I give to my daughter Elizabeth Sims, & then my debts to be paid & the money divided between my son Benjamin Wall & my daughter Elizabeth Sims.

Ex.   William Sims, Michael Wall

Wit.   Ben Chapman, Lewis Jackson, John Hunt

Probate indicates that William Sims qualified with John Sims his security.

319-(514) Appraisal of the personal estate of Jesse Abernathy dec'd. Included was negro wench Jenny. Signed by Liles Abernathy excr. Appraised by Charles King, Nathan(x)Pepper, John Hardaway. Returned to Court 28 Jul 1777.

320-(514) Will of William Robinson Sr   25 Mar 1777   25 Aug 1777

Of Meherrin Parish. "being now old and weak"

To my wife - lend to her the bed & furniture where she now lies, also negroes Hannah & David, as long as she is my widow; also the house of the house & plantation & a third part of the livestock, etc; after her widowhood, to be divided between my 2 sons Littleberry & William.

To my son Littleberry - negroes Judy & Charles; also Doroty & Darcas, & Peter for whom I have given a deed of gift to him; also give to him Old Hannah.

To my son William - the plantation where I now live & its land after my wife is no longer my widow; also negroes Lucy, Patty, Joseph, Judy Lucy's child, & Isaac Lucy's child.

Other provisions.

Ex.   my 2 sons Littleberry Robinson & William Robinson

Wit.   Joshua Dewberry, William Peebles, Ann(x)Peebles, Ambrose Jones

Probate indicates that Littleberry Robinson qualified with James Young his security.

321-(516) Will of John(x)Hagood   13 May 1777   22 Sep 1777

Of St Andrews Parish.

To my wife - give to her for life the plantation & land where I now live on the north side of Totero Creek; also a third of my stock, 1 feather bed & furniture, etc.

To my son John - 5 shillings.

To my son Benjamin - a tract of land on the south side of Totero Creek joining Collier; also 1 feather bed.

    To my son Randal - a tract of land where I now live on the north side of Totero Creek joining Collier; also 1 feather bed & furniture; should he die without issue, then the land is to be sold & the money divided among my 3 daughters.

    To my daughter Elizabeth Collier - 1 colt.

    To my daughter Mary Hagood - 1 mare, 1 feather bed & furniture.

    To my daughter Rebecca Hagood - 1 colt.

    The remainder of my estate is to be sold to pay my debts.

Ex.   Benjamin Hagood, Randal Hagood

Wit.   Lewis Collier, Elizabeth(x)Collier, Mary(x)Archer

Probate indicates that Benjamin Hagood qualified with Spence Waddy & James Dugger his securities.

322-(517) Will of John Walpole   7 Nov 1776   22 Sep 1777

"Sick and Weak in Body"

    To my wife Elizabeth - lend to her for life or widowhood all my negroes, namely, Matt, Paul, Charles, Robin, Pleasant, Matthew; after her death or marriage, I give the sd negroes & their increase to be divided between my 2 children at age 21.

    The money due my estate to be laid out in a tract of land for my wife to have for life or her widowhood & then the sd land to be sold & the money divided between my 2 children at age 21.

Ex.   my wife Elizabeth Walpole, my brother Thomas Walpole

Wit.   Edmund Webb, William Pilkinton, William(x)Smith

Probate indicates that Thomas Walpole qualified with James Mason his security.

323-(518) Will of James Wall Jr   15 Nov 1777   24 Nov 1777

Of Meherrin Parish. "Sick and Weak"

    To my aunt Agness Wall - the use of 1 room in my old house for her life & my excrs to supply her "with the necessaries of Life" during her life.

    To my wife - give to her for her life the use of the land where I now live joining the Glebe Tract, Robinson's Branch, & also joining the land mentioned in my father's will to be devised to Robert Jones on the east side of Halifax Road & south side of Great Swamp.

    To my son Michael - the land devised to my wife for her life, after her death.

    Since "there is a probability that my said Wife is with Child," then, if a boy, I give him the residue of the land devised to me by my father with the Glebe Land; should the child be a girl, then I give the sd lands to my son Michael.

    To my wife - the use of a third part of my slaves for life, except my negro fellow Will & his mother Sue; my excr to sell these 2 slaves.

    The residue of my slaves to be divided between my 2 children Mary & Michael & the unborn child should there be one.

    Should all my children die underage & before marriage, then I bequeath the use of their portions & the use of all my lands to my wife during her life & after decease to my cousin Peter Gray Wall son of James Wall & Sarah Wall.

    My wife is to be guardian to all my children, but as soon as my sons are age 10, then the Rev Mr

Fanning or my cousin James Wall to take the guardianship of my sd sons.

    Other provisions.

Ex.   my wife Mary Wall, my friends James Wall the older, Seymour Powell, my brother-in-law
       James Mason

Wit.   Mary Smith, Seymour Powell, David Rosser, Daniel Fisher

Probate indicates that James Wall, Seymour Powell & James Mason qualified with Sterling Edmunds, Douglass Wilkins & George Walker their securities.

324-(521) Will of Charles Edwards   25 Sep 1777   24 Nov 1777

    To my son Matthew - 1 shilling.

    To my son John - the land now in his possession.

    To my daughter Mary Edwards - £10.

    To my 4 boys Benjamin, William, Jacob & Lewis - the rest of my land to be divided among them, but not to be sold until the youngest comes of age.

    To my daughter Sary Rawlings - £10.

    To my wife - lend to her the rest of my estate during her widowhood & then to be divided among the following children: Benjamin Edwards, William Edwards, Jacob Edwards, Lewis Edwards, Hannah Edwards, Rebeccah Edwards, Jemima Edwards, Jean Edwards, Susannah Edwards.

Ex.   Benjamin Edwards, William Edwards

Wit.   James Blick, Benja(x)Edwards, William Edwards, Hannah(x)Edwards

Probate indicates that Benjamin Edwards qualified with John Edwards his security.

325-(522) Appraisal of the estate of John Hagood dec'd. Included was 1 negro fellow Bristo. Appraised by William Harrison, James Dugger, Spence Waddy. Returned to Court 24 Nov 1777.

326-(522) Appraisal of the estate of Joseph Phillips dec'd 29 Sep 1777. Appraised by Thomas Claiborne, Lewis Hicks, Robert Hicks. Returned to Court 24 Nov 1777.

327-(524) Appraisal of the estate of William Slate dec'd. Appraised as by court order dated Mar 1777 by David Rosser, William Davis, Ben Cheatham. Returned to Court 24 Nov 1777.

328-(524) Sale of the estate of William Slate dec'd by Robt Slate admr. No buyers named. Returned to Court 24 Nov 1777.

329-(525) Will of James(x)Yarbrough   28 Oct 1777   22 Dec 1777

Of Meherrin Parish. "weak of Body"

    To my wife Mary - lend to her the use of my land & plantation where I now life during her life.

    To my son William - the sd land & plantation after the death of his sd mother Mary.

    To my daughter Amy Yarbrough - 1 bed & furniture.

    The rest of my estate to be for the use of my sd wife Mary during her life & then to be divided between my sd son William & my sd daughter Amy Yarbrough.

Ex.   my son William Yarbrough & my wife Mary Yarbrough

Wit.   Sterling Harwell, Wm Yarbrough, Samuel Yarbrough

Probate indicates that Mary Yarbrough qualified with William Yarbrough & Sterling Harwell her securities.

330-(526) Appraisal of the estate of Ann Moseley dec'd as by court order dated 24 Nov 1777. Appraised by William Holloway, John Poarson, Daniel Hugg, John Moseley. Returned to Court 22 Dec 1777.

331-(1) Appraisal of the estate of Samuel Harwell 8 Nov 1777. Noted were amounts paid to Dr Stark, & James Whitman. Appraised by Buckner Harwell, John Rideout, Robert Gee Jr. Returned to Court 26 Jan 1778.

332-(1) Appraisal of the estate of Rebecca Wall dec'd. Noted was William Simms' cattle. Appraised by Lockett Mitchell, John Prince, Edmund Wilkins. Returned to Court 26 Jan 1778.

333-(2) Will of William(x)Dailey Sr   28 Jun 1777   26 Jan 1778
"very weak in body"
    To my wife Frances - lend to her 1 bed & furniture for her lifetime, also the plantation where I now dwell, also 8 cows, 2 mares, etc, & at her death or marriage the estate not given in legacies to be sold & the money divided among all my children then living.
    To my eldest daughter Elizabeth Malone - 1 cow & calf.
    To my daughter Molley Dailey - 1 cow & calf.
    To my daughter Salley Dailey - 1 cow & calf.
    To my daughter Pattey Dailey - 1 cow & calf.
    To my son William - the plantation where he now dwells with the third part of 320 acres.
    To my son Dennis - the third part of sd land where my son William now lives; 1 bed & furniture.
    To my son Benjamin - the plantation where Silvanus Shelton now lives with the third of sd land; 1 bed & furniture.
    To my son Arthur - the great barn & all the land I own in this place excepting the plantation & 100 acres where I now dwell; 1 desk, 1 gun, 1 bed & furniture.
    To my son Edmund - the plantation where I now dwell with 100 acres; also 1 chest & table.
    All the money due me to be received, my debts paid & the remainder to "be returned to my wife in order to Supply her & my little Children."
    Other provisions.
Ex.   George Malone, Sack Pennington
Wit.   James Marshall, Sack Pennington, William Robertson
Probate indicates that the excrs qualified with Charles Hicks & James Marshall their securities.

334-(4) Account for the estate of Isaac Row Walton by Littleberry Robinson. Named:

Thos Burnett Jr	Thomas Graham	Walter Peter
John Carter	Grey	Littleberry Robinson
Bowler Dobbins	Henry Haley	David Sills
Drury Dunn	Patrick Hall	John Spraberry
N. Edwards & Son	Charles Heathcock	Mrs Elizabeth Walton
Nathaniel Edwards Jr	Henry Lee	James Walton
The Rev Mr Emmerson	Allan Love	John Walton
Daniel Fisher	Allan Love & Co	Thomas Williams
William Forgerson	Elias Morgan	

Noted were the sale of negro Jamey, the hire of negro Herculas.
    Audited by Sterling Edmunds, William Walker. Returned to Court 26 Jan 1778.

335-(5) Will of Richard Thompson   30 Mar 1777   23 Feb 1778
      All my estate to be divided between my brother William Thompson & my sister Elizabeth Morris wife of James Morris.
Wit.   Katharine Moody, Sarah Wall, James Wall
James Morris was granted administration with the will annexed with James Mason his security.

336-(6) Will of James Fletcher   20 Nov 1777   23 Feb 1778
"sick & Weak"
      To my wife Middleton - 1 side saddle; lend to her negroes Will, Beck, Old Hannah, & Lewis, during her life, 2 feather beds & furniture, a cow & calf, etc, & the liberty to clear & to tend half the upper part of the land I bought from Thomas Clanton on the east side of Thomas's Branch; also lend to her the land & plantation where I now live.
      To my son James - all the land I bought from Thomas Clanton between Brown & the westward road; also negroes Jupiter & Anthony, 1 mare, etc.
      To my son John - the land I bought from Charles Leath; also 25 acres on this side of Thomas's Branch; also negroes Jack & his wife Bett, 1 feather bed & furniture, etc.
      To my son Richard - all the lands I bought from Edward Crews, Benjamin Clanton & Thomas Clanton on the north side of the westward road; also negroes Sam & Sue, 1 bed & furniture, etc.
      To my son Nathan - all the land I bought from Isaac Ledbetter on the east side of Fletcher's Branch to Rattle Snake Branch, joining Myrick & Manning; also negroes Hannah & Burwell; etc.
      To my son Owen Myrick Fletcher - the land & plantation I now live on; also negroes Bob & Milley, 1 bed & furniture, etc.
      To my daughter Rebecca Lashley - negroes Jim & Frank.
      To my daughter Betsey Fletcher - negroes Lewis & Lid, 2 cows & calves.
      To my daughter Middleton Fletcher - negroes Beckey & Eppraim, 2 cows & calves.
      To my daughter Mary Fletcher - negro girl Pugg, £50.
      At my wife's decease, the remainder of my estate to be sold & the money divided between my 2 sons Nathan & Owen Myrick Fletcher & my 3 daughters Mary, Betsey & Middleton Fletcher.
      Other provisions.
Ex.   my son-in-law John Lashley, my son James Fletcher
Wit.   Isham Rives, William King, William ...?
[Note: The will also has the date 13 Nov 1777.]

337-(7) Will of James Britt   5 Oct 1776   23 Feb 1778
      To my brother John - my feather bed & furniture during his lifetime & after his death then to his daughter Sarah Britt; also to my sd brother John, I give the rest & residue of my estate after my debts are paid.
Ex.   my brother John Britt
Wit.   Isham Lundy, William Lundy, James(x)Lundy

338-(8) Will of William Edwards   24 Jul 1776   23 Mar 1778
      To my wife - during her lifetime I give her the plantation where I now live to be divided from the ordinary & the lands, joining the river above the bridge, the stable built for Tearwright, the main

road from Hickses Ford, Daniel Fisher, Great Branch, Dr William Starke; also give to her absolutely the negroes & their increase which I received with her from her father; also give to her the use of half my household & kitchen furniture, etc; also negroes Esther, Aggey & her children, Ephraim, Mulatto Charles, Stephen, Abraham, during her widowhood.

To my daughter Rebecca Webb - negro girl Grace.

To my daughter Sarah Edwards - £500 & her choice of my negro girls not over age 12.

To my daughter Anne Edmund Edwards - £500 & her next choice of girls not over age 12.

To my son Benjamin - the land & plantation devised to me by my brother Nathaniel Edwards dec'd, being 2000 acres, 400 part of which I bought from Graves Eairs & is patented in my name to him.

To my son Nathaniel - the lands on the south side of Meherrin River below Hicks's Ford.

To my son Isaac - at age 21, I give him the other part of my land on which is the tavern & store joining where I [now] live, but the rents thereof to be divided between my 2 sons Benjamin & Nathaniel; should sd Isaac die before age 21, then his lands to go to my son Nathaniel & the tavern rented for the joint benefit of Benjamin & Nathaniel.

The residue of my property I give to my 3 sons Benjamin, Nathaniel & Isaac; since "I would choose my sons to be useful members of Soicety rather than wealthy," my friends the Rev Mr William Fanning & Col Allen Jones to be the guardians of my 3 boys to form their minds & manner "so as to render them a Credit to the County."

Other provisions.

Ex.   The Rev William Fanning, Col Allen Jones, Col Fredrick McLin, James Wall Jr, Walter Peter

Codicil. 24 Jul 1776. Since my wife may be with child & should she bring a son, then my excrs to lay out £1000 to be conveyed to the sd son, put out at interest for his benefit, that my estate then divided equally among 4 instead of 3 sons; should the child be a daughter, then she to receive £500 & a negro age 6 or 7. I also give to my son Nathaniel the land I purchased from Joseph Kidd. I also give to my son Benjamin after my wife's decease the land given to my sd wife for life; should sd Benjamin die before my wife or under age 21, the I give the sd land to my son Isaac. This dated 25 Feb 1778 & witnessed by Edmund Wilkins, Seymour Powell, Daniel Fisher.

Codicil. My excrs may sell my slave Christopher to Charles Williamson or Lewellin Williamson "or any other person he may Choose for a Master so as the price be not less than four hundred pounds." This witnessed by Edmund Wilkins, Seymour Powell, Daniel Fisher.

Probate indicates that Daniel Fisher & Seymour Powell testified to the handwriting, that the excrs qualified with Daniel Fisher & Richard Elliott their securities.

339-(10) Will of Daniel Huff   19 Apr 1773   24 Nov 1777
Of Meherrin Parish.

To my 2 youngest sons Lewis & James - all the land I now possess being 460 acres; James to have the plantation & houses where I now live & Lewis the other part, the line to join Hogg Pen Branch; should my son James die without heir, then my son Reubin to inherit his part; should my son Lewis die without heir then my son Phillomon to inherit his part.

To my wife Mary - my personal estate during her lifetime or widowhood & after her decease or marriage, my debts are to be paid & my estate to be divided among all my children & my grand-

daughter Tabitha Huff to have an equal part at that time with my own children.
Ex.   my wife Mary Huff, my son Daniel Huff
Wit.   John Hammack, Daniel Burnett
A further probate occurred 23 Mar 1778 when Mary Huff qualified with William Holloway her security.

340-(12) Will of Thomas Lambert   26 Dec 1776   23 Mar 1778
     To my wife - lend to her all my estate during her life or widowhood & at her death or marriage to be disposed of as follows:
     To Stephen Morgain - negro man Jacob, 1 bed & furniture, half my stock, & should sd Stephen die without issue, then William Kirke to have this legacy.
     To William Kirke - all the rest of my estate at my wife's death or marriage.
Ex.   William Kirke
Wit.   James Tarpley, Thomas(x)Upchurch, Henry Martin
Probate indicates that the sd excr qualified with Christopher Dameron & Samuel Dameron his securities.

341-(12) Will of William Gower   29 Aug 1775   27 Apr 1778
"Sick and Weak"
     To my wife Ann - the use of all my personal estate; should my estate be in debt, then my land may be sold & any remainder to go to my sd wife.
Ex.   my wife Ann Gower, Fredrick Maclin
Wit.   William Brent, Paul Tatum
Probate indicates that the excrx was dec'd, that Fredrick Maclin qualified with Peter Pelham Jr his security.

342-(13) Will of Mary(x)Brown   17 Apr 1778   27 Apr 1778
"very sick"
     To my daughter Frances Brown - my old mare.
     To my son Burwell Brown - my colt.
     To my 3 youngest daughters - £30 to be equally divided.
Ex.   my friend John Macklin
Wit.   Thomas Fielding, Rebecca Thweatt, John Macklin
Probate indicates that the excr qualified with John Jones his security.

343-(14) Will of John Simms   12 May 1778   25 May 1778
Of St Andrews Parish. "very Sick & Weak"
     To my son William - negroes Jamey & Doctor in lieu of the money that came from the Jacksons.
     To William Randolph - negro boy Claiborne.
     To Ellick Williams - negro boy Moses.
     To William Pinch - negro boy Ransome.
     To my wife Honour - all my other estate both real & personal during her life or widowhood to support her & to raise her small children.

To my son John - my land & plantation where I now live at the death or marriage of his mother; also negroes Aggy & Tempe.

To my son Fredrick - £200 to purchase him land.

To my son Benjamin - £200.

To John Lightfoot - 1 cow & calf.

The remainder of my estate to be divided among my 5 youngest children, namely, Mary Randolph, John Sims, Fredrick Simms, Sarah Simms, & Benjamin Simms, at their mother's death or marriage.

Other provisions.

Ex.   my wife, William Randolph, Peter Randolph

Wit.   Thomas Rivers, Jehu Peeples, Hubbard Peeples

Probate indicates that William Randolph & Peter Randolph qualified with Thomas Rivers & Douglass Wilkins their securities.

344-(15) Will of Isaac Jones   30 Apr 1777   23 Mar 1778

To my daughters Martha & Franky Robinson - at my wife's death, I give them land joining Hickory Run, Buchanan & myself, Piney Branch.

To my brother Peter Jones - all the land & plantation where he now lives above the Piney Branch.

To my son William - all the land in the fork of Piney Branch where he now lives.

To my wife - lend to her for life all the remainder of the land & plantation where I now live & at her death I bequeath the sd land & plantation to my son William.

To my wife Hannah - the rest of my estate.

Ex.   my wife

Wit.   Hugh Williams, Benjamin Jones, Jones Makenny

A further probate 25 May following indicates that the sd excrs qualified with Benjamin Jones her security.

345-(16) Appraisal of the estate of Thomas Lambert dec'd. Included were [negroes] James, Jacob, Prince, Jamey, Nann. Appraised by Charles Haskins, Hugh Williams, John Haskins. Returned to Court 25 May 1778.

346-(17) Will of Thomas Adams   5 Apr 1778   25 May 1778

"Sick & Weak"

After my debts are paid, my estate is to be sold except for such for the clothing of my son James.

To my son James - all the money from the sale of my estate & whatever is due me from notes, bonds, & accounts.

Should my sd son James die before maturity, then half of the money to be vested in the right of David Moss under whose care I wish him to be until he comes of age, & the other half to be vested in the right of my brother James Adams' children & my sister Sarah Williamson dec'd's children.

Ex.   David Moss, Henry Nicholson

Probate indicates that Drury Lanier & Henry Nicholson testified to the will, that the sd excrs qualified with John Dugger & John Dugger Jr their securities.

347-(18) Will of Benjamin Warren   17 May 1778   22 Jun 1778
"sick & Weak in Body"

To my son John - 100 acres on the north side of Spring Branch.

To my son Benjamin - the land & plantation where I now live of 485 acres on the south side of Spring Branch; also 125 acres which I bought from Jesse Tatum; also my still but reserving to my son John Warren the use of it; also all my negroes: Jack Sr, Jack Jr, Roger, Daniel, Dick, Bob, Nan, Rose, Fanny & Jenny; also all my livestock, etc, & he to pay £150 to each of my children John Warren, Martha Jackson, Rebeckah Hyde, Hannah Ogborn, Rittah Harris, Elizabeth Lashley.

To my grandchildren the children of my daughter Martha Jackson by her husband Mark Jackson - slaves Buck, Phillis, David, Frank, Jennen, Nann, & Judy, as their parents shall direct at their decease.

To Edward Wesson Jr son of Edward Wesson Sr - 40 acres on the south side of Martins Branch.

My son Benjamin to be free for his legacy "& enjoy the same as Man at full age," & should he die without heir then the land to descend to John Warren, & the rest of his estate then to descend to my 5 daughters Martha Jackson, Rebecah Hide, Rittah Harris, Hannah Ogborn & Elizabeth Lashley.

Ex.   my 2 sons John Warren & Benjamin Warren

Wit.   William Wesson, Sarah(x)Wright, Martha(x)Wesson

Probate indicates that the sd excrs qualified with John Powell, Drury Collier & Joseph Mason their securities.

348-(19) Will of John(x)Gibbs   1 Apr 1776   22 Jun 1778
"Sick & Weak of Body"

My land & plantation & my negro Annerky to be sold to pay my debts if needed.

To my son Stephen - my young mare.

To my son John - my other young mare.

To my wife Elizabeth - all the remainder of my estate.

To my granddaughter Betsey Gibbs - 1 cow & calf "when my Wife thinks she stands in need of it."

Ex.   my wife, William Pennington

Wit.   William Bishop, Reuben Ray

349-(20) Account 1770 - 1775 for the estate of John Gilliam dec'd by Mary Gilliam admrx. Named:

Richard Booker	Richd Kello	Seymour Powell
Thomas Evans	Gowner Owen	Ravenscraft
William Gilliam's estate	John Peebles	Lewis Tyas
Peter Harwell	Edward Pettiway	Mildred Willis' excr
Richard Hill	Hincha Pettiway	Mrs Wythe
Robert Jackson	Capt Powell	
James Jones		

Noted was Seymour Powell who was late guardian.

Audited by William Clack, John Hicks. Returned to Court 22 Jun 1778.

350-(21) Appraisal of the estate of John Simms dec'd as by court order dated May 1778. Included were negroes:

Aggy	Caesar	James	boy Ransom
wench Bett	Claiborne	Mial	man Sharper
Bob	boy Doctor	Moses	
Brister			

Also included were negro wench Beck & 2 children, wench Pegg & 1 child, wench Moll & 1 child, 1 boy (not named). Returned to Court 24 Aug 1778.

351-(25) Appraisal of the estate of Edward Major dec'd. Appraised by William Pritchett, John Gilliam, Mason Bishop. Returned to Court 24 Aug 1778.

352-(26) Appraisal of the estate of Benjamin Warren dec'd as by court order dated Jun 1778. Included were negroes:

Bob	Fanny	Nanny	Rose
Daniel	Jack	Penny	
Dick	Jack	Roger	

Appraised by John Powell, Thomas Claiborne, Hubbard Hobbs, Paul Hartwell. Returned to Court 24 Aug 1778.

353-(27) Will of Silvanus Stokes   15 May 1778   24 Aug 1778
"very sick & Weak in Body"

    To my daughter Sukey Stokes - 4 negroes Sampson, Cate, Cumbo & Jamey Booker; also a bed & furniture, a chest of drawers.

    To my son Thomas - the land I now live on; also 4 negroes Linson, Daphney, Nancey & Nanny; also give to him 1 other negro girl Amy & to pay his sisters £20 each; also 1 bed & furniture, etc.

    To my son William - a tract of land in Sussex Co; also 5 negroes Levina, Bob, Casar, Frank, & Sarah; also give to him 1 other negro Ben Pompy, my son Thomas to keep the 3 last named until my son William is age 18; also 2 beds & furniture, etc.

    To my daughter Molly Hamlin Stokes - 4 negroes Moll, Ingram, Phillis, George & Janey, a bed & furniture, a chest of drawers.

    To my daughter Dolly Stokes - 4 negroes Hannah, Sally, Little Frank & Allen; 1 bed & furniture, a chest of drawers.

    To my daughter Hellen Walker Stokes - 4 negroes Lucy, Daniel, Phebe & John; a bed of furniture & £50.

    All the rest of my estate to be divided among my then living children.

    Other legacies & provisions.

Ex.   John Flood Edmunds, John Jones, my son Thomas Stokes
Wit.   John Jones, Lewis Williams, Hamlin Freeman
Probate indicates that Thomas Stokes qualified with Hamlin Freeman, John Sturdivant & John Hicks his securities.

354-(28) Appraisal of the estate of William Dailey dec'd as by court order dated Jan 1778. Appraised by William Gee, Thomas Steagall, James Marshall. Returned to Court 28 Sep 1778.

355-(29) Account for the estate of William Dailey dec'd by George Malone & Sack Pennington excrs. Named: Frances Dailey widow, John Dailey, Molly Dailey, Love & Company, Silvanus Shelton.
   Audited by Aaron Haskins, Christ' Haskins. Returned to Court 28 Sep 1778.

356-(30) Inventory of the estate of William Robinson Sr 24 Dec 1777 by Littleberry Robinson excr. Included were negroes:

girl Annerky	Dorothy	girl Jemima
boy Ben	girl Fanny	man Peter
boy Cato	woman Hannah	Young Hannah
Darkas	boy Isaac	
man David		

Returned to Court 28 Sep 1778.

357-(31) Appraisal of the estate of Edward Holloway dec'd 20 Sep 1776. Included were [negroes]: Bett, Bridgett, Charles, Daniel, Hannah, Jude, Moses.
   Returned to Court 26 Oct 1778.

358-(33) Appraisal of the estate of Daniel Huff dec'd 23 Jul 1778 as by court order dated 1778. Included was negro Dinah. Appraised by William Holloway, William Gunn, John Barker. Returned to Court 26 Oct 1778.

359-(36) Appraisal of the estate of James Yarbrough dec'd 1778. Returned to Court 26 Oct 1778.

360-(37) Will of George Finch   29 Sep   26 Oct 1778
Of Meherrin Parish. "Sick & Weak in Body"
   To my son James - 1 cow & calf.
   To my daughter Elizabeth Finch - 1 cow & calf.
   To my son John - 1 cow.
   To my son George - 1 young heifer.
   To my son William - 1 young heifer with calf.
   To my son Gerrat - 1 heifer.
   Jesse Davis should taken my 2 youngest sons & they have 6 hogs out of my estate.
   Other legacies.
Ex.   Jesse Davis, William Smith Gadding
Wit.   Thomas Fielding, William(x)Smith Gadding
Probate indicates that the sd excrs refused to qualify; further probate 22 Feb 1779 indicates that John Parham was granted administration with the will annexed with Fredrick Davis his security.

361-(38) Appraisal of the estate of Charles Edwards dec'd. Appraised by Samuel Harwell, Benjamin Blick, Cuthbert Smith. Returned to Court 26 Oct 1778.

362-(39) Appraisal of the estate of Francis Epps dec'd 30 Sep 1778. Included were negroes: boy Charles, woman Doll, man Guy, boy John, man Ned, man Phill, man Pompey.

Signed by Phebe Epps admrx. Appraised 30 Sep 1775 as by court order dated Sep 1775 by Nathaniel Mabry, Burrel Grigg, William Dunn. Returned to Court 23 Nov 1778.

363-(41) Will of Christopher Mason   26 Mar 1773   23 Nov 1778
"Very sickly & Weak"

To my son Joseph Mason - 4 shillings sterling.

To my daughter Elizabeth Speede & her husband Lewis Speede - lend to them for life negro girl Amey & her increase; after their decease, sd girl & her increase to go to all the children of my sd daughter Elizabeth Speede.

To my wife Sarah - all my lands of 900 acres; also my slaves, livestock, etc.

Ex.   my friend Owen Myrick, my wife Sarah Mason, my brother David Mason, my son Joseph Mason

Wit.   James(x)Yarbrough, James Williams, Thomas House, Mary(x)Yarbrough

Probate indicates that Owen Myrick & Joseph Mason qualified with William Holloway & Hartwell Marratte their securities.

364-(43) Appraisal of the estate of William Morris dec'd 12 Feb 1778. Appraised by William Raney, Jone Williams, Peter Willis, Daniel(x)Fowler. Returned to Court 23 Nov 1778.

365-(44) Will of John Maclin   5 Jan 1779   25 Jan 1779
"Sick & Weak of Body"

To my wife Mary - lend to her for life all the land on the north side of Lanes Branch, including the plantation where I now live, with the slaves Selah, Dick, Pender, Frank, Jack, Patt & Giles; also 3 feather beds & furniture, etc.

To my daughter Mary Maclin - slaves James, Nanny, Bess, Arthur, Moll, Lewis, Bowling; also 12 cattle, 10 sheep, 1 feather bed & furniture, etc; but should she die before age 21, then what I have given her to be given to my daughter Jane, & if they both die before marriage or age 21, I give the same to be divided between my 2 sons Edmund & Irwin.

To my daughter Jane Maclin - slaves Giles, Lidia, Miner, Doll, Esther, Sarah & Pleasant; should she die before age 21, then what I have given her to be given to my daughter Mary Maclin; should they both die before marriage or age 21, I give the same to be divided between my 2 sons Edmund & Irwin.

To my 2 sons Edmund & Irwin - slaves Jack, Frank, Dick, Pender, Hague, Judy, Patt, Celia, Fountain, Bob, Sarah, Amey, Nanny; should either of them die before age 21 or marriage, then the survivor to have the sd slaves.

To my son Edmund - the land on the north side of Lanes Branch & half the land I may be entitled to "over the Mountains."

To my son Irwin - the land on the south side of Lanes Branch & half the land I may be entitled to "over the Mountains."

    To Ezebel Jackson - 1 sorrel mare.

    All my estate left to my wife at her decease to be divided between my 2 sons Edmund & Irwin.

Ex.   my brothers Thomas Maclin & William Maclin, my friend Alexander Watson

Wit.   Thomas Maclin, William Maclin, Timothy(x)Reading, James Parham, Lucy Maclin

Probate indicates that Thomas & William Maclin qualified with Fredrick Maclin & William Batte their securities.

366-(46) Will of James Morris   3 Dec 1778   25 Jan 1779

"sick and weak of Body"

    To my wife Elizabeth - lend to her a third part of my land & plantation where I now live during her life; lend to her negro fellow Bob, 1 bay mare, 1 feather bed & furniture, etc; after her decease I give the sd negro fellow Bob & the personal estate to my son William.

    The remainder of my estate to be sold, my debts paid, & then £100 to my son William, & the remainder to go to my daughter Rhode Morris & my daughter Amey Morris; should either die before age 21 or they marry, then the dec'd's estate to be divided between my other children.

Ex.   Capt John Vinson, my father Thomas Morris

Wit.   Gracey Morris, Thomas Morris, James Wardin, Joshua Vinson

Probate indicates that Thomas Morris qualified with Nathaniel Malone & Robert Powell his securities.

367-(47) Will of Thomas Davis   30 Nov 1778   22 Feb 1779

Of Meherrin Parish. "sick and weak"

    After debts are paid, I wish the rest of my estate sold & the money divided among my brothers & sister John Davis, Fredrick Davis, Jesse Davis, & Martha Rosser.

Ex.   Fredrick Davis, Sterling Harris

Wit.   Lewis Thorp, Peyton Harris, James Harris

Probate indicates that Fredrick Davis qualified with John Pritchett & Lewis Thorp his securities.

368-(48) Appraisal of the estate of Christopher Mason dec'd. Included were negroes Jack, Mingo, Peg, Phillis. Appraised by Lewis Hicks, Herwood Crany, Thomas Betty. Returned to Court 28 Jun 1779.

369-(49) Appraisal of the estate of Thomas Howell dec'd 28 Aug 1778. Appraised by Peter Randle, Briggs Goodrich, Beverley Randle. Returned to Court 28 Jun 1779.

370-(51) Will of Francis Stainback   3 Apr 1778   28 Jun 1779

Of St Andrews Parish.

    To my wife Mary - lend to her all my estate real & personal during her lifetime.

    To my son Francis - all my land & plantation; also negroes Peter, Patience & her young child Lewis, 1 feather bed & furniture, etc.

    To my daughter Mary Abernathy - negro boy Bob.

    To my daughter Susanna Hartwell - negroes Nan & Charles, £40.

To my *[blank]* Sally Hancock - negro Isham.

To my daughter Elizabeth Stanback - negroes Ned & Holly; 1 feather bed & furniture.

To my daughter Anne Hunt - negroes Cary & Hubbard; 1 feather bed & furniture.

To my daughter Rebecca Wilson - £40.

"I intend no more for my son Littleberry Stainback's heirs than what they are possessed with."

My stock at my wife's death to be divided among Mary Abernathy, Susanna Hartwell, Elizabeth Stainback, Anne Hunt & Francis Stainback.

To my *[blank]* Mary Stainback - negro Bett, 1 feather bed & furniture.

My household furniture & plantation utensils & all that is not mentioned to be divided among my 3 youngest children Elizabeth Stainback, Anne Hunt & Francis Stainback.

Ex.   Richard Hartwell, Turner Hunt

Wit.   Thomas Rivers, Jenny(x)Stainback

Probate indicates that the sd excrs qualified with Paul Hartwell & Benjamin Hancock their securities.

371-(52) Appraisal of the estate of William Davis dec'd 17 Dec 1778. Included were negroes: girl Frank, boy George, Jack, boy Ned. Also included were Tab & child Jeremiah.

Appraised by Peterson Thweatt, Archable Dancy, Eades Smith. Returned to Court 28 Jun 1779.

372-(56) Will of Daniel(x)Williams   19 Nov 1778   28 Jun 1779

"sick & weak of Body"

To my wife Sarah - my whole estate & she to settle or to dispose of to maintain my wife & children.

Ex.   my wife

Wit.   William Bailey, John Williams, William Blalock, William Denton

Probate indicates that the sd excrx qualified with William Blalock & William Denton her securities.

373-(57) Account 1778 for the estate of William Morris dec'd. Named:

Fields ...?	Col Jones	William Simms
Benjamin Blick	Henry Morris Jr	Thomas Stith
William Brodnax	Henry Morris Sr	William Wall
John Clack	Peter Pelham	Mary Williams
Howell Eldridge	Henry Rawlings	Peter Williams
Briggs Goodrich	Thomas Saunders	

Audited by Henry Merritt, Thomas Lundie, Thomas Rivers. Returned to Court 28 Jun 1779.

374-(57) Will of Mary(x)Ledbetter   23 Nov 1778   26 Jul 1779

"sick and weak in Body"

2 hogsheads of tobacco that I left in the hands of my son Isaac Ledbetter "when I moved down to the place where I now live" to be sold with enough of my estate to my pay debts.

To my eldest son Isaac - negro fellow Thomas, £5.

To my son George - all my land on the south side of Little Creek up to Nathan Harris's land, joining Duglas's High Hill, Rattlesnake Creek, Jordan's road; also negro boy Herculas.

Since there is likely to be a contract between my daughter Mary the late wife of John Bradley dec'd & my son Richard Ledbetter, then if my sd daughter gives to my son Richard a title to land on Broad River in North Carolina where John Bradley dec'd formerly lived, then I give my land & plantation not already given away to my sd daughter, but should she make no title to my sd son Richard, then I give the sd land & plantation to my sd son Richard.

To my son Richard - negro girl Pegg.

To my daughter Elizabeth Williams - negro boy Ned.

To my daughter Mary the late wife of John Bradley dec'd - negro fellow Sissax, wench Junes, & boy Woodley.

To my granddaughter Mary Bradley - negro or mulatto girl Doll.

To my daughter Sarah Mirick - £300.

To each of my 3 daughters - 1 deep dish & pewter basin.

Other provisions.

Ex.   my son George Ledbetter, my daughter Mary Bradley
Wit.   Gideon Harris, Patience(x)Lane, Catharine(x)Harris

375-(59) Will of John Parham   8 May 1779   26 Jul 1779
"very sick & weak in Body"

To my wife Sarah - £200, her life in the plantation where I now live; lend to her slaves Davy, Sarah, Lucy; also lend to her 1 bed & furniture, 6 cows & calves, etc.

To my son James - all my lands; should he die before age 21 or before he has an heir, then the land to be divided among my then surviving children; also give to him slaves Toney, George, Roger, Fib, Liddia; should he die before age 21 or has an heir, then the sd slaves to be divided as aforesaid.

To my daughter Betsey Parham - slaves Jacob, Fillis, Skipper, Thom; should she die before she comes of age or marries, then sd negroes to be divided between my daughters Salley & Polly Parham.

To my daughter Sally Parham - slaves Silvia, Dick, Winney; should she die before she comes of age or marries, then sd negroes to be divided between Betsey & Polly.

To my daughter Polley Parham - slaves Member, Orange, Moll; should she die before she comes of age or marries, then sd negroes to be dived between Betsey & Sally Parham.

All my bonds & accounts to be divided among my children James, Betsey, Sally & Polly Parham.

All my estate not otherwise given away [be kept] in the plantation where I now live until my son James is age 21, the profits thereof to support my sd wife & all my children.

At the death of my sd wife Sarah, I give to Betsey Parham negro girl Sarah, to Sally Parham negro wench Lucy, to Polly Parham negro boy Davy.

Other legacies & provisions.

Ex.   my friend John Turner, my son James Parham, my wife Sarah Parham
Wit.   Nathaniel Hicks, Thomas Lewellin, Saml Davis, Martha(x)Wilson

Probate indicates that John Turner & Sarah Parham qualified with Nathaniel Hicks their security.

376-(61) Appraisal of the estate of Silvanus Stokes Sep 1778. Included were negroes:

Amey	Casar	Daniel	George
Ben Pompy	Cate	Daphney	Hannah
Bob	Cumbo	Frank	James Booker

Janey	Moll Ingram	Phillis	Sarah
Linson	Nancy	Sally	Toney
Livina	Nanny	Sampson	
Lucy	Phibi		

Noted were bonds on Dancy Staindley, Lewis Williams, Burwell Thweatt.

Appraised by Thomas Merritt, Joseph Ezell, Hamlin Freeman. Returned to Court 26 Jun 1779.

377-(67) Appraisal of the estate of Robert Clark 7 May 1774. Included was negro Jone. Appraised by Peter(x)Clark, Henry Clark, Fredrick Davis. Returned to Court 26 Jun 1779.

378-(68) Appraisal of the estate of Joshua Clark dec'd as by court order dated 23 Jan 1775. Included were negroes woman Phillis, Moll, Grace, Dick.

Appraised by John Pritchett, John Brown, George Wyche. Returned to Court 26 Jul 1779.

379-(70) Account 1775 for the estate of Joshua Clark dec'd. Named:

Benjamin Binum	Jacob Harris	John Pritchett
William Blunt	Jeston Knot	Dr Ridley's estate
H. Clark	Susanna Mitchell	Ed Rowell
Henry Clark	Norflet	Dr Stark
Joshua Clark	Henry Peebles	Thomas Tomlinson
Hailey Dupree	John Peterson	John Wilkerson
Thomas Dupree	William Peterson	Captain Wyche
Charles Gilmour	Anne Pitman	

Also noted was Nathaniel Clark's orphans.

Signed by Peter Clark excr. Audited by Briggs Goodrich, James Tomlinson. Returned to Court 26 Jul 1779.

380-(71) Will of Deadmond Rowe   2 Mar 1779   26 Jun 1779

Of St Andrews Parish. "weak of Body"

To my brother John - £400.

My wearing clothes & my saddle & bridle to be sold.

To Susanna Green - 1 pair of silver shoe buckles, 1 pair of silver stave buttons.

To William Clack Jr - 1 silver stock buckle, 1 hat, 3 silver dollars.

Ex.   my friends Thomas Merriott, William Clack

Wit.   Ezebel Merriott, John Patrick, Betty Clack

Probate indicates that Thomas Merriott refused to qualify; that William Clack qualified with Thomas Merriott his security.

381-(72) Will of John Gresham   31 Dec 1778   26 Jun 1779

To my wife Christianna - the use of the land & plantation where I now live, as also the labor of all my negroes, & also the use of all my personal estate after paying my debts.

To my son Anthoney - negro boy Tom at the death or marriage of my wife.

To my son Ambross - negro boy George at the death or marriage of my wife.

To my daughter Patty Barnes - negro girl Jude at the death or marriage of my wife, 1 bed & furniture, 2 cows & calves, £30.

To my daughter Mary - negroes Booker & Hannah at the death or marriage of my wife, also 2 bay horses, 1 bed & furniture, 2 cows & calves, & the liberty to live in my dwelling house until she marry.

To my grandson Anthony Gregorey Gresham - £70 after the death or marriage of my wife.

To my son Assa - after the death or marriage of my wife, I give him the land & plantation where I now live; also negroes Brister, Harry & Alce, 2 mares, the rest of my personal estate not given away.

Ex.   my son Anthoney Gresham & Assa Gresham
Wit.   William Harrison, Henry Harrison, James Marshall
Probate indicates that the sd excrs qualified with John Jones & Burwell Thweatt their securities.

382-(73) Inventory of the estate of Francis Stainback dec'd 10 Jun 1779. Included were 12 negroes:

Betty	Holly	Lewis	Patience
Bob	Hubbard	Nan	Peter
Cary	Isham	Ned	
Charles			

Signed by Turner Hunt & Richard Hartwell excrs. Returned to Court 23 Aug 1779.

383-(74) Will of Peterson Thweatt   25 Aug 1779   27 Sep 1779
"very sick & weak in body"

To my wife Rebeca - lend to her during her widowhood all my estate except my negro Long Fib & her 2 children Peg & Anthoney; these I wish to be sold to discharge my debts.

All the remainder of my estate to be kept on the plantation & the profits to support my wife & children; after her death or marriage, I wish my estate to be divided between my son John Peterson Thweatt & the child my wife is now pregnant with if a son; if not, I give all my land to my son John Peterson Thweatt & the remainder of my estate to be divided between them; if either die before age 21, my estate to go to the other; should both die before age 21 or marriage, then my estate to be divided among my brothers James Thweatt & Thomas Thweatt, & my sisters Tabitha Hamilton, & Sarah Mitchell.

Ex.   my wife Rebecca Thweatt, my brother James Thweatt, my friend John Turner
Wit.   Sam Davis, Archable Dancy, Mary(x)Slate, Sally(x)Davis
Probate indicates that James Thweatt qualified with John Hamlinton & Robert Rivers his securities.

384-(75) Will of Benjamin(x)Edwards   20 Aug 1779   27 Sep 1779

To my son Charles - all my land.

To my wife - lend to her the rest of my estate during her widowhood & then to my divided between my son Charles & daughter Polly Edwards.

Ex.   Benjamin Blick
Wit.   Ichabad Marshall, James Blick
Probate indicates the sd excr qualified with James Blick his security.

385-(76) Will of Elizabeth(x)Hurst   31 Aug 1777   27 Sep 1779
"very sick & weak of Body"

To my daughter Sally Hurst - 2 feather bed & furniture, 2 suit of curtains, 6 pewter plates, my books, etc, & all the remainder of my estate; should she die before she marriages or is under age, then the above sd estate to go to my son William Blanks.

I leave 20 shillings of the money that is due me to school my grandson James Blanks.

Ex.   John Maclin
Wit.   Thomas Morris, Rebecca Sims

Probated further on 25 Oct following, it was noted that the excr was dec'd; Thomas Cocke was appointed administrator with the will annexed with Daniel Fisher & Peter Pelham Jr his securities.

386-(77) Account for William Gower dec'd by John Maclin dec'd. Named:

Isaac Adams	Samuel Harwell	Susanna Russell
Sarah Adams	Thos Johnson	William Smith
Benjamin Bass	Thomas Jordan	Zachariah Smith
Jesse Berryman	Fredrick Maclin	Paul Tatum
William Brunt	John Peebles Jr	James Vaughan
John Deen	Scarbrough Penticost	William Vaughan Jr
William Goodrum	John Prince	John Whittington
Buckner Harwell	Robert Rivers	

Signed by Fredrick Maclin. Audited by John Cocke, Daniel Fisher. Returned to Court 27 Sep 1779.

387-(78) Account 1779 for the estate of Thos Adams dec'd by Henry Nicholson & David Moss excrs. Named were Edwd Marks, Mr Ruffin. Returned to Court 27 Sep 1779.

388-(79) Appraisal of the estate of William Harrup dec'd 8 Sep 1779. Signed by Jonathan Harrup admr. Returned to Court 27 Sep 1779.

389-(80) Sale of the estate of William Harrup dec'd. Buyers:

Elisha Clark	Michael Lane	Joseph Proctor Jr
John Crews	Henry Morris	Richard Proctor
Elizabeth Harrup	Littleberry Overby	Henry Rawlings
Jonathan Harrup	John Parrish	John Rawlings
John Jones	Joseph Proctor	

Signed by Jonathan Harrup admr. Returned to Court 27 Sep 1779.

390-(81) Inventory of the estate of Henry Jones. Signed by Barnabas Jones excr. Returned to Court 22 Nov 1779.

391-(81) Will of Gabriel(x)Harrison   12 Jun 1779   22 Nov 1779

To my son Nathaniel - negro boy Harry.

To my son James - negro boy Bob.

All my land to be sold & equally divided between my 2 sons Nathaniel & James.

To my daughter Janie Harrison - negro girl Fanny.

To my daughter Sarah Anne Harrison - negro girl Visey.

To my wife - negroes Peter, Grace, Betty, Tom, & all the rest of my estate after my debts are paid "& for her to raise the Children."

Ex.   my wife Sarah Anne Harrison

Wit.   James Blick, Benjamin Blick, John Gladish

Probate indicates that the sd excrx qualified with Benjamin Blick & James Blick her securities.

392-(82) Inventory of the estate of Richard Caudle 6 Apr 1771. Included were negroes: James, Jane Milly, Ned, Sam, Sarah, Silivia.

Signed by Thomas Morris excr. Returned to Court 22 Nov 1779.

393-(83) Will of John Warren   31 Oct 1779   22 Nov 1779

"very sick and weak"

To my daughter Elizabeth - negro man Jack, girl Milly.

To my son Merriott - negro man Bob, boy Isham.

To my son John - negro boy Allen, girl Jenny.

To my son William - negro wench Else, girl Amey.

To my son Thomas - £300 VA to be put at interest at my death; also negro girl Silvia.

To my wife Sarah - the use of my negro fellows Bob, Jack, Allen & Else, during her life & then to fall to the above named children; also give to her the use of all my lands in this county to sell as she shall think fit during her life or widowhood; should she die or marry after selling the sd land & before she purchases, then that money to be put at interest & divided among my children as they arrive to age 18; or, should she die or marry possessing sd lands, then the land to be sold & divided among my sons Merriott, John, William, & Thomas; my filly should be for the use of my wife & she should raise 5 colts for my 5 children & that my daughter Elizabeth Warren should have first choice & so on according to their births.

I leave the warrant I have for 1000 acres in Kentucky to the discretion of my executors to be sold & divided among my 4 sons at age 18.

Other legacies & provisions.

Ex.   my father-in-law Thomas Merriott, my brother-in-law Mark Jackson, my brother-in-law
        Gedion Harris, my wife Sarah Warren

Wit.   John Bailey, Benjamin Warren, Elizabeth(x)Smith

Probate indicates that Thomas Merriott, Mark Jackson & Sarah Warren qualified with John Rose & Benjamin Warren their securities.

394-(85) Will of Peter(x)Brooks   2 Nov 1779   22 Nov 1779

My debts to be paid & the remaining part of my estate I leave to my wife Sarah during her life & at her death I give it to Sterling Gawf.

Ex.   Sterling Gawf

Wit.   Richard(x)Massey, Travis Griffis

Probate indicates that the sd excr qualified with Richard Massey & Travis Griffis his securities.

395-(86) Account 1779 for the estate of Silvanus Stokes dec'd by Thomas Stokes excr. Named: Dolley Stokes, Helen W. Stokes, Molley H. Stokes, Sukey Stokes, Thomas Stokes, William Stokes.
   Returned to Court 24 Jan 1780.

396-(86) Will of John Hardiway   9 Dec   24 Jan 1780
   To my daughter Frances Caudle - negroes Little Tom, Daniel, Burwell, Harry, Sue, Sterling.
   To my son Marcum - negroes Great Tom, Isbell, Sam, Little Hannah, Bob, Frank.
   To my daughter Sarah Hardiway - negroes Pat, Lucy, Liddia, James, Sall, Lewis.
   To my daughter Nancey Hardiway - negroes Nutty, Cloriss, Lett, Little Peter, Old Hannah, Old Lewis.
   The rest of my estate to be divided among my wife Mary Hardiway, my son Hartwell Hardiway & daughter Rebecca Hardiway.
   Other legacies.
Ex.   my son Marcum Hardiway, William Caudle
Wit.   William Harrison, Rose(x)Stewart, James Owen
Probate indicates that William Caudle qualified with John Jones & William Harrison his securities.
[Note: The will is dated 9 Dec "in the fourth year of our Commonwealth."]

397-(87) Appraisal of the estate of John Gresham dec'd as by court order dated Jul 1779. Included were negroes: girl Alce, boy Booker, fellow Brister, boy George, girl Hannah, boy Harry, girl Jude, boy Tom.
   Appraised by William Pennington, Sack Pennington, James Marshall. Returned to Court 28 Feb 1780.

398-(89) Will of Hugh Love   28 Apr 1779   28 Feb 1780
Of Meherrin Parish.
   To my wife Elizabeth - give to her for life the land on Evans Creek where Mary Hulen now lives & after her death to be divided among my 3 sons Edward, John & William; also negro fellows Joe & Cato, boy Arthur, & woman Sarah, & after my wife's decease they to be divided among all my children; also the use of all my household furniture & livestock & after her death to be divided among my children.
   While my wife lives single, the estate is to be kept together & the children maintained out of its profits; should she marry before the children come of age, then ⅔ of the personal estate to be sold & the money divided among all my children & my executor then to manage my children & their estates.
   To my wife - £100 "out of my Stock in Trade with Messʳˢ McCall Elliott & Co.
   To my son Edward - negroes Hampton, Ben, Nancey & Hesther; also £100 from my stock in trade; should he die before age 21 or marriage or has issue, then this legacy to be divided among my surviving children.
   To my daughter Mary Love - negro fellows Casar & Will, girl Phebe, & boy Davy; also £100 to be raise out of my stock in trade; should she die underage or before she marries or has issue, then this legacy to be divided among my surviving children.
   To my son John - negro fellow Primus, boy Jerrey, girl Amy, woman Fanny; £100 to be raised

out of my stock in trade; also a pair of shoes & 3 silver buckles, & a gold broach; should he die before he is age 21 or marries or has issue, then this legacy to be divided among my surviving children.

To my son William - negro woman Hannah, woman Milly, girl Martin, fellow Dick, boy Booker; also £100 to be raised out of my stock in trade; also "a pair of set knee buckels and a set gold broach."

Other legacies & provisions.
Ex.   my brother Allan Love, my nephew John Love
Wit.   Nathaniel Roberson, Charles Floyd, Edward Walker
Probate indicates that Allen Love qualified with Beverly Brown & Nathaniel Roberson his securities.

399-(91) Appraisal of the estate of Peterson Thweatt dec'd 1 Nov 1779. Included were 15 negro fellows, wenches & children (not named); also negroes Fibby, Peg & Anthony, who were sold.
Appraised by David Rosser, Edward Smith, John Turner. Returned to Court 28 Feb 1780.

400-(92) Will of Thomas(x)Camp   29 Jan 1780   28 Feb 1780
"sick and weak"
To my wife Salley - all my estate both real & personal to maintain my 3 children Nancey Camp, Polly & Betty Camp, during my sd wife's life, & at her death my estate to be divided among my 3 named children.
Ex.   my friends William Goodrich, Churchil Anderson, John Camp
Wit.   Edward Goodrich Jr, Littleton Williamson, Margret(x)*[blank]*
Probate indicates that the sd excrs qualified with Oliver Day & Henry Mangum their securities.

401-(93) Will of Edith(x)Britt   27 Jan 1780   27 Mar 1780
Of Meherrin Parish.
To my son Charles Ledbetter - negro fellow Herculas; 1 white mare.
To my son Drury Ledbetter - negro boy James; 1 gray horse.
To my son Henry Ledbetter - all the money I have & that I have on demand; also 6 hogs, 1 mare.
To my granddaughter Edith Harris - 1 blue "chints" gown, 1 blue damask gown, 1 cotton gown.
To my daughter Elizabeth Rawlings - all my clothes to be divided among her 4 children Molly, Elizabeth, Fanny & Nancey; also give to my sd daughter £10.
All the rest of my estate to be sold & divided among Charles Ledbetter, Henry Ledbetter, Drury Ledbetter, & the fourth part of the amount to be divided among Henry Walton, Daniel Walton & David Walton.
Ex.   my son Henry Ledbetter, Charles Smith
Wit.   John Howell, Thomas(x)Walton, Elizabeth(x)Blalock

402-(94) Appraisal of the estate of Thomas Davis dec'd. Included were negroes Harry, Phib & Will. Signed by Fredrick Davis excr.
Appraised by John Pritchett, James Tomlinson, John Parham. Returned to Court 27 Mar 1780.

403-(95) Appraisal of the estate of Gabriel Harrison dec'd. Included were negroes: wench Betty, boy Bob, girl Fanny, wench Grace, boy Harry, fellow Peter, boy Tom, girl Visey.

Appraised by Nathaniel Harrison, Benjamin Blick, Charles Harrison. Returned to Court 26 Jun 1780.

404-(97) Will of John(x)Hill   1 Dec 1779   26 Jun 1780
Of Meherrin Parish.
"much afflicted in body"
     To my wife Frances - lend to her my plantation & land where I live during her life or widowhood & after her death or marriage I will my land & plantation to be sold & the money equally divided among my 3 sons, John, Robert & Richard Hill; give to her 1 feather bed & furniture, 2 mares.
     To my son Robert - 1 feather bed & furniture.
     To my son John - 1 feather bed & furniture.
     To my daughter Hannah Hill - 1 feather bed & furniture.
     To my daughter Allis Woodard - 10 shillings.
     To my daughter Frances Hathcock - 10 shillings.
     To my son Robert - my set of coopers tools.
     To my son Richard - 1 black mare.
     To my son Robert - my gun.
     To my wife - my stock of hogs.
     Other legacies & provisions.
Ex.   my 2 sons John & Robert Hill
Wit.   John Brewer, William Avent, Thomas Brewer
Probate indicates that Robert Hill qualified with Henry Walton his security.

405-(99) Will of Mary(x)Adams   5 Jan 1774   26 Jun 1780
Of St Andrews Parish. "infirm of body"
     To my son Isaac Adams - 1 feather bed & furniture, 2 iron pots & hooks, etc.
     To my granddaughter Sarah Adams - negro woman Peg, 1 flax wheel; "This I give to my son Isaac Adams for to maintain me during my life."
Ex.   My son Isaac Adams
Wit.   Avris Wilkerson, Edward(x)Adams Jr
Probate indicates that the witnesses were dead, that Joel Wilkinson testified to the handwriting of Avris Wilkinson who witnessed & wrote the sd will, that Isaac Adams stated that he found the sd will in his father's house after his death; Isaac Adams was granted administration with the will annexed with William Adams his security.

406-(100) Appraised of the estate of John Warren dec'd. Included were negroes: lad Allen, child Amy, wench Alse, fellow Jack, girl Jenny.
     Appraised by Thomas Claiborne, William Blalock, Robert Hicks. Returned to Court 26 Jun 1780.

— to be continued —

...? 1,9,173
...?, Fields 373
...?, Frederick 243
...?, James 173
...?, John 1
...?, Margret 400
...?, Mary 276
...?, Robert 1,41,173
...?, Thomas 91
...?, William 336
...?, Zebulin 123

-A-
Abernathy, Charles 217
Abernathy, Clarissa 310
Abernathy, David 217,302,310
Abernathy, Jesse 132,310,319
Abernathy, John 6
Abernathy, Liles 310,319
Abernathy, Mary 370
Abernathy, William 301
Adams, Ann 125
Adams, David 143
Adams, Edward Jr 405
Adams, Henry 185
Adams, Isaac 386,405
Adams, John 346
Adams, Mary 405
Adams, Peter 125
Adams, Sarah 386,405
Adams, Thomas 346
Adams, Thos 387
Adams, William 125,405
Adams, Wm 249
Adamson, James 176
Addams, Rubin 165
Alexander 96
Alfriend, Shadrack 297
Allan, Anne 55
Allan, James 14,262
Allan, Thomas 55
Allen, James 298
Allen, John 24

Allen, William 303
Ambrose, John 136
Anderson, Churchil 400
Anderson, George 74,129,130
Anderson, Henry 238,300
Anderson, John 282
Anderson, Mary 25
Andrews, Anna 159
Andrews, Benjamin 159
Andrews, Benjamin Forden 222
Andrews, Clabon 159
Andrews, David 5,159
Andrews, Drury 5
Andrews, Elizabeth 159
Andrews, Jesse 159
Andrews, John 159
Andrews, Joseph 135,159,187,
  224
Andrews, Mary 159
Apperson, Daniel 300
Archer, Mary 321
Atherton, Jepthah 257
Atkeison, John 167,171
Atkins, Absalom 14
Atkinson 119
Atkinson, Absalom 222
Atkinson, John 123
Atkinson, Roger 124
Austin, John 280
Avant, William 44
Avent, John 114
Avent, William 404
Averiss, William 208
Avoris, William 21

-B-
Bailey, Frances 152
Bailey, Henry 115,167
Bailey, John 224,393
Bailey, Robert 13,21,60,316
Bailey, William 372
Bailey, Wm 280
Bailey, Wm Jr 280

Baind, James 176
Baird, Elizabeth 3
Baker, Richard 77
Baley, Henry 166
Balfour, James 68,102,111,170
Ballard, Jno 123,136,143
Ballard, John 75,77,175,281
Ballard, John Jr 89,90,284
Bank, Richard 225
Barker, John 47,358
Barlow, John 216
Barlow, Wm 257
Barner, John 131
Barnes, Hannah 159
Barnes, Jacob 199
Barnes, Patty 381
Barns, Stephen 317
Barrow, William 197,293
Bass, Benjamin 79,162,386
Bass, Burwell 282
Bass, Drury 282
Bass, Henry 296
Bass, James 62
Bass, Mary 62,278
Bass, Samuel 282
Bass, Thomas 62
Bass, Thos 278
Bates 248
Bates, Henry 248
Batte, Hannah 14
Batte, William 365
Battes, William 121
Battle, Thomas 44
Batts 165
Batts, William 123
Beck, John 306
Bedingfield, Thomas 31
Bedingfield, Thos 114
Belcher, James 75
Belches, James 44
Bell, Alexander 14
Bell, Richard 123
Belshire, Elizabeth 77

Bennett, Benjamin 105
Bennett, James 92
Bennit, James 209
Bennit, Reuben 198
Bennitt, James 4
Bennitt, Joseph 135
Bennitt, Martha 287
Bennitt, Reuben 135
Bennitt, William 77
Bennitt, Wm 129
Benson, Benjn 175
Berryman, Jesse 386
Betty, Sarah 71
Betty, Thomas 132,368
Betty, William 71
Binum, Benjamin 379
Birchet, Drury Jr 7
Birchett, Elizabeth 121
Birchett, Grief 153
Birchett, Robert 108
Bird, James 75
Bird, Wm 259
Birdsong, John 253
Birdsong, Mary 158
Bishop, James 134
Bishop, Jarimy 134
Bishop, John 134,167
Bishop, Joseph 91,223,263
Bishop, Mary 134
Bishop, Mason 300,351
Bishop, Mathew 223
Bishop, William 44,134,172,
  192,300,348
Bishop, Wm 257
Bittle, John 199
Blackley, Russell 91
Blalock, David 116
Blalock, Elizabeth 401
Blalock, William 116,372,406
Blan, Peter 96
Bland, Jno 136
Bland, John 114
Bland, Richard 136

Bland, Theoderick 136
Bland, Theodorick 45
Blanks, Eliza 192
Blanks, Elizabeth 192
Blanks, Henry 223
Blanks, Ingram 40,44,192
Blanks, James 192,205,385
Blanks, John 192
Blanks, Mary 192
Blanks, Nancy 192
Blanks, Nicholas 91
Blanks, Richard 44,168,192,
  261
Blanks, Suckey 192
Blanks, William 385
Blanks, Wm 192
Blick 157
Blick, Benja 151
Blick, Benjamin 4,107,132,157,
  273,279,361,373,384,391,403
Blick, Benjn 264
Blick, James 384,391
Blick, Mary 108
Blick, Thomas 108,128,135,
  151
Blow, John 257
Blow, Samuel 257
Blunt, William 379
Blunt, Wm 265,280
Booker, Richard 349
Booth, George 181,225,304
Booth, Giliam 181
Booth, Gilliam 304
Booth, John 22,181,285
Booth, Lucy Gilliam 181
Booth, Nanch 181
Booth, Rebecca 181,304
Booth, Reuben 22,42,304
Booth, Reubin 181
Booth, Thomas 181
Booth, Wm 181
Boseman, Winford 158
Boseman, Winney 158

Bosman, Wm 229
Boswell, William 48
Bowdin, Jno 257
Bowls, ...? 2
Boy, James 218
Bracey, Thomas 131
Bradley, John 374
Bradley, Mary 374
Bradley, Pat 96
Bradley, Patt 91
Branscom, John 274
Branscom, Richard 274
Branscom, Sarah 274
Branscom, Thomas 274
Branscomb, Richard 197,293
Branscomb, Richd 258
Brayham, John 206
Brent, William 93,341
Brent, Wm 126,279
Brewer 165
Brewer, Alley 209
Brewer, Alse 212
Brewer, Frances 121
Brewer, George 209,219
Brewer, George Jr 211,212
Brewer, Henry 185
Brewer, John 14,70,109,114,
  127,150,180,184,185,212,219,
  258,404
Brewer, Nicholas 209,219
Brewer, Thomas 404
Brewer, Urvin 121
Brewer, William 52,130,215
Brewer, Wm 106,209
Briggs, Betsy 292
Briggs, Frederick 153
Briggs, Gray 96,132,135,176,
  257
Briggs, Henry 153
Briggs, Howell 292
Briggs, Jesse 292
Briggs, Robert 266
Briggs, Saml 292

Briggs, Samuel 25
Briggs, Tho 153
Briggs, Thomas 255,292
Britt, Edith 401
Britt, James 337
Britt, John 337
Britt, Sarah 337
Broadnax, Anne 45
Broadnax, William 45
Brodnax, Edward 45
Brodnax, John 45,296
Brodnax, William 45,303,373
Brooks, Elisha 244
Brooks, Peter 14,143,394
Brooks, Sarah 130,143,394
Brown 75,336
Brown, Beverly 7,110,315,398
Brown, Burwell 296,342
Brown, Daniel 7
Brown, Frances 110,342
Brown, Francis 110
Brown, Henry 259,282
Brown, Jere 132
Brown, Jeremiah 219,229,232
Brown, Jesse 303
Brown, John 110,220,282,378
Brown, Lewis 110
Brown, Mary 121,296,342
Brown, Philemon 242
Brown, Richard 110
Brown, Sarah 7
Brown, Urvin 117,222,231,296
Brown, William 7,75,99,110,
  220
Brown, Wm 233
Bruce, John 92
Brumbelow, Frances 119
Brumbelow, Jessee 119
Brunt, William 386
Buchanan 344
Buchanan, James 44,111
Buchanan, Neil Sr 132
Buchanan, Niel 136

Buckhanan, Wm 221
Buckner, Charles 136
Burch, Jane 88
Burch, Richard 84,88,244,267
Burch, Richard Jr 84,88
Burch, Richd Jr 267
Burdge, Alexr 287
Burdge, Frederick 120
Burdge, Nathl 148
Burgess, Frederick 273
Burnett, Daniel 339
Burnett, Jesse 136
Burnett, Joseph 137
Burnett, Thomas 156
Burnett, Thos Jr 334
Burnitt, Daniel 15
Burnitt, Deborah 15
Burnitt, Joice 15
Burnitt, Joice Jr 15
Burnitt, Joice Sr 15
Burnitt, Lucy 15
Burnitt, Richard 15,19
Burrell, Benjamin 220
Burrow, Philip 96
Burt, Wm 259
Butler, Mr 191
Butler, Thomas 88,191,210,
  216,310
Butt, Jesse 282
Butt, Sucky 110
Butterworth, Charles 108,151
Buttes, Thomas 232
Butts, Jesse 125
Butts, John 96,243
Bynum, Ben 97
Bynum, Benja 129,142
Bynum, Benjamin 14,77,83,285
Bynum, Drury 199,265
Bynum, Elizabeth 265

-C-
Cagebrook, Mary 170
Cain, George 257

Camp, Betty 400
Camp, John 400
Camp, Nancey 400
Camp, Polly 400
Camp, Salley 400
Camp, Thomas 186,400
Campbell, Mary 159
Carlos, John 9
Carlos, Mathew 132
Carrell, Daniel 118
Carrell, Daniel 127
Carrell, George 118
Carrell, Sandal 118
Carroll, Daniel 31
Carter, Charles 66
Carter, George 66,104
Carter, James 44
Carter, John 66,75,238,334
Carter, Joseph 92,93,239,243
Carter, Lucy 66
Cary, Edward 77
Cary, Miles 114
Cato, Daniel 50,193,211,232
Cato, John 232
Cato, Sterling 24,178
Cato, William 114
Catoe, Daniel 123,282
Catoe, Daniel Sr 282
Catoe, Sterling 282
Catoe, Sterlling 129
Caudle, Charles 41
Caudle, Frances 396
Caudle, John 41,310
Caudle, Mary 41
Caudle, Richard 41,392
Caudle, Richd 17
Caudle, Susanna 41
Caudle, William 41,396
Chambless, Henry 52
Chambless, Lucy 49
Champbell, Colin 242
Champbell, Collin 242
Champbell, Mary 242

Champbell, Robert 209,212, 242,260
Champbell, Walter 242
Chapman 136
Chapman, Anne 247
Chapman, Ben 318
Chapman, Benjamin 26,136
Chapman, Elizabeth 26
Chapman, Isabellear 26
Chapman, John 26,92,216,247, 251
Chapman, John Hamblin 26
Chapman, John Hamlin 26
Chapman, Mary 247
Chapman, Will 136
Chapman, William 26,69,246, 247,308
Chapman, Wm 268
Chappell, Nanny 239
Cheatham, Ben 109,122,327
Cheatham, Joseph 280
Cheek, Ann 25
Christian, Wm 225
Clack, Benjn 282
Clack, Betty 380
Clack, Drury 179
Clack, Eldridge 30,234
Clack, Elisha 38,278
Clack, George 38,278
Clack, Henry 179
Clack, James 234,278,282
Clack, John 28,69,91,128,132, 135,176,216,234,242,246,264, 278,373
Clack, Joshua 179
Clack, Mary 234
Clack, Milley 179
Clack, Nathaniel 179
Clack, Patty 278
Clack, Peter 14,179
Clack, Prudence 278
Clack, Randle 278
Clack, Rebaca 179

Clack, Robert 179
Clack, Simon 74,179
Clack, Sue 179
Clack, William 15,42,98,181, 216,349,380
Clack, William 42
Clack, William Jr 380
Clack, Willie 179
Clack, Winehfield 179
Clack, Wm 21
Clack, Wm 123,230,234,242, 246,282
Claiborne, Thomas 326,352, 406
Clanton, Benjamin 336
Clanton, Charles 228
Clanton, Edward 228,252,306
Clanton, Thomas 75,215,228, 306,309,336
Clanton, Thoms 306
Clark, Elisha 48,389
Clark, George 48
Clark, H. 379
Clark, Henry 377,379
Clark, Joshua 378,379
Clark, Nathaniel 379
Clark, Peter 77,175,377,379
Clark, Robert 377
Clark, Simon 129
Clark, William 224
Clarke, Deliah 150
Clarke, Dudley 164
Clarke, Elisha 151,303
Clarke, George 305
Clarke, Henry 129,130,150
Clarke, Joshua 129,130
Clarke, Mial 150
Clarke, Peter 129,150
Clarke, Robert 129,150
Clarke, Simon 130
Clarke, Susannah 150
Clarke, Willey 150
Clarke, Winifred 129

Clary, Benjamin 280
Clary, Harrod 195,202
Clary, Harwood 75
Clayton 36
Clayton, Brittain 301
Clayton, George 88,301
Clayton, John 301
Clements, Amey 125
Clements, Thomas 125
Clifton, Dorcas 311
Clifton, Richard 142
Clinch 75
Clinch, C. 177
Clinch, Christopher 75,176,228
Clinch, Edward 75
Clinch, Mary 75,177,228
Clinch, Wm 183
Coaker, James 14
Cock, Lemuel 280
Cock, Richard 171
Cocke, Anne 111
Cocke, Brazure 25
Cocke, Frances 25
Cocke, Henry 20
Cocke, James 25
Cocke, John 111,386
Cocke, John Jr 111
Cocke, Lemuel 111
Cocke, Martha 25
Cocke, Peter 155
Cocke, Richard 57,111
Cocke, Thomas 25,111,385
Cocke, William 25
Coleman, Daniel 75
Coleman, Jno 124
Coleman, John 36,37,85,124
Coleman, Susannah 25
Colleir, Jno 137
Colleir, Nancy 133
Collier 321
Collier, Amos 56
Collier, Ann 63
Collier, Charles 39,46,63,101,

132,180,184,185
Collier, Drury 44,347
Collier, Elizabeth 321
Collier, George 180,185,186
Collier, Henry 180,186
Collier, Howell 224
Collier, Isaac 63,64,67
Collier, John 180,185,186
Collier, Jon 180
Collier, Lewis 181,304,321
Collier, Lucy 185
Collier, Mary 83
Collier, Myhill 63
Collier, Thomas 63,91,210
Collier, Vines 63,101
Colony, William 171
Connelly, William 44,91
Cook, Burwell 178
Cook, Drury 102,178,282
Cook, Elinor 259
Cook, Elizabeth 178
Cook, Hen 285
Cook, Henry 178,259,282
Cook, John 14,178,231
Cook, Mary 178,259
Cook, Salley 259
Cook, Sarah 178
Cook, Thomas 178,259
Cook, William 75
Cook, Wm 123
Cooke, Betty 231
Cooke, Burrell 231
Cooke, John 240
Cooper, George 280
Cooper, John 280
Cooper, William 5
Cordle, Richard 218
Corner, James 279
Corral, Rebeccah 171
Courtney 20
Courtney, Clack 143
Courtney, Dr 98
Courtney, Prudence 278

Covington, Wm 213
Cramore, Jane 282
Cranfield, Thomas 303
Cranfurd, Thomas 31
Crany, Herwood 368
Crawford, Thomas 132,136
Crawson, John 176
Crews, Edward 336
Crews, John 305,389
Crook, Joseph 190
Crowder, James 80
Crowder, Sarah 80
Crutchfield, James 26
Culver, Rebeccah 154

-D-
Dailey, Arthur 333
Dailey, Benjamin 333
Dailey, Dennis 333
Dailey, Edmund 333
Dailey, Frances 333,355
Dailey, John 355
Dailey, Molley 333
Dailey, Molly 355
Dailey, Pattey 333
Dailey, Salley 333
Dailey, William 333,354,355
Dailey, William Sr 333
Dameron, Bartholomew 146
Dameron, Christopher 340
Dameron, Samuel 340
Damron, Bartholomew 25
Dancey, Archd 102
Dancy, Archable 371,383
Daniel, Isham 91
Daniel, Sarah 110
Davis, Benjamin 95
Davis, Charles 78,109
Davis, Edmond 71
Davis, Federick 109
Davis, Frederick 231,269
Davis, Fredk 150
Davis, Fredrick 360,367,377,

402
Davis, Henry 75
Davis, Jesse 360,367
Davis, Jessee 109
Davis, John 95,109,367
Davis, Martha 95
Davis, Mary 95,132,286
Davis, Matthew 297
Davis, Nancy 95
Davis, Sally 383
Davis, Sam 383
Davis, Saml 375
Davis, Samuel 55
Davis, Thomas 109,259,367,
402
Davis, William 95,96,109,122,
249,327,371
Davis, Wm 101,248
Day, Oliver 185,400
Dean, Thomas 9
Deardan, George 256
Dearding, George 225
Deen, John 386
Dellihay, Arthur 126
Dellihay, Edmond 126
Dellihay, Sarah 126
Dellilhay, John 126
Deloney, Henry 284
Dennis, Henry 300
Denton, Benjamin 103
Denton, James 103
Denton, Jesse 308
Denton, Jessee 103
Denton, John 103,169,170,308
Denton, Thomas 103,169,170
Denton, William 372
Dewberry, Joshua 165,285,320
Dewberry, Thomas 267
Dickson, Jonathan 14
Dillard, John 80
Dillard, Mary 80
Dillehay, Arthur 162
Dittisfor, John 240

Dixon, William 77
Dobbin, Bowler 174
Dobbins, Bowler 75,334
Dobbins, John 119
Dobbins, Moses 119,153
Dobie, John 285
Dobin, Bowler 176
Doby, Hannah 80
Doby, Jno 143
Doby, John 58,80,81
Doby, Nathaniel 80
Doby, William 80,81
Dobyns, Anne 119
Dobyns, Betty 119
Dobyns, Charles 119
Dobyns, John 119
Dobyns, John Batten 119
Dobyns, Moses 119
Dobyns, Rachel 119
Donald, Alexander 132
Donaldson, Benjamin Chap man 269
Dorson, John 139
Douglass, John 132
Douglass, William 132
Drew, John 256
Drury 36
Drury, Stephen 45,242
Duggar, John 119
Dugger, James 321,325
Dugger, John 4,346
Dugger, John Jr 346
Dugger, John Sr 105
Duglas 374
Duke, John Taylor 91,224
Duncan, Charles 91,96
Dungion, John 167
Dunkley 267
Dunkley, Henry 275
Dunkley, John 190,225
Dunkley, Martha 275,279
Dunkley, Moses 225
Dunlap, Archibald 280

Dunlop, James 114
Dunn, ...? 2
Dunn, Betty 2
Dunn, David 2,17
Dunn, Drury 2,158,334
Dunn, Frances 2
Dunn, Ishmael 2,68
Dunn, Molly 2
Dunn, William 2,134,362
Dupree, Elizabeth 269
Dupree, Hailey 379
Dupree, Haley 59,97,150
Dupree, Henry 269
Dupree, John 59,199,222
Dupree, Lewis 179,188,222, 282
Dupree, Mary 269
Dupree, Rebecca 269
Dupree, Robert 59
Dupree, Robt 142
Dupree, Thomas 269,379
Dyer, James 75

-E-
Eairs, Graves 338
Eaton, Thomas 75
Eaves, Thomas 295
Edmds, Col 256
Edmonds, Nicholas 225
Edmunds, Charles 313
Edmunds, Gray 75
Edmunds, Henry 25,153,270
Edmunds, Howell 77
Edmunds, Jno Flood 145
Edmunds, John 107,191
Edmunds, John Flood 15,25,75, 353
Edmunds, Nicholas 25
Edmunds, Sterling 36,37,57, 270,279,323,334
Edmunds, Thomas 36,37,153
Edmunds, Thos 124,279
Edmunds, Wm 114

Edmundson, John 279
Edwards 36
Edwards, Ann 57
Edwards, Anne 4,5,57,135
Edwards, Anne Edmund 338
Edwards, Arthur 303
Edwards, Benjamin 33,105, 107,157,324,338,384
Edwards, Charles 5,107,151, 157,324,361,384
Edwards, Charles Jr 4
Edwards, Charles Sr 5
Edwards, Chs Jr 135
Edwards, Elizabeth 33
Edwards, Hannah 324
Edwards, Isaac 33,57,137,338
Edwards, Jacob 324
Edwards, Jane 57
Edwards, Jean 324
Edwards, Jemima 324
Edwards, Jesse 94
Edwards, Jno 151
Edwards, John 5,157,324
Edwards, John Jr 135
Edwards, Lewis 324
Edwards, Mary 324
Edwards, Mathew 135
Edwards, Matthew 324
Edwards, Mrs 303
Edwards, N. 334
Edwards, Nathaniel 33,57,75, 77,338
Edwards, Nathaniel Jr 26,33, 65,334
Edwards, Nathl 114,136,143
Edwards, Nathl Jr 14
Edwards, Polly 384
Edwards, Rebecca 33
Edward, Rebeccah 324
Edwards, Sarah 57,338
Edwards, W. 238
Edwards, William 14,26,33, 57,67,72,77,80,111,136,157,

170,324,338
Edwards, Wm 100,129,130, 143,145,178
Eldridge, Howell 373
Eliott, Martha 244
Eliott, Richard 25
Elliot, Richd 88
Elliott, McCall 398
Elliott, Richard 37,136,181, 310,338
Elliott, William 14,77
Elliott, Wm 229
Ellis, Cabell 280
Ellis, Caleb 280
Ellis, Jonathan 280
Ellis, Joseph 114
Elzey, John 14
Embry, ...? 244
Embry, Elizabeth 244
Embry, Ermin 244
Embry, Henry 244
Embry, Martha 84,85,124,244
Embry, Mary 244
Embry, Sarah 244
Embry, William 244
Emmerson, Arthur 12,31
Emmerson, Mr 334
Emmery, Mary 62
Eppes, Francis 303
Eppes, Wm 114
Epps, Edward 39
Epps, Francis 362
Epps, Phebe 362
Epps, Wm 282
Esell, Thomas 44
Evans, Thomas 349
Evans, William 14,45,75,123, 179,282
Eves, Graves 136
Eyeres, Col 257
Ezell, Joseph 376
Ezell, William 14

-F-
Fanning, Mr 323
Fanning, William 72,338
Farguson, William 67
Fawn, Elizabeth 134
Fear, William 44
Fennell, Elizabeth 139
Fennell, Hardy 282
Fennell, Isham 139,269
Fennell, John 139
Fennell, Mary 130,179
Fennell, Mildred 179
Fennell, Sith 139
Fennil, Isham 189
Fennil, John Jr 188
Fennill, John Jr 189
Field, Mr 257
Fielding, Thomas 342,360
Fields, Theophilus 219
Finch, Elizabeth 360
Finch, George 360
Finch, Gerrat 360
Finch, James 360
Finch, John 360
Finch, Joseph 285
Finch, William 360
Finney, Jno Austin 261
Fisher, D. 136,137,257
Fisher, Daniel 7,14,44,45,72, 75,103,114,123,133,136,199, 210,215,314,323,334,338,385, 386
Fisher, Edward 107,136,157
Fisher, James 164,279
Fisher, Mr 107,157
Fletcher, Betsey 336
Fletcher, James 336
Fletcher, John 53,228,336
Fletcher, Mary 336
Fletcher, Middleton 336
Fletcher, Nathan 336
Fletcher, Owen Myrick 336
Fletcher, Richard 336

Floid, Morris 282
Floid, Thos 282
Floide, Josiah 194
Floyd, Charles 82,398
Floyd, Joseph 39
Floyd, Josiah 39
Forester, Martin 75
Forgason, William Sr 293
Forgerson, William 334
Fort, Henry 107
Fortune, William 303
Foster, Elizabeth 121
Foster, Simon 91
Fowler, Daniel 305,364
Fox, John 253
Fox, Noona 253
Fox, Sarah 253
Fox, Thomas Avent 253
Fox, William 39,100,253,254, 289
Freeman, Edward 141,156
Freeman, Hamlin 353,376
Freeman, Peter 156,295
Fryer, William 167
Fuqua, Mary 262
Fuqua, Samuel 262
Furgason, Wm 274

-G-
Gadding, William Smith 360
Gadsen, Christopher 92
Garner, Richard 185
Garner, William 165,185
Gatt, James 265
Gawf, Sterling 394
Gea, Tabitha 22
Gee, Charles Jr 80
Gee, Elizabeth 80
Gee, Henry 80
Gee, John 257
Gee, Robert 96,279
Gee, Robert Jr 331
Gee, Tabitha 248

Gee, William 2,22,87,354
Geer, Patty 12
Geer, William 12
Gholson, Thos 278
Gholston, Thomas 136
Gibbs, ...? 43
Gibbs, Betsey 348
Gibbs, Elizabeth 348
Gibbs, John 348
Gibbs, Stephen 348
Gilcrist, Jas 280
Gilham, John 186
Gilliam 136
Gilliam, Amy 227
Gilliam, Elizabeth 158
Gilliam, John 18,270,349,351
Gilliam, Martha 227
Gilliam, Mary 18,349
Gilliam, William 158,349
Gilmour, Charles 379
Gladish, John 391
Gladish, Martha 132
Glover, Elizabeth 39
Goalston, John 164
Goen, James 143
Going, Drury 141
Goldsberry, John B. 126
Goldston, John 279
Goodrich, Benjamin 103
Goodrich, Briggs 55,75,91,136,
   276,369,373,379
Goodrich, Edward 91,203,
   287,316
Goodrich, Edward Jr 274,400
Goodrich, William 293,400
Goodrich, Wm 274
Goodrum, James 93
Goodrum, William 386
Goodwin, James 121
Goodwin, Judith 121
Goodwin, Nancy 121
Goodwin, Peter 118
Gordan, Charles 164

Gordan, Elizabeth 164
Gordan, Samuel 91
Gorden, Charles 279
Gordon, Samuel 257
Gower, Abell 96
Gower, Ann 341
Gower, William 96,341,386
Graham, Thomas 334
Granwood, Abner 164
Gray, Ann 221
Gray, Archibald 221
Gray, Etheldred 280
Gray, John 75,176,221
Gray, Joseph 257
Gray, Lucy 75
Gray, Watson 221
Green, Frederick 136
Green, Susanna 380
Green, William 75
Greenhill, Joseph 315
Greenway, James 303
Greenwood, Abner 146,279
Gresham, Ambross 381
Gresham, Anthoney 381
Gresham, Antony Gregorey 381
Gresham, Assa 381
Gresham, Christianna 381
Gresham, Jno 149
Gresham, John 381,397
Gresham, Mary 381
Grey 334
Griffin, Thomas 36
Griffin, Thomas Buckland 37
Griffin, William 36
Griffis, Thomas 295
Griffis, Travis 394
Griffith, Thomas 295
Grigg, Burrel 78,167,362
Grigg, Burrill 115
Grigg, Frederick 167
Grigg, Samuel 171
Grubbs, Hensley 153
Gulley, Patty 291

Gun, Hannah 43
Gunn, Thomas 91
Gunn, William 358
Gunter, David 225
Guter, John 282

-H-
Hagood, Benjamin 321
Hagood, Gresham 61
Hagood, John 321,325
Hagood, Mary 321
Hagood, Mordicai 61
Hagood, Randal 321
Hagood, Rebecca 321
Haley, Henry 97,334
Haley, James 97
Hall, Dixon 38,61
Hall, Hugh 38,48,303
Hall, James 262
Hall, Mary 38
Hall, Mr 303
Hall, Nathan 71
Hall, Patrick 54,55,234,334
Hall, Rebecca 92
Hall, William 38
Hamilton, Andrew 136
Hamilton, James 63
Hamilton, Jno 136
Hamilton, John 18,170
Hamilton, Tabitha 383
Hamilton, William 63
Hamlinton, John 383
Hammack, John 339
Hammond, Elizabeth 214
Hammond, John 213
Hammond, William 213
Hancock, Benjamin 370
Hancock, Sally 370
Hancocke, Robert 80
Hanson, Richard 137,283
Hardaway, John 319
Hardie, Richard 77
Hardin, William 228

Hardiway, Hartwell 396
Hardiway, John 396
Hardiway, Marcum 396
Hardiway, Mary 396
Hardiway, Nancey 396
Hardiway, Rebecca 396
Hardiway, Sarah 396
Haregrove, Benjamin 135
Hargrove, Benja 157
Hargrove, Benjamin 107
Harper, Joseph 279
Harring, Daniel 77
Harris, Catharine 374
Harris, Edith 401
Harris, Elizabeth 180
Harris, Gedion 393
Harris, Gideon 276,374
Harris, Harris 374
Harris, Henry 91
Harris, Jacob 282,379
Harris, James 185,367
Harris, Joseph 158
Harris, Kathrine 276
Harris, Nathan 24
Harris, Peyton 367
Harris, Rittah 347
Harris, Sterling 367
Harrison 96,141
Harrison, Benja Jr 127
Harrison, Benjamin 167,239,
  246
Harrison, Charles 403
Harrison, Col 63
Harrison, Daniel 239
Harrison, Dolley 205
Harrison, Elizabeth 239
Harrison, Gabriel 391,403
Harrison, Henry 381
Harrison, James 127,205,226,
  261,391
Harrison, Janie 391
Harrison, Jeaney 110
Harrison, Joseph 239,243

Harrison, Nathaniel 120,391,
  403
Harrison, Nathiniel 271
Harrison, Patty 239
Harrison, Rebecca 205
Harrison, Sarah 205
Harrison, Sarah Anne 391
Harrison, Simmons 239
Harrison, Thomas 16,44,132,
  205,261
Harrison, William 16,17,41,68,
  86,239,325,381,396
Harrison, Wm 94,218,261
Harrup, Elizabeth 389
Harrup, Jonathan 388,389
Harrup, Mining 164
Harrup, William 388,389
Hartwell, Paul 352,370
Hartwell, Richard 26,75,370,
  382
Hartwell, Saml 174
Hartwell, Susanna 370
Harwell, Absalom 277,302
Harwell, Anna 31
Harwell, Anne 277
Harwell, Betsey 132
Harwell, Buckner 331,386
Harwell, Cassander 31
Harwell, Cassandra 132
Harwell, Elizabeth 31,132
Harwell, Frederick 132
Harwell, Greif 31,132
Harwell, James 31,131,132,
  217,302
Harwell, John 267
Harwell, Mark 132
Harwell, Mason 56,132
Harwell, Mourning 31,132
Harwell, Peter 349
Harwell, Richard 132
Harwell, Sally 31,132
Harwell, Samuel 31,132,271,
  277,331,361,386

Harwell, Sterling 329
Haskins, Aaron 355
Haskins, Charles 345
Haskins, Chrisr 355
Haskins, Christopher 300
Haskins, John 345
Hathcock, Frances 404
Hawkins, Daniel 285
Hay, Richard 141
Hay, Richard Jr 143
Hayes, Richard Jr 156
Haynes, Anthony 57
Hays, John 267
Heathcock, Charles 334
Henia(?), John 208
Hensley, Joseph 92
Hicks, Ben 132,138
Hicks, Charles 333
Hicks, George 10
Hicks, James Sr 46
Hicks, John 349,353
Hicks, Judith 63
Hicks, Lewis 326,368
Hicks, Nathaniel 296,375
Hicks, Nathl 117,206
Hicks, Robert 128,204,326,406
Hicks, Sarah 10,30
Hide, Rebecah 347
Hightower, Charnel 208
Hightower, Charnel Sr 214
Hightower, Jno 146
Hightower, John 279
Hightower, Rawleigh 304
Hightower, Rawley 279
Hightower, Sarah 208
Hightower, Thomas 315
Hightower, Thos 146
Hill, Frances 404
Hill, Hannah 404
Hill, John 180,185,186,404
Hill, Mary 181
Hill, Richard 349,404
Hill, Robert 404

Hines, Ann 269
Hines, David 83,269,311
Hines, Sarah 269
Hines, Sterling 269
Hinton, James 66,136
Hix, Nathiniel 240
Hix, Nathl 231
Hobbs, Hubbard 352
Hobbs, John 279
Holloway, Edward 357
Holloway, William 75,306,
  309,330,339,358,363
Holloway, Wm 146,182
Holt, Elizabeth 25
Holt, Henry 185
Holt, Thos 280
Hood, Reuben 175
Hoomes, John 303
Hopkins, Sarah 245
Horsburgh, Alexander 132
Horton, Amos 77
House 248
House, James 44
House, John 44,116
House, Jordan 138
House, Laurance 167
House, Lawrance 44,116
House, Lucy 116
House, Mary 116
House, Rebecca 116
House, Saml 138
House, Samuel 116
House, Thomas 363
House, William 116
Howard, Catey 175
Howard, Henry 20,280
Howard, Jane 175
Howard, John 77,175
Howard, Kathrine 77
Howard, Mary 175
Howard, Rachel 175
Howard, Robert 77
Howard, Saml 175

Howell, John 401
Howell, Thomas 55,369
Howse, Laurence 288
Huckebay, Charles 43
Huff, Daniel 47,339,358
Huff, James 339
Huff, Lewis 339
Huff, Mary 339
Huff, Phillomon 339
Huff, Reubin 339
Huff, Tabitha 339
Huff, William 3,53,75
Hugg, Daniel 330
Hulen, Mary 398
Huling, Edmund 71
Huling, Edward 82
Huling, Mary 71
Hunnicutt, Wm 262
Hunt, Anne 370
Hunt, Elizabeth 228
Hunt, John 212,318
Hunt, Turner 370,382
Hunter, Wm 257
Hurst, Elizabeth 40,385
Hurst, Penny 40,299
Hurst, Pen^y. 261,267
Hurst, Sally 385
Hurst, Sarah 204
Hyde, Milly 49
Hyde, Rebeckah 347
Hyde, Richard 215
Hynes, Charles 303

                    -I-
Ingram, Barthm 279
Ingram, Benjamin 22,98,248,
  283
Ingram, Elizabeth 22
Ingram, George 22,98,248
Ingram, Hannah 98,248
Ingram, James 22,42,98,248,
  250,267
Ingram, Jeremiah 98,248

Ingram, Jesse 248
Ingram, John 84,155,248,279,
  316
Ingram, John Jr 98,250
Ingram, Joseph 22,61,248
Ingram, Joshua 22,248
Ingram, Richard 22,248
Ingram, Salley 98
Ingram, Samuel 248
Ingram, Thomas 216
Ingram, William 98
Irby, Anthony 219
Irby, Mrs 314

                    -J-
Jackson 96,343
Jackson, Amy 61,287
Jackson, Bethiah 216,241
Jackson, Daniel 216,241
Jackson, Ezebel 365
Jackson, Henry 132
Jackson, Henry Jr 118
Jackson, James 132
Jackson, John 92,216,241
Jackson, John Jr 216
Jackson, Lewis 216,318
Jackson, Mark 55,118,347,393
Jackson, Martha 347
Jackson, Peter 55,136
Jackson, Raif 216
Jackson, Robert 349
Jackson, Samuel 216
Jackson, Susanna 51
Jackson, Thomas 96,216
Jackson, Thos 91
Jameson, Dr 257
Jarrot, Nick 216
Jean, William 19,75
Jeans, Wm 132
Jeeter, John 14,282
Jeffres, Winehfield 179
Jeffries, Elizabeth 179
Jeter, John 129,291,298

Johnson, Ann 287
Johnson, Arthur 195
Johnson, Benja 154
Johnson, David 228
Johnson, Henry 195
Johnson, James 61,158,180,185
Johnson, Jno 129,130
Johnson, John 55,195,202,209,
  232,285
Johnson, Mary 253
Johnson, Moses 49,52,228
Johnson, Nathiniel 195,202
Johnson, Sarah 228
Johnson, Tabitha 195
Johnson, Thomas 55,151
Johnson, Thos 386
Johnson, William 287
Johnson, Wincey 195
Jones, Allan 57
Jones, Allen 338
Jones, Ambrose 320
Jones, Barnabas 390
Jones, Benjamin 344
Jones, Britain 55
Jones, Col 373
Jones, Frederick 225
Jones, Hannah 344
Jones, Henry 390
Jones, Isaac 344
Jones, Jacob 258
Jones, James 146,349
Jones, James Seeroant(?) 66
Jones, John 41,91,95,98,107,
  157,181,216,251,257,277,314,
  342,353,381,389,396
Jones, Joseph 283
Jones, Joshua 114
Jones, Lewelling 208,225
Jones, Michael 132
Jones, Mordecai 314
Jones, Nathaniel Thomas 244
Jones, Peter 108,214,301,344
Jones, Rebecca 57

Jones, Robert 323
Jones, Robt 256
Jones, Sara 23
Jones, Sarah 225
Jones, Thomas 225
Jones, William 132,344
Jones,Robt 102
Jordan 374
Jordan, Thomas 386
Jorden, Wm 280
Jordon, Burrel 59
Jordon, Drury 59
Jordon, Hannah 59
Jordon, Jenny 59
Jordon, Sarah 83
Jordon, Thomas 59
Jourdan, John 136
Jude, John 75
Judkins, Charles 75
Judkins, Jorden 280

-K-
Kannedy 157
Kee, James 280
Kelley, Jiles 267,279
Kello, Richd 349
Kellow, Richard 257
Kelly 36
Kelly, Richard 136
Kelton, Richard 96
Kenneday 107
Kent, Edward 244
Kidd, Joseph 338
Kimball, William 75
King, Charles 319
King, George 317
King, James 285
King, Joseph 216
King, Nathiniel 199
King, William 336
Kirke, William 340
Kirkland, Ann 262
Kirkland, Benjn 262

Kirkland, Elizabeth 262
Kirkland, Richard 157
Kirkland, Richd 107
Kirkland, Thomas 262
Kirkland, Wm 262
Knight, Joel 282
Knight, John 91
Knight, William 14,44
Knight, Wm 285
Knot, Jeston 379
Knot, Justain 129
Knott, Jefton(?) 179
Knott, Justain 130
Knott, Justin 282

-L-
L...?, William 89
Laffoon, Nathaniel 136
Lambert, John 31
Lambert, Thomas 340,345
Lane, Michael 389
Lane, Patience 374
Lane, Simon Jr 185
Lang, George 132
Lanier, Benjamin 194,256
Lanier, Buckner 132
Lanier, Burwell 232
Lanier, David 132
Lanier, Drury 346
Lanier, Elizabeth 88
Lanier, Henry 178
Lanier, James 265,282
Lanier, John 39
Lanier, Lemuel 132
Lanier, Lemuell 226
Lanier, Lewis 96,279
Lanier, Mary 39,178
Lanier, Nicholas 45
Lanier, Richard 146,164,279
Lanier, Robert 216,279,283
Lanier, Robin 164
Lanier, Sarah 39
Lanier, Thomas 93,216

Lanier, William 45,164
Lanier, Wm 88,279
Lashley, Elizabeth 347
Lashley, John 336
Lashley, Rebecca 336
Lashley, William 237
Lashley, Wm 215
Lashly, John 75
Lasy, Philemon 266
Lattimore, John 275
Laurance, Ann 167
Laurance, John 167,168,171, 172
Laurance, Robert 36
Laurance, Thomas 166,168
Laurance, Thomas Sr 167
Lawrance, Richard Littlepage 36
Lawrence, Anness 134
Lawrence, Jesse 134
Lawrence, John 134
Leath, Charles 336
Ledbetter, Charles 55,401
Ledbetter, Drury 24,401
Ledbetter, George 24,374
Ledbetter, Henry 24,401
Ledbetter, Isaac 75,336,374
Ledbetter, Mary 24,374
Ledbetter, Richard 374
Ledbetter, William 75
Lee, Henry 197,334
Lee, Peter 32
Letbetter, George 276
Letbetter, John 195
Letbetter, Mary 276
LEWELLIN - cf. Llewellin
Lewellin, Thomas 375
Lewis, Zebulon 273
Lifsey, Anne 102
Lifsey, Benjamin 102
Lifsey, Jane 102
Lifsey, John 102,219
Lifsey, Marthy 102

Lifsey, Rebeckah 102
Lifsey, Wm 102
Lightfoot 246
Lightfoot, John 343
Linch, James 75
Linch, John 176
Lindsey, James 266
Lindsey, Thomas 207
Lindsey, William 234,315
Lindsey, Wm 248
Little, John 265
Littlepage, Richard 119
Llewellin, Thos 294
Locke, Richard 132
Loftain, John 132
Loftin, John 56
Long, Joseph 44
Love, Alan 215
Love, Allan 43,71,99,131,136, 151,224,267,334,398
Love, Allen 75,98
Love, Edward 398
Love, Elizabeth 71,398
Love, Hugh 71,99,398
Love, John 398
Love, Mary 398
Love, William 398
Lovesay, John 285
Lovesey, John 114
Low, Thos 282
Lowd, Anne 178
Loyd, John 36
Loyd, William 132
Lucas, Becky 308
Lucas, Betty 111
Lucas, Charles 104
Lucas, Charles Jr 313
Lucas, Charles Sr 313
Lucas, Edmund 313
Lucas, Elizabeth 44
Lucas, Frederick 313
Lucas, John 308,312
Lucas, Nathaniel 313

Lucas, Rebecca 308,313
Lucas, Sally 308
Lucas, Samuel 137,308,312
Lucas, Tabitha 313
Lucas, William 308
Lucas, William Jr 312
Lucy, Burrel 216
Lucy, Burwell 91
Lucy, Phillemon 207
Lucy, Robert 124
Lundie, Isham 188
Lundie, Mr 124
Lundie, Robert 206
Lundie, Thomas 36,37,151,373
Lundie, Thos 145
Lundy, Isham 121,337
Lundy, James 337
Lundy, William 289,337
Lyall, Thomas 246

-M-
Mabry, Anne 91
Mabry, Braxton 11
Mabry, Daniel 91,96,201
Mabry, Hinchey 33,57,91,96, 136,203
Mabry, James Jr 91
Mabry, Joel 9,18,64,91
Mabry, Jordan 31
Mabry, Joshua 9,31,91
Mabry, Mary 24
Mabry, Nathaniel 40,91,96,166, 172,362
Mabry, Nathl 113,201,299
Mabry, Seth 11
Mackintire, John 282
Macklin, John 342
Macl...?, William 13
MACLIN - cf Mclin
Maclin, Amy 173
Maclin, Capt 257
Maclin, Edmund 365
Maclin, Elizabeth 125,173

Maclin, Federick 151
Maclin, Frederick 9,67,125, 173,203,239
Maclin, Fredrick 341,365,386
Maclin, Fredk 123
Maclin, Frizzell 279
Maclin, Henry 190,225,267
Maclin, Irwin 365
Maclin, James 44,103,130,144, 169,170,173
Maclin, Jane 365
Maclin, John 12,96,125,136, 173,174,203,216,224,226,267, 296,365,385,386
Maclin, John Jr 86
Maclin, Lucy 365
Maclin, Mary 365
Maclin, Susannah 173
Maclin, Thomas 12,125,173, 365
Maclin, William 42,60,125, 173,178,365
Maclin, Wm 21,149,173,181, 250
Macling, Frederick 91
Macling, James 91
Major, Edward 351
Makenny, Jones 344
Mallerby, John 209
Malloby, John 44
Malone, Anne 133
Malone, Drury 39
Malone, Elizabeth 333
Malone, George 333,355
Malone, Nathaniel 86,299,366
Malone, William 133
Mangum, Henry 400
Manning 336
Manning, Catharine 140
Marchall, Ichabod 126
Maritt, Henry 244
Maritt, Mary 244
Marks, Edward 176

Marks, Edwd 387
Marratte, Hartwell 363
Marshall, Ichabad 384
Marshall, Isaac 5,108
Marshall, James 333,354,381, 397
Marshall, John 250
Marshall, Samuel Jr 284
Marshall, Samuell 250
Martin 119
Martin, Abraham 220
Martin, Henry 220,340
Martin, James 257
Martin, Mary 220
Martin, William 220
Martin, Wm 266
Mason, Avey 141
Mason, Charles 88,267
Mason, Christopher 3,80,200, 222,253,363,368
Mason, David 75,80,92,102, 114,123,137,143,363
Mason, Davis 136
Mason, James 16,133,157,167, 171,322,323,335
Mason, John 88
Mason, Joseph 347,363
Mason, Mary 80,88
Mason, Richard 88,141,185
Mason, Samuel 157
Mason, Sarah 363
Mason, William 136
Mason, Xpher 31,116
Massey, Anne 23,35
Massey, Elizabeth 100
Massey, Hezekiah 23
Massey, John 23,24
Massey, Richard 23,58,143,394
Massey, Tabitha 23
Massey, Thomas 14,100,143
Massey, William 14,23,55,112, 143
Massey, Wm 100,285

Massie, John 35,285
Massie, Thos 285
Mathews 119
Mathews, Charles 214
Mathis, Betty 140
Mathis, Charles 147
Mathis, Elizabeth 140
Mathis, Susannah 140
Mathis, William 140
Mathis, Wm 164
Matthews, Susannah 255
Matthis, John 99
McClary, John 77
McKeney, Morgan 225
McKinny, John 61
McLemore, James 311
McLemore, John 311
Mclin, Fredrick 338
Medearis, John 97
Meggott, Samuel 303
Meggs, Thomas 209
Megs, Nathaniel 132
Melton, Isaac 167
Melton, John 115
Melton, Mary 115
Merriott, Ezebel 380
Merriott, Thomas 82,380,393
Merritt 36
Merritt, ...? 36
Merritt, Henry 373
Merritt, Martha 25
Merritt, Mary 279
Merritt, Thomas 376
Merritt, Thos 225
Merritt, William 25,88,132
Metcalf, Anthony 257
Middlemost, Archd 136
Miller, Jacob 164
Miller, John 255
Milnear 14
Minetree, Archibald 3
Minetree, Mary 3
Minter, John 99

Mirick, Sarah 374
Mitchel, Dorothey 144
Mitchel, William 98
Mitchell, Ann 144
Mitchell, Elizabeth 179
Mitchell, Henry 129
Mitchell, Jno 151
Mitchell, John 13,60,61,181,
 287
Mitchell, Locket 144
Mitchell, Lockett 160,332
Mitchell, Mary 144,230
Mitchell, Olph 230
Mitchell, Richard 61
Mitchell, Sarah 43,383
Mithcell, Susanna 379
Mitchell, Thomas 144,160
Mitchell, William 230
Mitchell, Wm 264
Miz'd, Avas 154
Miz'd, Edy 154
Mize, Jeremiah 154
Moody, Ann 180
Moody, Katharine 335
Moody, Kirby 179,199,282
Moore, Isham 91
Moore, Martha 23
Moore, Mary 86
Moore, Thomas 61,193
Moore, Tobias 196,232
Mooring, Benjn 280
Morass, Thomas 41
Morgain, Stephen 340
Morgan, Elias 55,334
Morgan, Ellic 176
Morgan, Humphrey 285
Morgan, John 282
Morgan, Mary 223
Moris, Robt 155
Morris 36
Morris, Amey 366
Morris, Chiseland 114
Morris, Elizabeth 335,366

Morris, Gracey 366
Morris, Henry 36,151,389
Morris, Henry Jr 373
Morris, Henry Sr 373
Morris, James 335,366
Morris, John 285
Morris, Mrs Richard 132
Morris, Rhode 366
Morris, Ricd 272
Morris, Richard 148
Morris, Susanna 148
Morris, Thomas 16,40,44,134,
 166,192,205,212,237,366,385,
 392
Morris, Thos 102,113,201,261
Morris, Thos Sr 307
Morris, William 364,366,373
Morriss, Henry 91,96
Morriss, Susannah 272
Moseley, Ann 330
Moseley, Benjamin 306
Moseley, John 330
Moseley, Levy 306
Moseley, Robert 19
Moseley, Samuel 306
Moseley, William 306,309
Mosely, Benjamin Sr 75
Mosely, Elizabeth 15
Mosely, Isaac 75
Mosely, Robert 15
Mosely, Samuel 75
Mosely, William 75
Moss, David 346,387
Moss, Henry 279
Moss, Kathrine 68
Mounger, Henry 24,32,51
Munger, Henry 276
Myrick 336
Myrick, Matthew 75
Myrick, Owen 53,174,182,195,
 202,288,317,363
Myrick, William 3

-N-
Na...?, Reuben 39
Nance, Isham 39
Nance, John 39
Nance, Reuben 39,99
Nance, Tabitha 39
Nance, William 39,46
Nash, John 37,275
Nash, Mary 275
Nelson, Frances 77
Nelson, Nicholas 199
Nelson, Secretary 137,163,219,
 281
Nevison, John 72
Nevison, Mr 257
Newell, John 75
Newsom, Nathl 314
Newsom, Wm 257
Niblett, John 155
Nicholson, Henry 75,346,387
Nicholson, James 280
Nicholson, Nathiniel 183
Nicholson, Rebecca 120
Nicholson, Robert 120
Nicolson, Henry 216
Nicolson, Rebecca 273
Nicolson, Robt 273
Nipper, John 39
Nix, Nathl 282
Nolley, Daniel 216
Nolly, ...miah(?) 144
Nolly, Daniel 67
Nolly, Lucy 144
Nolly, Nehemiah 216,241
Norfleet 14
Norfleet, Cordal 14
Norflet 379
Norflet, Cordial 199
Northcross, James 137,238
Northcross, Martha 137
Northcross, Mary 137
Northross, Richard 168
Nott, Amy 179

-O-

Odonnally, James 285
Ogbon, John 263
Ogborn, Hannah 347
Ogborne, Benjamin 155
Ogborne, Charles 155
Ogborne, Harry 155
Ogborne, James 155
Ogborne, John 155
Ogborne, Mathew 155
Ogborne, Tabitha 155
Ogborne, William 155
Ogbourn, Josiah 223
Ogburn, John 96
Ogburne, William 223
Oliver, Fanny 25
Oliver, James 20,40,44,170,
  261
Oliver, John 25
Overby, Littleberry 389
Owen, Gowner 349
Owen, Grenow 7
Owen, Gronow 28
Owen, James 396
Owen, John Loyd 7
Owen, Jona 7
Owen, Richard Brown 7
Owen, Robert 7
Owen, Wm 230

-P-

Page, Elizabeth 159
Paisance, Jn 198
Parham 79,91,96,162
Parham, Betsey 375
Parham, Butts 96
Parham, Frances 222,229
Parham, James 206,222,229,
  236,365,375
Parham, John 222,229,240,
  360,375,402
Parham, Lewis 209,212,257
Parham, Matthew 91,173,229

Parham, Patty 49
Parham, Polly 375
Parham, Rebeca 173
Parham, Salley 375
Parham, Sarah 375
Parham, William 44,104,137,
  222,229
Parham, Wm 235,261
Park, Richd 256
Parker, Elizabeth 153
Parker, Jane 153
Parker, John 153,270
Parker, Nancy 153
Parker, Starling 153
Parker, Sterling 153
Parker, Thomas 153
Parker, William 153
Parrish, John 389
Parrish, Thomas 5,126
Parsons, William 36
Patarson, Capt 257
Patrick, John 380
Pattain, John 236
Patten, John 235
Pattillo, Anne 132
Pattillo, Austin 132
Pattillo, Nancy 132
Pearson, John 75,309
Peeblees, Jno 143
Peebles, Ann 320
Peebles, Frances 83
Peebles, Henry 83,379
Peebles, John 14,77,83,231,
  349
Peebles, John Jr 14,76,77,386
Peebles, John Sr 74
Peebles, Joseph 76
Peebles, Robert 83
Peebles, William 320
Peeples, Ann 100
Peeples, Betty 178
Peeples, David 282
Peeples, Ephraim 282

Peeples, Hubbard 343
Peeples, Jehu 343
Peeples, John 96,239
Peeples, Joseph 135
Peeples, Robert 282
Peete, Dr 257
Peete, Thomas 14,20,75,228
Peete, Thos 261
Peirce, John 14,77
Pelham, Peter 133,157,373
Pelham, Peter Jr 136,144,341,
  385
Pendie, Mr 257
Pendlton, Mr 136
Penn, Mary 146
Penn, Moses 146
Penn, Philip 147
Penn, Phillip 146
Penn, Thomas 146,147
Pennington, Benjamin 132
Pennington, David 261
Pennington, Sack 333,355,397
Pennington, William 348,397
Penticost, Scarbrough 108,151,
  386
Peoples, Betty 178
Peoples, David 91,159,178
Peoples, Hubard 178
Peoples, Jehue 178
Peoples, Jno 129
Peoples, John 91,114,123,265
Peoples, Joseph 91
Peoples, Robert 129,130
Peoples, William 285
Pepper, Nathan 302,319
Person 14
Person, Benja 176
Person, Colin 311
Person, John 182,209
Person, Philip 311
Person, Thomas 34,163
Person, Thos 281
Person, Will 265

Persons, John 219
Peter, John 44
Peter, Walter 44,136,137,261, 334,338
Peterson, Batt 14,179,282
Peterson, Batte 77
Peterson, Briggs 114
Peterson, Jno 114
Peterson, John 14,114,229, 282,285,379
Peterson, Mrs 114
Peterson, William 77,379
Peterson, Wm 142
Petterson, Batt 114
Pettiway, Edward 349
Pettiway, Hincha 349
Pettway, Amelia 9
Pettway, Amelia Pettway 11
Pettway, Cecilia 9,11
Pettway, Edward 9,11
Pettway, Edward Jr 27,29
Pettway, Elizabeth 9
Pettway, Frances 9,11,29
Pettway, Hinchey 9,18,64
Pettway, John 9,11,27
Pettway, Mary 9,11
Pettway, Robert 11,308,313
Petway, John 91
Phenix, John 225
Phillips, Elizabeth 315
Phillips, John 32
Phillips, Joseph 315,326
Phipps, Joseph 135
Phips, Joseph 51,55,61
Phips, Sarah 287
Phips, William 13,60
Pilkinton, Richard 305
Pilkinton, William 322
Pinch, William 343
Pincham, Elizabeth 300
Pincham, Peter 300
Pincham, Samuel 300
Pinnell, Wm 267

Pitman, Anne 379
Pitts, Walter 232
Poarch, Joshua 176
Poarch, Solomon 282
Poarson, John 330
Poetress, Joshua 176
Pondrey, Moses 216
Pool, Alexander 98
Pope, Matthew 77
Powel, Margret 209
Powell, Capt 349
Powell, Frances 114
Powell, James 193,196,209, 219,232
Powell, Jno 154
Powell, John 210,347,352
Powell, Leonard 137
Powell, Robert 16,68,366
Powell, Seymour 57,114,294, 323,338,349
Powell, William 102
Powell, Wm 219
Powers, Lydia 317
Powers, Sarah 317
Preston, Owen 280
Price, John 41,68,94
Price, Joseph 68
Price, Mary 68
Price, William 68,86
Pride, Halcot 257
Pride, Wm 129
Prince, Andrew 282
Prince, John 332,386
Prince, Rebecca 103
Prince, Rebeccah 170
Pritchett, John 179,282,367, 378,379,402
Pritchett, William 351
Procter 136
Procter, Benjamin 157
Procter, Thomas 159
Proctor 36
Proctor, Ambrus 285

Proctor, Benjamin 5,107
Proctor, Joseph 303,389
Proctor, Joseph Jr 389
Proctor, Nicholas 5
Proctor, Richard 389
Proctor, Robert 260
Proctor, Sarah 159
Proctor, Thomas 187,260
Purdie, Georg 265
Purdie, George 137

-Q-
Quarles, Catharine 255
Quarles, James 140,146,255
Quarles, John 140,161,275,279, 292
Quarles, Moses 95,146,164, 255,292
Quarles, William 140
Quarls, John 255
Quarls, Lewis 255

-R-
Rae, James 280
Ragsdale, John 91
Ramsay, Richard 140
Ramsey, Catharine 221
Ramsey, Richard 161
Randall, Josiah 176
Randle, Anne 51
Randle, Barnet 55
Randle, Barnett 51
Randle, Beverley 369
Randle, Coalby 51,55
Randle, Elizabeth 51
Randle, Jeconias 195
Randle, John 51,55
Randle, Josiah 215
Randle, Oney 51
Randle, Peter 369
Randle, William 54,55,65,69
Randle, William Sr 51
Randolph, Mary 343

Randolph, Peter 343
Randolph, William 343
Raney, William 234,364
Raney, Wm 144
Ransom, James 257
Ravenscraft 349
Ravenscroft, Thomas 15
Rawlings, Elizabeth 401
Rawlings, Fanny 401
Rawlings, Hannah 2
Rawlings, Henry 373,389
Rawlings, John 389
Rawlings, Molly 401
Rawlings, Nancey 401
Rawlings, Sary 324
Ray, Reuben 348
Read, Anna 255
Read, Anner 140
Read, Elizabeth 255
Read, James 75
Read, Jno 146
Read, John 140,255,260
Read, Lewis 140,255
Read, Mary 140,255
Read, Molley 140
Read, Peter 75
Read, Robert 140,255
Read, Sarah 161
Read, Thomas 140,161,255
Read, William 140
Read, Wm 255
Reading, Timothy 365
Reavis, David 75
Reavis, James 75
Redding, William 125
Reives 14
Reives, George 14,229
Reives, Mary 59
REN - cf Wren
Ren, Betty 253
Ren, Wm 261
Renn, John 20,205
Renn, Mary 103

Richardson, Nathaniel 110
Richardson, Thomas 164
Richardson, William 110
Richardson, Wm 110,274
Richerson, Anne 279
Rideout, John 331
Rideout, William 164
Ridley, Dr 379
Ridley, James 209
Ridley, James D. 212
Ridley, James Day 14,26,75,
   102,136,137,142,232
Ridley, Mary 33,57
Rieves, Thomas 164
Rivers, John 91
Rivers, Robert 383,386
Rivers, Thomas 62,343,370,
   373
Rivers, Wm 185
Rives 153
Rives, Ben 100
Rives, Benja 121
Rives, Benjamin 100,109,117,
   233,289,291
Rives, Elizabeth 289
Rives, Federick 198
Rives, Franke 100
Rives, George 100,112,285
Rives, Hannah 269
Rives, Harmon 231,291
Rives, Isham 336
Rives, Jno 123
Rives, John 80,289,298,314
Rives, Moses 282
Rives, Nancy 314
Rives, Robert Jr 56
Rives, Sarah 100,178
Rives, Simon 285
Rives, Thomas 153
Rives, Thos 279
Rives, Timothy 233
Rives, William 100,291
Rives, Wm 231,233,285

Road, Ann 223
Roberson, Isaac 116
Roberson, John 91
Roberson, Nathaniel 36,398
Roberson, William 91,96
Roberts, Jane 300
Roberts, Mary 300
Roberts, Michael 14,114,123
Roberts, Rebecca 300
Roberts, Samuel 300
Roberts, Thomas 300
Roberts, Willis 256
Robertson 136
Robertson, John 31,132
Robertson, Littleberry 23,24
Robertson, William 132,333
Robins, Lucy 253
Robinson 75,216
Robinson, Edward 128,136,
   151,247
Robinson, Elisha 223
Robinson, Elizabeth 248
Robinson, Franky 344
Robinson, Henry 278
Robinson, John 14,158,247,251
Robinson, Littleberry 32,136,
   320,334,356
Robinson, Littlebury 276
Robinson, Lucy 253
Robinson, Martha 344
Robinson, Mary 278
Robinson, Mrs 314
Robinson, Thomas 223
Robinson, William 320
Robinson, William Sr 320,356
Rodgers, John 24
Rogers, Anne 153
Rogers, Wm 153
Roland, Jesse 285
Rollings 278
Roper, David 25,146,147,292
Roper, John 237
Rose, Absalom 294

Rose, Elizabeth 75
Rose, John 287,393
Rose, John Jr 61,242
Ross, John Jr 187
Rosser, Benjamin 286
Rosser, David 109,122,286,
  323,327,399
Rosser, Elizabeth 286
Rosser, James 129,286
Rosser, John 83,106,286,307
Rosser, John Jr 184
Rosser, Martha 367
Rosser, Patty 109
Rosser, Sarah 286
Rosser, Thomas 286
Row, Dedmund 95
Rowe, Deadmond 380
Rowe, John 380
Rowell, Benjamin 14,253
Rowell, Ed 379
Rowell, Edward 14,114
Rowell, Edwd 282
Ruffin, Benjn 257
Ruffin, John 311
Ruffin, John Jr 199
Ruffin, Mr 387
Ruffin, Robert 234
Russell 9
Russell, Jno 149
Russell, John 224
Russell, Richard 224
Russell, Susanna 386

        -S-
Sadler, Charles 36
Sadler, Thomas 187
Samford, Hannah 223
Samford, Urvin 223
Samford, William 223
Samford, William Sr 223
Sandifur, Limelick 167
Saunders, Thomas 373
Scarborough, Edward 2,17

Scarborough, Lewis 278,303
Schell, Nathiniel 183
Scoggin, Wm 267
Scott, Joseph 199
Scott, Thomas 229
Seaton, John 55
Seawell, Benjamin 10
Seawell, Benjamin Jr 10,63
Seawell, Benjamin Sr 10
Seawell, Joseph 10
Seawell, Lucy 10
Sebrell, Nathl 280
Sewell, Benjamin 216
Sexton, Mary 110
Shackleford, Richard 20
Shalton, John 257
Shalton, Thomas 185
Shearling, John 282
Shehorn, Wilson 23
Shell, William 43
Shelton, Silvanus 333,355
Shepherd, Thos 232
Short, John 301
Short, Thos 277
Short, William Sr 6
Short, Wm 145
Sills, David 2,141,334
Simmons, Benja Sr 125
Simmons, Benjamin 145
Simmons, Ermine 145
Simmons, Henry 6,36,96,145,
  257
Simmons, Sarah 223
Simmons, Thomas 6,31,37,145,
  257
Simmons, Wm 262
Simms, Adam 251
Simms, Bartlet 246
Simms, Benjamin 343
Simms, Burrell 246
Simms, Burwell 246
Simms, Fredrick 343
Simms, George 246

Simms, Honour 343
Simms, John 30,343,350
Simms, Milington 246
Simms, Nathl 246
Simms, Sarah 343
Simms, William 246,332,343,
  373
Simms, Zachariah 246
Simons, Charles 45,132
Sims, Adam 67,76,246
Sims, Burrell 55
Sims, David 133
Sims, Elizabeth 133,318
Sims, George 268,276
Sims, Isaac Row 276
Sims, John 65,67,69,318,343
Sims, Rebecca 385
Sims, Sarah 276
Sims, William 67,133,136,318
Singleton, Charles 210
Singleton, Michael 315
Singleton, Phill 210
Singleton, Phillip 198
Singleton, Thos 210
Sisson, John 67
Sisson, Sarah 24
Sisson, Stephen 73,216
Sisson, Thomas 10
Slate, Mary 383
Slate, Robt 328
Slate, William 327,328
Smith, Aaron 200
Smith, Ambrose 197
Smith, Benjamin 86
Smith, Charles 55,401
Smith, Cuthbert 361
Smith, David 9
Smith, Eades 122,282,371
Smith, Eads 109,249
Smith, Edward 86,399
Smith, Elizabeth 63,86,393
Smith, Hannah 86
Smith, Harwood 92

Smith, Joel 144
Smith, John 209,248,285
Smith, Josiah 63,101
Smith, Lucy 86
Smith, Mary 221,323
Smith, Moses 91,200,261
Smith, Nicholas 142
Smith, Pheeby 200
Smith, Rebecca 86
Smith, Richard 86
Smith, Robert 209
Smith, Roger 70,258
Smith, Ruth 9
Smith, Sarah 86
Smith, Susannah 200
Smith, Tabitha 86
Smith, Thomas 114,200
Smith, Thos 102
Smith, William 4,5,63,75,135,
   200,285,322,386
Smith, Wm 267
Smith, Zachariah 386
Solomon, Betty 143
Solomon, James 143
Sones, John 253
Speede, Elizabeth 363
Speede, Lewis 363
Spence, John 14
Spraberry, John 334
Spraborough, Ann 165
Spraborough, Archelous 165
Spraborough, James 165
Spraborough, John 165
Spraborough, Jothen 165
Sprabrough, Jas 185
Sprabrough, John 186
Spratly, Wm 280
Stainback, Francis 370,382
Stainback, Jenny 370
Stainback, Littleberry 370
Stainback, Mary 370
Staindley, Dancy 376
Stake, Wm 137

Stanback, Elizabeth 370
Stanback, Frederick 264
Stanback, George 230,261
Stanback, Litt 135
Stanback, Thomas 230
Stanback, Wm 230
Standback, George 230
Stark, Dr 331,379
Stark, Robert 210
Starke, William 338
Starke, Wm 136
Stead, John 15
Steagall, Elizabeth 98
Steagall, George 87,304
Steagall, Thomas 22,354
Steed, John 132
Steed, Nathanael 19
Step, Susannah 179
Stewart, Charles 296,314
Stewart, Elizabeth 314
Stewart, James 40,44,405
Stewart, Rebecca 314
Stewart, Richd 314
Stewart, Rose 41,396
Stewart, Sally 314
Stith 119
Stith, Aristotle 37
Stith, Buckner 36,164
Stith, Buckner Jr 120,273
Stith, Buckner Sr 271
Stith, Charlotte 37
Stith, Drury 36,37,148,271,301
Stith, Edmunds 36,37
Stith, Elizabeth 36,37,120
Stith, Griffin 257
Stith, Howell 37
Stith, John 36
Stith, Katherine 37
Stith, Mariania 120
Stith, Martha 120
Stith, Sarah 37
Stith, Tho 130,132,148
Stith, Thomas 28,31,36,37,88,

   120,132,151,273,373
Stith, Thos 110,256,271,277,
   279
Stith, William 75,300
Stith, Wm 155,263
Stokes, David 276
Stokes, Dolley 395
Stokes, Dolly 353
Stokes, Drury 115,171
Stokes, Helen W. 395
Stokes, Hellen Walker 353
Stokes, Molley H. 395
Stokes, Molly Hamlin 353
Stokes, Sarah 276
Stokes, Silvanus 46,82,194,
   353,376,395
Stokes, Sukey 353,395
Stokes, Tempy 278
Stokes, Thomas 353,395
Stokes, William 353,395
Stone, Elizabeth 87
Stone, Frances 255
Stone, Thomas 37,207
Strange, Elizabeth 61
Strange, John 287
Strange, Owen 316
Strange, Stephen 61
Stundy, John 267
Sturdivant, John 353
Sullivant, Charles 55
Sullivant, Richard 89,90
Swanson, John 55
Sykes, Benja 298
Sykes, Benjamin 100

-T-
Tarkill, George 176
Tarpley, Edna 110
Tarpley, James 25,340
Tatum, Edward 75,79,126
Tatum, Jesse 347
Tatum, Joseph 96
Tatum, Nathaniel 162

Tatum, Paul 341,386
Tatum, Peter 79
Taylor, Daniel 248,287
Taylor, Henry 136
Taylor, John 282
Taylor, Rebeca 176
Taylor, Richard 132,137,279
Taylor, Robt 246
Taylor, William 199
Tazewell, Henry 145,314
Tazewell, Littleton 92,257
Tazwell 257
Tazwell, John 257
Tazwell, Sophia 257
Tearwright 338
Tewell, Jane 297
Tewell, John 297
Tewell, Matthew 297
Tewell, Samuel 297
Thomas, Peter 31
Thomas, Richard 217
Thomas, Richd 218
Thomas, Thomas 207
Thomlinson, Thomas 14
Thompson, Richard 335
Thompson, William 335
Thompton, Wm 204
Thornton, William 91,98,230
Thornton, Wm 242,245
Thorp, Joshua 14
Thorp, Lewis 367
Thower, Hezekiah 131,138
Threadgill, Annabel 87
Threadgill, George 87
Threadgill, John 22,87
Threadgill, Randolph 87
Threadgill, Thomas 87
Threadgill, William 87
THROWER - cf Thower
Thrower, Hezchiah 47
Thweat, Thomas 114
Thweatt, Burwell 376,381
Thweatt, James 383

Thweatt, John 121
Thweatt, John Peterson 383
Thweatt, Judith 121
Thweatt, Peterson 371,383,399
Thweatt, Rebeca 383
Thweatt, Rebecca 342
Thweatt, Thomas 383
Thweatt, Wm 257,265
Tiller, Major 123
Tillman, Anne 51
Tillman, George 191
Tillman, John 191
Tillman, Mary 191
Tillman, Richard 55
Tilloe, John 199
Tilman, John 91
Tilman, Richard 75
Timms, Amos 242
Tippit, John 98
Tippitt, John 248
Tomblinson, John 189
Tomlinson, James 74,123,129,
  130,282,379,402
Tomlinson, John 23,123,282,
  285
Tomlinson, Lucas 282,289
Tomlinson, Rebecca 286
Tomlinson, Sarah 179
Tomlinson, Thomas 379
Tompkins, Joseph 86
Tompson, Amy 95
Tompson, John 92
Tompson, Peter 95
Tooke, Joseph 14
Troter, James 91
Trotter, James 63,64
Troughton, Andrew 44,230
Troughton, James 230
Truett(?), Henry 157
Tucker, Wood 91,239
Tuke, Joseph 285
Tulley, Wm 146
Turbyfill, John 242

Turbyfill, John Jr 242
Turnbull, Charles 75
Turnbull, George 267
Turnbull, Robert 75
Turner, Arthur 50,123,311
Turner, Donaldson 269,311
Turner, Elizabeth 269
Turner, Henry 289
Turner, Jennitt 142
Turner, Jno 129,130,142
Turner, John 142,163,281,282,
  286,296,311,375,383,399
Turner, Milly 311
Turner, Pattsey 142
Turner, Rebeccah 142
Turner, Simon 221
Turner, Thomas 311
Turner, Thomas Jr 269
Turner, William 142,199
Turner, Wm 114
Twitty, George 87,132
Twitty, Mary 245
Twitty, Molly Jr 245
Twitty, Thomas 199,245
Twitty, Thomas Jr 245
Twitty, Thos Jr 224
Tyas, Lewis 349

-U-
Underwood, Elizabeth 58,141
Underwood, Jno 143
Underwood, John 58
Underwood, Sammons 141
Underwood, Thomas 141,156
Underwood, William 141
Upchurch, Thomas 340

-V-
Vaughan 36
Vaughan, Charles 279
Vaughan, David 279
Vaughan, Elizabeth 248
Vaughan, James 386

Vaughan, Penrod 171
Vaughan, William 55
Vaughan, William Jr 386
Vaughan, Wm 178
Vaughn, David 164
Vaughn, Mary 227
Vaughn, William 114,204
Vaughn, Wm 227
Verell, Wm 92
Vinsent, Aaron 285
Vinsent, Peter 209
Vinson, James 129
Vinson, John 58,196,211,232, 247,366
Vinson, Joshua 366
Vinson, Moses 193,196,232, 259
Vinson, Thomas 50,123,253, 254,259

-W-
Waddy, Spence 321,325
Wade, James 61
Wade, Thomas 310
Wager, Elizabeth 44
Waldin, Mathew 201
Waldon, Mary 44
Walker 36
Walker, Benjamin 39
Walker, Edward 398
Walker, George 271,279,283, 323
Walker, James 45
Walker, R. 132
Walker, Thomas 244
Walker, William 132,170,171, 181,334
Walker, Wm 277
Wall, Agness 323
Wall, Benjamin 318
Wall, David 267
Wall, George 139,231
Wall, Henry 244,282

Wall, Isaac 244
Wall, James 33,66,83,92,104, 106,111,114,136,137,139,242, 296,323,335,
Wall, James Jr 44,50,66,123, 238,286,294,296,307,323,338
Wall, James Sr 323
Wall, Jammy Sr 136
Wall, John 92,242,267
Wall, John Jr 92
Wall, Mary 231,240,286,323
Wall, Michael 92,173,318,323
Wall, Peter Gray 323
Wall, Rebecca 209,257,318,332
Wall, Sarah 323,335
Wall, William 139,318,373
Wallace, John 62
Waller, Benjn 92
Wallton, Isaac Row 32
Wallton, John 24,55,65
Walpole, Elizabeth 322
Walpole, John 322
Walpole, Thomas 322
WALTON - cf Wallton
Walton, Daniel 24,401
Walton, David 24,401
Walton, Drury 24
Walton, Elizabeth 24,276,334
Walton, Fanny 24
Walton, Henry 24,401,404
Walton, Isaac Row 24,268,276, 334
Walton, James 334
Walton, John 268,276,334
Walton, Nancey 24
Walton, Thomas 401
Wammock, Wm 282
Ward, Benjamin 300
Wardin, James 366
Ware, Peter 136
Ware, Thomas 55
Warren, Benjamin 54,347,352, 393

Warren, Elizabeth 393
Warren, John 288,347,393,406
Warren, Merriott 393
Warren, Sarah 393
Warren, Thomas 393
Warren, William 393
Warthin, Richard 39
Washington, Sarah 228,280
Washington, Thomas 183,228
Washington, Thos 182,280
Watkins, Wm 257
Watlington, John 257
Watson, Alexander 9,11,120, 132,308,365
Watson, Alexr 143
Watson, Lucretia 9,11
Watson, William 9,87
Weaver, Thomas 75
Webb, Edmund 306,322
Webb, Elizabeth 158
Webb, John 158
Webb, Micah 158
Webb, Rebecca 338
Weldon, Daniel 96
Weldon, John Chavis 190
Wesson, Edward Jr 347
Wesson, Edward Sr 347
Wesson, Martha 347
Wesson, William 347
Westbrook, Saml 114
Westbrookes, Honour 221
Westmoreland, Isham 279
Whealer, Benjamin 54
Whealer, Benjamin Sr 51
Whitby, John 75
White, George 43
White, Henry 280
White, John 43
White, Samuel 43,47
White, Sarah 43
White, William 43
Whiteley, Benja 155
Whiteley, Benjamin 155

Whitman, James 331
Whittington, Frederick 78,170, 171
Whittington, Howell 78,205
Whittington, John 78,103,169, 170,267,386
Wiggins, Samuel 198
Wilkerson, Avris 405
Wilkerson, John 379
Wilkes, Joseph 94
Wilkins, Douglass 67,323,343
Wilkins, Duglass 274
Wilkins, Edmund 67,133,279, 332,338
Wilkins, Rebecca 67
Wilkins, Tabitha 67
Wilkinson, Jno 124
Wilkinson, Joel 405
Wilkinson, John 14,114
Williams 119
Williams, Benja 113,171,205, 299
Williams, Benjamin 44,172,287
Williams, Betsey 99
Williams, Charles 49
Williams, Christopher 49
Williams, Daniel 49,372
Williams, Elizabeth 99,374
Williams, Ellick 343
Williams, Frances 245
Williams, Frankey 49
Williams, Frederick 99
Williams, Henry 229,282
Williams, Hew 216
Williams, Hugh 119,140,147, 161,223,225,255,275,279,292, 344,345
Williams, James 99,116,363
Williams, Jane 49,52
Williams, Jno 149,152
Williams, John 99,245,278,279, 372
Williams, Jonathan 220

Williams, Jone 364
Williams, Lazarus 61,287
Williams, Lewis 353,376
Williams, Mary 61,287,373
Williams, Matthew 287
Williams, Nicholas 287
Williams, Peter 14,278,373
Williams, Robert 282
Williams, Rowland 49
Williams, Sarah 372
Williams, Seth 49
Williams, Silas 99
Williams, Susannah 99,245
Williams, Susanny 245
Williams, Thomas 185,334
Williams, Thomas Harris 75
Williams, William 99,116,224, 287,290
Williams, Wyatt 155,245
Williamson, Charles 10,30,103, 338
Williamson, Exum 117
Williamson, Henry 282
Williamson, James 282
Williamson, Jesse 163,281
Williamson, John 91,106
Williamson, Joseph 91,123
Williamson, Judith 10
Williamson, Lewellin 338
Williamson, Lewis 14,75,233
Williamson, Littleton 400
Williamson, Robert 123,274, 282
Williamson, Sarah 346
Williamson, Thomas 265,285
Willie, John 91
Willis, Augustine 136
Willis, Elizabeth 57
Willis, Francis 14
Willis, Jacob 275
Willis, John 44,257
Willis, Mildred 349
Willis, Peter 364

Wilson, Henry 275,283,284
Wilson, James 275
Wilson, Jeremiah 75
Wilson, John 275,283
Wilson, Lucy 180
Wilson, Martha 375
Wilson, Nicholas 280
Wilson, Rebecca 370
Winfield, Joel 194
Winfield, John 267
Winfield, Joshua 39,63,132
Wiott, Hubbard 280
Wmson, John 106
Wommacke, Wm 188
Wood, Reuben 77
Wood, Thomas 206
Wood, William 97
Woodard, Allis 404
Wooddall, James 212
Woodow, Frank 124
Woodroof, George 295,303
Woodroof, John 180
Woodroof, Richard 180
Woodrough, Richard 184
Woolsey, Joel 317
Woolsey, John 51,55
Woolsey, Randle 51
Wortham, Anne 3
Wortham, Ch...? 3
Wortham, Charles 3
Wortham, Edward 3
Wortham, Elizabeth 3
Wortham, James 3,8,53,75
Wortham, John 3
Wortham, Lucy 3
Wortham, William 3
Wray, Benjamin 154
Wray, Frances 154
Wray, James 154
Wray, John 136,154
Wray, Mary 154
Wray, Nathaniel 55,154
WREN - cf Ren

Wren, John 113,171
Wren, Wm 129
Wrenn, Francis 171
Wrenn, Joel 171
Wrenn, John 78
Wrenn, Joseph 225
Wrenn, Mary 78
Wrenn, Robert 78
Wrenn, Thomas 78
Wrenn, William 44
Wright, Elizabeth 110
Wright, Jeremiah 146
Wright, John 119,279
Wright, Mary 119
Wright, Mr 257
Wright, Robt 146
Wright, Samuel 288
Wright, Sarah 347
Wright, Solomon 71
Wright, Uriah 68
Wyche, Captain 379
Wyche, Elizabeth 269
Wyche, George 50,77,123,179,
229,237,253,269,282,296,307,
378
Wyche, John 102,282
Wyche, Nancy 269
Wyche, Nathiniel 209,212,269
Wyche, Nathl 269
Wyche, Patience 278
Wyche, Peter 123
Wyche, Rebecca 269
Wyche, Sarah 313
Wyche, Winny 67
Wynne, Solomon 279
Wythe, Mrs 349

-Y-
Yarbrough, Amy 329
Yarbrough, James 329,359,363
Yarbrough, Mary 329,363
Yarbrough, Samuel 329
Yarbrough, William 329

Yeargin, Samuel 176
Young, Francis 12,14,28,33,
76,107,157,198
Young, James 320
Young, Lucy 198
Young, Michaiel 198
Young, Michaiel Cadle 227
Young, Michaiel Cadle Sr 198
Young, Michaiel Jr 198
Young, Mychaiel Cadle 227
Young, Temperance 198
Young, Thomas 198

-Z-
Zacharie, John 248

...? Embry 244

Agness Wall 323
Allis Woodard 404
Alse Brewer 212
Amelia Pettway 9
Amelia Pettway Pettway 11
Amey Clements 125
Amey Morris 366
Amy Gilliam 227
Amy Jackson 61,287
Amy Maclin 173
Amy Nott 179
Amy Tompson 95
Amy Yarbrough 329
Ann Adams 125
Ann Cheek 25
Ann Collier 63
Ann Edwards 57
Ann Gower 341
Ann Gray 221
Ann Hines 269
Ann Johnson 287
Ann Kirkland 262
Ann Laurance 167
Ann Mitchell 144
Ann Moody 180
Ann Moseley 330
Ann Peebles 320
Ann Peeples 100
Ann Road 223
Ann Spraborough 165
Anna Andrews 159
Anna Harwell 31
Anna Read 255
Annabel Threadgill 87
Anne Allan 55
Anne Broadnax 45
Anne Chapman 247
Anne Cocke 111
Anne Dobyns 119
Anne Edwards 4,5,57,135
Anne Harwell 277

Anne Hunt 370
Anne Lifsey 102
Anne Lowd 178
Anne Mabry 91
Anne Malone 133
Anne Massey 23,35
Anne Pattillo 132
Anne Pitman 379
Anne Randle 51
Anne Richerson 279
Anne Rogers 153
Anne Tillman 51
Anne Wortham 3
Anner Read 140
Anness Lawrence 134
Avas Miz'd 154
Avey Mason 141

Becky Lucas 308
Bethiah Jackson 216,241
Betsey Fletcher 336
Betsey Gibbs 348
Betsey Harwell 132
Betsey Parham 375
Betsey Williams 99
Betsy Briggs 292
Betty Camp 400
Betty Clack 380
Betty Cooke 231
Betty Dobyns 119
Betty Dunn 2
Betty Lucas 111
Betty Mathis 140
Betty Peeples 178
Betty Ren 253
Betty Solomon 143

Cassander Harwell 31
Cassandra Harwell 132
Catey Howard 175
Catharine Harris 374
Catharine Manning 140
Catharine Quarles 255

Catharine Ramsey 221
Cecilia Pettway 9,11
Charlotte Stith 37
Christianna Gresham 381
Clarissa Abernathy 310

Deborah Burnitt 15
Deliah Clarke 150
Dolley Harrison 205
Dolley Stokes 395
Dolly Stokes 353
Dorcas Clifton 311
Dorothey Mitchel 144

Edith Britt 401
Edith Harris 401
Edna Tarpley 110
Edy Miz'd 154
Elinor Cook 259
Eliza Blanks 192
Elizabeth Andrews 159
Elizabeth Baird 3
Elizabeth Belshire 77
Elizabeth Birchett 121
Elizabeth Blalock 401
Elizabeth Blanks 192
Elizabeth Bynum 265
Elizabeth Chapman 26
Elizabeth Collier 321
Elizabeth Cook 178
Elizabeth Dupree 269
Elizabeth Edwards 33
Elizabeth Embry 244
Elizabeth Fawn 134
Elizabeth Fennell 139
Elizabeth Finch 360
Elizabeth Foster 121
Elizabeth Gee 80
Elizabeth Gibbs 348
Elizabeth Gilliam 158
Elizabeth Glover 39
Elizabeth Gordan 164
Elizabeth Hammond 214

Elizabeth Harris 180
Elizabeth Harrison 239
Elizabeth Harrup 389
Elizabeth Harwell 31,132
Elizabeth Holt 25
Elizabeth Hunt 228
Elizabeth Hurst 40,385
Elizabeth Ingram 22
Elizabeth Jeffries 179
Elizabeth Kirkland 262
Elizabeth Lanier 88
Elizabeth Lashley 347
Elizabeth Love 71,398
Elizabeth Lucas 44
Elizabeth Maclin 125,173
Elizabeth Malone 333
Elizabeth Massey 100
Elizabeth Mathis 140
Elizabeth Mitchell 179
Elizabeth Morris 335,366
Elizabeth Mosely 15
Elizabeth Page 159
Elizabeth Parker 153
Elizabeth Pettway 9
Elizabeth Phillips 315
Elizabeth Pincham 300
Elizabeth Randle 51
Elizabeth Rawlings 401
Elizabeth Read 255
Elizabeth Rives 289
Elizabeth Robinson 248
Elizabeth Rose 75
Elizabeth Rosser 286
Elizabeth Sims 133,318
Elizabeth Smith 63,86,393
Elizabeth Speede 363
Elizabeth Stanback 370
Elizabeth Steagall 98
Elizabeth Stewart 314
Elizabeth Stith 36,37,120
Elizabeth Stone 87
Elizabeth Strange 61
Elizabeth Turner 269

Elizabeth Underwood 58,141
Elizabeth Vaughan 248
Elizabeth Wager 44
Elizabeth Walpole 322
Elizabeth Walton 24,276,334
Elizabeth Warren 393
Elizabeth Webb 158
Elizabeth Williams 99,374
Elizabeth Willis 57
Elizabeth Wortham 3
Elizabeth Wright 110
Elizabeth Wyche 269
Ermin Embry 244
Ermine Simmons 145
Ezebel Jackson 365
Ezebel Merriott 380

Fanny Oliver 25
Fanny Rawlings 401
Fanny Walton 24
Frances Bailey 152
Frances Brewer 121
Frances Brown 110,342
Frances Brumbelow 119
Frances Caudle 396
Frances Cocke 25
Frances Dailey 333,355
Frances Dunn 2
Frances Hathcock 404
Frances Hill 404
Frances Nelson 77
Frances Parham 222,229
Frances Peebles 83
Frances Pettway 9,11,29
Frances Powell 114
Frances Stone 255
Frances Williams 245
Frances Wray 154
Francis Brown 110
Franke Rives 100
Frankey Williams 49
Franky Robinson 344

Gracey Morris 366

Hannah Barnes 159
Hannah Batte 14
Hannah Doby 80
Hannah Edwards 324
Hannah Gun 43
Hannah Hill 404
Hannah Ingram 98,248
Hannah Jones 344
Hannah Jordon 59
Hannah Ogborn 347
Hannah Rawlings 2
Hannah Rives 269
Hannah Samford 223
Hannah Smith 86
Helen W. Stokes 395
Honour Westbrookes 221

Isabellear Chapman 26

Jane Burch 88
Jane Cramore 282
Jane Edwards 57
Jane Howard 175
Jane Lifsey 102
Jane Maclin 365
Jane Parker 153
Jane Roberts 300
Jane Tewell 297
Jane Williams 49,52
Janie Harrison 391
Jean Edwards 324
Jeaney Harrison 110
Jemima Edwards 324
Jennitt Turner 142
Jenny Jordon 59
Jenny Stainback 370
Joice Burnitt 15
Joice Burnitt Jr 15
Joice Burnitt Sr 15
Jona Owen 7
Jothen Spraborough 165

Judith Goodwin 121
Judith Hicks 63
Judith Thweatt 121
Judith Williamson 10

Katharine Moody 335
Katherine Stith 37
Kathrine Harris 276
Kathrine Howard 77
Kathrine Moss 68

Lucretia Watson 11
Lucretian Watson 9
Lucy Burnitt 15
Lucy Carter 66
Lucy Chambless 49
Lucy Collier 185
Lucy Gilliam Booth 181
Lucy Gray 75
Lucy House 116
Lucy Maclin 365
Lucy Nolly 144
Lucy Robins 253
Lucy Robinson 253
Lucy Seawell 10
Lucy Smith 86
Lucy Wilson 180
Lucy Wortham 3
Lucy Young 198
Lydia Powers 317

Margret ...? 400
Margret Powel 209
Mariania Stith 120
Martha Bennitt 287
Martha Cocke 25
Martha Davis 95
Martha Dunkley 275,279
Martha Elliott 244
Martha Embry 84,85,124,244
Martha Gilliam 227
Martha Gladish 132
Martha Jackson 347

Martha Merriett 25
Martha Moore 23
Martha Northcross 137
Martha Robinson 344
Martha Rosser 367
Martha Stith 120
Martha Wesson 347
Martha Wilson 375
Marthy Lifsey 102
Mary ...? 276
Mary Abernathy 370
Mary Adams 405
Mary Anderson 25
Mary Andrews 159
Mary Archer 321
Mary Bass 62,278
Mary Birdsong 158
Mary Bishop 134
Mary Blanks 192
Mary Blick 108
Mary Bradley 374
Mary Brown 121,296,342
Mary Cagebrook 170
Mary Campbell 159
Mary Caudle 41
Mary Champbell 242
Mary Chapman 247
Mary Clack 234
Mary Clinch 75,177,228
Mary Collier 83
Mary Cook 259
Mary Davis 95,132,286
Mary Dillard 80
Mary Dupree 269
Mary Edwards 324
Mary Embry 244
Mary Emmery 62
Mary Fennell 130,179
Mary Fletcher 336
Mary Fuqua 262
Mary Gilliam 18,349
Mary Gresham 381
Mary Hagood 321

Mary Hall 38
Mary Hardiway 396
Mary Hill 181
Mary House 116
Mary Howard 175
Mary Huff 339
Mary Hulen 398
Mary Huling 71
Mary Johnson 253
Mary Lanier 39,178
Mary Ledbetter 24,374
Mary Letbetter 276
Mary Love 398
Mary Mabry 24
Mary Maclin 365
Mary Marritt 244
Mary Martin 220
Mary Mason 80,88
Mary Melton 115
Mary Merritt 279
Mary Minetree 3
Mary Mitchell 144,230
Mary Moore 86
Mary Morgan 223
Mary Nash 275
Mary Northcross 137
Mary Penn 146
Mary Pettway 9,11
Mary Price 68
Mary Randolph 343
Mary Read 140,255
Mary Reives 59
Mary Renn 103
Mary Ridley 33,57
Mary Roberts 300
Mary Robinson 278
Mary Sexton 110
Mary Slate 383
Mary Smith 221,323
Mary Stainback 370
Mary Tillman 191
Mary Twitty 245
Mary Vaughn 227

Mary Waldon 44
Mary Wall 231,240,286,323
Mary Williams 61,287,373
Mary Wray 154
Mary Wrenn 78
Mary Wright 119
Mary Yarbrough 329,363
Middleton Fletcher 336
Mildred Fennell 179
Mildred Willis 349
Milley Clack 179
Milly Hyde 49
Milly Turner 311
Molley Dailey 333
Molley H. Stokes 395
Molley Read 140
Molly Dailey 355
Molly Dunn 2
Molly Hamlin Stokes 353
Molly Rawlings 401
Molly Twitty Jr 245
Mourning Harwell 31,132
Mrs Edwards 303
Mrs Irby 314
Mrs Peterson 114
Mrs Richard Morris 132
Mrs Robinson 314
Mrs Wythe 349

Nancey Camp 400
Nancey Hardiway 396
Nancey Rawlings 401
Nancey Walton 24
Nancy Blanks 192
Nancy Booth 181
Nancy Colleir 133
Nancy Davis 95
Nancy Goodwin 121
Nancy Parker 153
Nancy Pattillo 132
Nancy Rives 314
Nancy Wyche 269
Nanny Chappell 239

Noona Fox 253

Oney Randle 51

Patience Lane 374
Patience Wyche 278
Pattey Dailey 333
Pattsey Turner 142
Patty Barnes 381
Patty Clack 278
Patty Geer 12
Patty Gulley 291
Patty Harrison 239
Patty Parham 49
Patty Rosser 109
Penny Hurst 40,299
Phebe Epps 362
Pheeby Smith 200
Polly Camp 400
Polly Edwards 384
Polly Parham 375
Prudence Clack 278
Prudence Courtney 278

Rachel Dobyns 119
Rachel Howard 175
Rebaca Clack 179
Rebeca Parham 173
Rebeca Thweatt 383
Rebecah Hide 347
Rebecca Booth 181,304
Rebecca Dupree 269
Rebecca Edwards 33
Rebecca Hagood 321
Rebecca Hall 92
Rebecca Hardiway 396
Rebecca Harrison 205
Rebecca House 116
Rebecca Jones 57
Rebecca Lashley 336
Rebecca Lucas 308,313
Rebecca Nicholson 120
Rebecca Nicolson 273

Rebecca Prince 103
Rebecca Robert 300
Rebecca Sims 385
Rebecca Smith 86
Rebecca Stewart 314
Rebecca Thweatt 342
Rebecca Tomlinson 286
Rebecca Wall 209,257,318,332
Rebecca Webb 338
Rebecca Wilkins 67
Rebecca Wilson 370
Rebecca Wyche 269
Rebeccah Corral 171
Rebeccah Culver 154
Rebeccah Edwards 324
Rebeccah Prince 170
Rebeccah Turner 142
Rebeckah Hyde 347
Rebeckah Lifsey 102
Rhode Morris 366
Rittah Harris 347
Rose Stewart 41,396
Ruth Smith 9

Salley Camp 400
Salley Cook 259
Salley Dailey 333
Salley Ingram 98
Salley Parham 375
Sally Davis 383
Sally Hancock 370
Sally Harwell 31,132
Sally Hurst 385
Sally Lucas 308
Sally Stewart 314
Sandal Carrell 118
Sara Jones 23
Sarah Adams 386,405
Sarah Anne Harrison 391
Sarah Betty 71
Sarah Branscom 274
Sarah Britt 337
Sarah Brooks 130,143,394

Sarah Brown 7
Sarah Cook 178
Sarah Crowder 80
Sarah Daniel 110
Sarah Dellihay 126
Sarah Edwards 57,338
Sarah Embry 244
Sarah Fox 253
Sarah Hardiway 396
Sarah Harrison 205
Sarah Hicks 10,30
Sarah Hightower 208
Sarah Hines 269
Sarah Hopkins 245
Sarah Hurst 204
Sarah Johnson 228
Sarah Jones 225
Sarah Jordon 83
Sarah Lanier 39
Sarah Mason 363
Sarah Mirick 374
Sarah Mitchell 43,383
Sarah Parham 375
Sarah Phips 287
Sarah Powers 317
Sarah Proctor 159
Sarah Read 161
Sarah Rives 100,178
Sarah Rosser 286
Sarah Simmons 223
Sarah Simms 343
Sarah Sims 276
Sarah Sisson 24
Sarah Smith 86
Sarah Stith 37
Sarah Stokes 276
Sarah Tomlinson 179
Sarah Wall 323,335
Sarah Warren 393
Sarah Washington 228,280
Sarah White 43
Sarah Williams 372
Sarah Williamson 346

Sarah Wright 347
Sarah Wyche 313
Sary Rawlings 324
Sophia Tazwell 257
Suckey Blanks 192
Sucky Butt 110
Sue Clack 179
Sukey Stokes 353,395
Susanna Caudle 41
Susanna Green 380
Susanna Hartwell 370
Susanna Jackson 51
Susanna Mitchell 379
Susanna Morris 148
Susanna Russell 386
Susannah Clarke 150
Susannah Coleman 25
Susannah Maclin 173
Susannah Mathis 140
Susannah Matthews 255
Susannah Morriss 272
Susannah Smith 200
Susannah Step 179
Susannah Williams 99,245
Susanny Williams 245

Tabitha Gea 22
Tabitha Gee 248
Tabitha Hamilton 383
Tabitha Huff 339
Tabitha Johnson 195
Tabitha Lucas 313
Tabitha Massey 23
Tabitha Nance 39
Tabitha Ogborne 155
Tabitha Smith 86
Tabitha Wilkins 67
Temperance Young 198
Tempy Stokes 278

Wincey Johnson 195
Winehfield Clack 179
Winehfield Jeffres 179

Winford Boseman 158
Winifred Clarke 129
Winney Boseman 158
Winny Wyche 67

...? 2,145,173,244

Aaron 275,283
Abby 51,54,253,278,
  296,305
Abigail 182
Abraham 32,33,43,47,
  51,52,54,57,65,76,82,
  338
Abram 24,49,234,308
Absolom 25
Aby 254
Adam 208
Agga 160
Agge 343
Aggey 338
Aggy 25,76,144,271,
  273,308,350
Alce 381,397
Alec 270
Aleck 308
Alicke 161
Allen 353,393,406
Alse 153,406
Ambross 239,243
Amca 9
America 69
Amey 25,43,110,363,
  365,376,393
Amy 18,47,57,81,82,
  86,139,227,244,249,
  253,254,271,273,353,
  398,406
Anake 19
Andrew 259
Andy 3
Anekey 242,244
Annakey 15,50,63,64,
  268
Annerky 348,356
Anthoney 383
Anthony 31,69,102,
  121,131,296,308,336,

399
Archer 33,69,203
Ariala 259
Arter 125,173
Arthur 80,81,82,242,
  275,284,289,298,365,
  398
Austin 278
Austine 269

Ball 6
Barbery 25
Barthshab 249
Batt 33,148
Batte 65
Beck 25,50,122,253,
  254,268,273,336,350
Beckey 336
Becky 177
Belinder 259
Ben 24,32,34,72,76,
  110,182,273,290,300,
  304,308,316,356,398
Ben Pompy 353,376
Bess 57,69,88,131,173,
  308,365
Bett 31,122,131,182,
  203,247,251,273,336,
  350,357,370
Betty 34,65,69,76,149,
  152,227,245,271,382,
  391,403
Black Moses 57
Boatswain 266
Bob 28,31,43,47,57,
  125,131,173,175,178,
  181,182,268,271,273,
  290,297,304,308,336,
  347,350,352,353,365,
  366,370,376,382,391,
  393,396,403
Bobb 17
Bobbin 18

Bocer 278
Boker 305
Booker 381,397,398
Bowling 125,365
Bowser 25
Brandon 57,158
Bridget 9,161,183
Bridgett 357
Brister 350,381,397
Bristo 325
Buck 6,347
Burwell 110,336,396
Butcher 177

Caesar 350
Cambridge 51,54
Cary 370,382
Casar 353,376,398
Cate 3,43,47,50,53,72,
  153,208,244,248,270,
  286,307,353,376
Cato 76,82,86,182,356,
  398
Cealah 34
Ceasar 82
Ceazer 248
Ceazor 244
Celia 365
Chaney 110
Charity 66,104
Charles 25,26,50,57,
  69,93,125,182,247,
  248,251,253,254,271,
  320,322,357,362,370,
  382
Cheney 25
Chloe 173,194,303,
  308
Chocolet 72
Christian 125
Christopher 338
Claiborne 343,350
Clarisa 183

Clarissia 57
Cloe 48,57,278
Cloriss 396
Collins 259
Cook 39,46
Criss 289,298
Cuba 308
Cue 227
Cuff 57
Cuffee 57
Cuffey 57
Cull 278,305
Cumbo 353,376
Cynthia 72
Cyrus 173

Dafney 183
Dan 254
Daniel 63,64,82,122,
  248,253,271,278,305,
  347,352,353,357,376,
  396
Daphney 31,64,131,
  353,376
Daphny 63
Darcas 320
Darcus 17
Darkas 356
Dava 160
Dave 63
Davey 144
David 117,140,203,
  273,320,347,356
Davy 9,110,248,317,
  375,398
Delee 304
Delsey 57,63
Dick 6,18,34,50,57,69,
  72,76,82,100,112,131,
  149,152,153,179,182,
  229,236,245,248,253,
  254,255,271,273,287,
  290,297,347,352,365,

375,378,398

Dicky 194

Dilcy 9

Dillo 244

Dilsey 64

Dinah 18,33,36,57,65,
76,82,95,110,112,131,
183,203,227,228,252,
253,254,271,308,358

Diner 100

Ding 110

Discey 11

Doctor 76,191,304,
343,350

Doll 9,24,32,39,110,
121,125,149,152,245,
287,290,300,362,365,
374

Donum 57,76

Dorcas 57,65

Dorcass 268

Dorcus 9,33,50

Dorothy 356

Doroty 320

Eady 63,63,64

Eagg 227

Easter 72

Elleck 255

Else 393

Emmanuel 39,46

Ephraim 57,338

Eppraim 336

Essex 65

Ester 160

Esther 144,338,365

Fanney 271

Fanny 131,173,316,
347,352,356,391,398,
403

Fax 32

Fed 76

Fib 49,100,112,308,
375

Fibb 246

Fibby 399

Fill 173

Fillis 19,34,158,179,
243,375

Flora 57,72,308

Fountain 365

Frances 43,286,307

Frank 24,25,32,36,39,
40,46,47,63,64,77,80,
81,86,88,109,122,131,
173,175,192,194,248,
253,254,271,308,336,
347,353,365,371,376,
396

Fred 289,290,304

Friday 278

Gambo 2,17

Gane 50

George 22,42,50,69,
73,102,110,149,152,
208,245,248,308,353,
371,375,376,381,397

Giles 365

Ginney 239

Gloster 194

Godfrey 31,57,131

Goliak 131

Grace 76,95,101,179,
208,227,234,338,378,
391,403

Grant 181

Great Frank 234

Great Jack 234

Great James 304

Great Jimmy 253,254

Great Lucy 69

Great Tom 304,396

Gundy 72

Guy 208,362

Hagar 247,251

Hague 365

Hal 66

Haley 308

Hall 18,83,203,248,
283

Hampton 82,398

Hamsheir 57

Hannah 33,39,46,50,
65,82,83,88,104,117,
125,173,182,266,269,
271,308,313,320,336,
353,356,357,376,381,
397,398

Harculus 24,32

Harray 244

Harris 76

Harry 9,39,46,63,64,
66,88,102,104,122,
173,275,308,314,381,
391,396,397,402,403

Harvey 208

Hector 18,203,227

Herculas 334,374,401

Hester 82

Hesther 398

Holley 275

Holly 283,370,382

Hubbard 370,382

Humphrey 88

Ingram 353

Isaac 34,51,54,72,173,
234,273,320,356

Isbell 396

Isham 76,248,370,382,
393

Isle of Wight 269

Jack 18,25,37,40,72,
73,76,80,81,88,109,
110,122,144,149,152,
173,192,208,227,228,
231,240,245,250,252,
269,271,273,278,305,
336,352,365,368,371,
393,406

Jack Jr 347

Jack Sr 347

Jacko 36

Jacko 271

Jacky 160

Jacob 9,34,69,72,139,
158,183,229,236,253,
254,269,340,345,375,

Jame 112

James 24,31,41,47,50,
63,64,95,131,140,183,
194,316,345,350,365,
392,396,401

James Booker 376

Jamey 102,271,334,
343,345

Jamey Booker 353

Jammie 72

Jammy 136

Jams 59

Jane 51,80,98,122,221,
243,289,298,392

Janey 110,249,286,
353,376

Jean 81

Jeen 101

Jeff 300

Jeffree 182

Jeffrey 34

Jem 43

Jemima 356

Jemmy 6,9,35,57,65,
82,88,231,240

Jenn 41

Jennen 347

Jenny 25,31,34,56,57,
73,208,250,310,319,
347,393,406

Jeremiah 371

Jerrey 398
Jerry 110
Jesse 152
Jim 34,179,181,248, 336
Jimm 203
Jimmy 23,32,69
Jinny 254
Jo 95
Joan 221,229,236
Joe 9,72,82,101,125, 271,308,398
John 18,271,353,362
Johnson 246,268
Jona 253
Jone 377
Joseph 73,320
Jude 24,36,46,357,381, 397
Judey 117
Judith 239,243,248
Judy 25,32,34,37,39, 88,102,110,149,155, 245,251,269,271,308, 316,320,347,365
June 110,178
Junes 374
Juno 173,278,305
Jupiter 273,336

King 34,57
Kitt 81

Lanes Branch 365
Lett 57,396
Letty 248
Levina 353
Lewis 31,80,81,86, 145,182,271,308,336, 365,370,382,396
Libbie 179
Lid 192,336
Lidd 40

Liddia 375,396
Lidia 57,365
Lilly 31
Limus 17
Linda 31,131
Linson 353,376
Little Ceazor 244
Little Frank 353
Little Hannah 396
Little James 304
Little Jenny 286,307
Little Jimmy 253
Little Jinny 254
Little Lucy 69
Little Mingo 244
Little Moll 144
Little Noll 160
Little Peter 396
Little Tom 304,396
Livina 376
London 289
Long Fib 383
Luce 39
Lucey 49
Luck 153
Luckenny 244
Lucy 24,25,32,34,46, 62,69,72,76,88,122, 178,194,228,253,254, 259,287,290,308,316, 320,353,375,376,396
Lusey 109
Lydia 208,308

Mace 18
Mag 36,271
Mago 57
Manser 178
Mar...? 8
Marandy 182
Mariah 25
Marma...? 3
Marrear 244

Martha 287
Martin 398
Mary 72,73,296
Mater 152,245
Mathew 121
Matt 15,19,24,32,149, 245,296,322
Matthew 37,322
Member 375
Meter 149
Mial 350
Mill 66
Milley 104,144,160, 173,203,271,336
Milly 36,41,57,63,64, 82,273,392,393,398
Mina 110
Miner 173,365
Mingo 76,80,81,144, 160,183,244,368
Moggy 122
Moll 43,47,80,81,121, 131,144,152,160,179, 208,231,240,242,244, 316,350,353,365,375, 378
Moll Ingram 376
Molley 271
Moroco 9
Moses 72,110,117, 182,248,275,283,343, 350,357
Mulatto Charles 338
Mureah 178
Murear 244
Murreah 72

Nackey 11
Nacksey 9
Nan 40,66,69,86,175, 177,192,234,248,253, 254,259,273,308,347, 370,382

Nancey 353,398
Nancy 376
Nann 15,17,19,24,128, 345,347
Nanny 57,72,271,308, 352,353,365,376
Nat 253,254
Natt 304
Ned 18,22,23,31,35, 41,42,57,65,117,121, 131,148,149,152,208, 245,273,304,313,362, 370,371,374,382,392
Nelley 244
Nero 203,308
Nick 63,64
Nutt 18,144,160
Nutty 227,396

Old Cuff 57
Old Dick 234
Old Donum 57
Old Hannah 83,320, 336,396
Old Jenny 307
Old Juno 91
Old Lewis 396
Old Lucy 57
Old Sarah 57
Old Solomon 283
Old Sue 304
Old Will 57
Oliver 48
Orange 375
Oro 203
Orpha 249
Orson 305

Pall 243
Pat 254,286,396
Patience 72,117,311, 370,382
Patt 3,8,18,25,34,57,

63,64,69,78,153,178,
181,227,231,239,240,
248,253,273,300,304,
307,316,365
Patty 139,320
Paul 268,322
Paymour 65
Peg 28,57,82,250,368,
383,399,405
Pegg 71,72,182,350,
374
Peggy 308
Pender 365
Penny 110,352
Peter 6,9,22,31,34,40,
50,57,71,82,86,100,
112,117,121,131,153,
181,182,183,192,248,
268,275,278,284,304,
305,308,316,320,356,
370,382,391,403
Peyton 308
Phebe 69,353,398
Pheby 82,131,153,275
Phib 52,222,402
Phibb 31
Phibby 63,64,275,283
Phibe 122
Phibi 376
Phil 86
Philic 88
Phill 248,362
Philladay 52
Phillis 15,25,39,40,46,
72,76,82,173,179,192,
239,247,251,275,283,
308,347,353,368,376,
378
Phoebe 286,307,314
Pleasant 322,365
Pompey 19,64,244,362
Pompy 6,15,18,63
Primus 82,117,398

Prin...? 2
Prince 345
Priss 66,104
Pugg 336
Punch 36,271

Que 18

Rachel 81,122,153,
178,270
Rachell 102
Ransom 350
Ransome 343
Rho...? 43
Rhoda 255
Rhode 140
Ricks 50
Rippin 203
Robert 18,57
Robin 24,32,110,208,
227,234,253,254,271,
286,307,322
Rochel 161
Roger 43,47,69,100,
112,183,229,236,246,
247,251,268,347,352,
375
Rose 3,34,47,72,80,
117,139,182,275,283,
347,352
Ruth 255

Sack 25
Sall 69,117,178,183,
194,242,251,271,316,
396
Sally 353,376
Sam 9,41,49,50,52,
69,112,114,158,161,
173,194,203,255,263,
275,283,336,392,396
Sambo 131
Sampson 273,353,376

Sarah 9,39,41,46,50,
57,72,86,88,144,160,
173,227,239,243,244,
247,249,271,300,353,
365,375,376,392,398
Scipio 271
Sebubbio 9
Sela 122
Selah 365
Sender 205,304
Shagg 203
Sharper 57,128,239,
243,350
Silvey 117
Silvia 41,69,173,182,
300,375,392,393
Simon 9,80,81,86,110,
178,228,252
Sissax 374
Skipper 229,375
Smith 278,305
Solomon 50,69,72,275
Southy 72
Staffor 57
Stafford 21,31,131,
181,304
Stephen 28,338
Steporey 308
Sterling 396
Stewart 76
Subbabo 227
Suck 86,128,308
Suckey 36,52,271
Sue 24,32,57,69,80,
98,173,182,249,250,
273,323,336,396
Sukey 308
Sunkey 271
Surry 183,269
Swan 300

Tab 95,109,173,371
Tabb 72,101,122,182

Taffey 102
Tarla 244
Temp 120,273
Tempe 343
Thom 375
Thomas 374
Tib 235
Tilder 6
Tillar 289
Tiller 298
Tim 57,117
Titus 69
Toby 286,307
Tom 18,21,25,37,57,
76,81,82,98,110,173,
181,203,239,243,248,
250,253,254,259,268,
269,271,278,308,381,
391,397,403
Toney 34,43,47,76,
194,229,236,253,254,
375,376
Tony 88,173

Umphrey 9
Ussry 9

Val 305
Van 270
Villag..? 80
Vilot 182
Viny 275
Violet 51,54
Visey 391,403
Voluntine 269,278

Weldon 183
Wil 305
Will 25,31,43,47,50,
65,69,72,76,82,110,
122,139,153,177,179,
182,211,247,251,270,
271,273,278,283,286,

304,308,314,323,336,
398,402
William 307
Win 112
Winney 18,39,46,100,
182,208,296,375
Winny 110
Woodley 69,374

Yellow Moses 57
York 50,128
Young Eaton 153
Young Hannah 356
Young Jimmy 24
Young Peg 28
Young Sifar 24
Young Sue 181,304
Younger 31,131

Zays 76

...? 3

Albemarle Parish 80
Amelia County 300
Anter Dam Swamp 192
Augusta 173

Beaver Pond Branch 155
Beaverpond Branch 36
Blue Stone branches 36
bridge road 155
Bristol Parish 301
Broad River 374

Cain Branch 179
Cattail Creek 23
Chapman Ford Tract 26
Charlotte County 301
Cold Water 246
Collin Creek 120
Congaree River 311
Cope's Creek 31
Couche's Run 36
Couches Run 120
court house 133,173,242

Deep Branch 246

Dinwiddie County 45,108,135,
   170,301
Dividing Branch 192,246
Duglas's High Hill 374
Duglass Run 274

Edgecombe County NC 230
Essex County 140
Evans Creek 398

Fisher's 37
Fletcher's Branch 336

Glebe Tract 323
Granville County 245,248

Grassey Pond road 133
Great Branch 244,338
Great Creek 278
Great Swamp 323

Halifax Road 323
Haw Branch 274
Hicke's Ford 111
Hickory Run 344
Hickses Ford 338
Hixes plantation 57
Hixes Swamp 205
Hogg Pen Branch 339
Hollow Branch 259
Hoods 3

Isle of Wight County 229

Jack's Branch 63
James River 3
Jones's Creek 36

Kentucky 393

Licks Bog 253
Little Creek 306,374
Little Meadow 192
Lizard Creek 306
Log House Branch 253
Loyd's branches 36
Lunenburg County 242,244,
   248

Martins Branch 347
Mecklenburg County 20,31,
   39,120,143,275,284,308
Meherin River 22,57
Meherrin 248
Meherrin Parish 3,12,24,26,39,
   71,83,99,100,102,116,139,154,
   178,179,180,200,246,247,248,
   274,286,296,306,318,320,323,
   329,339,360,367,398,401,404

Meherrin River 242,248,338
Metcalf's Swamp 57
Moores Swamp 9
Mountain Creek 275

Narrow Branch 274
North Carolina 3,110,230,245,
   248,265,374
Northampton Co NC 265

Old Shop Branch 246
ordinary 338
Otterdam Swamp 314
over the mountains 365

Piney Branch 344
Pittsylvania County 173
Pole Bridge Branch 246
Poplar Creek 198
Prince George County 3

Quag Branch 192
Quarrel Swamp 24,195
Quarter 153
Quarter plantation 139

R...? Creek 244
Rattle Snake Branch 336
Rattlesnake Creek 374
Roaring Rock 242
Robinson's Branch 323
Rocky Branch 24
Round Meadow 173
Russells tract 9

Saw Scaffold Branch 51
Second Branch 141
South Carolina 92
Southampton County 114,136,
   199,265,287,303,311
Spring Branch 179,347
St Andrews Parish 7,9,10,12,
   25,36,38,41,57,62,66,67,68,87,

88,103,110,115,119,125,126,
134,142,145,155,159,173,192,
198,205,227,230,234,239,242,
244,255,275,278,287,292,300,
321,343,370,380,405
Stoney Creek 45,153
Sturgeon Run 244
Sturgion Creek 37
Sturgion Run 36
Surry County 111,183,280
Sussex County 80,125,228,353

Tar Kiln Branch 24
Tarbrough 230
tavern 338
Thomas's Branch 336
Tomlin's Run 141
Totero Creek 321

Uper Spring Run 274

Wa...? Creek 244
westward road 336

York County 77

Continental Army 310

MERCHANTS
Atkinson 123
Bailey & Son 14
Cranfield mer. 303
Crawford & Co 136,143
Cunningham & Co 136
Dunlop & Co 92
Edwards & Co 111,123,136,143
Edwards & Son 75,77,114,334
Elliott & Co 398
Hamilton & Co 14,136
Love & Co 334,355
Person & Norfleet 14,77
Peter & Company 137
Purdie & Dixon 123
Stith & Clack 92
Taylor & Company 132
Young & Pocke 136

ordinary house 153

over the mountains 365

Reverend 28,36,37,72,124,151,257,323,334,338

Revolution 297